The Financial Advisor's Success Manual

How to Structure and Grow Your Financial Services Practice

David I. Leo, Founder
Street Smart Research Group LLC

Craig Cmiel, Co-Founder
Great Lakes & Atlantic Wealth Management & Advisory Partners LLC

AMACOM
AMERICAN MANAGEMENT ASSOCIATION
New York • Atlanta • Brussels • Chicago • Mexico City • San Francisco
Shanghai • Tokyo • Toronto • Washington, D.C.

Bulk discounts available. For details visit:
www.amacombooks.org/go/specialsales
Or contact special sales:
Phone: 800-250-5308
E-mail: specialsls@amanet.org
View all the AMACOM titles at: www.amacombooks.org

American Management Association: www.amanet.org

This publication is designed to provide accurate and authoritative information in regard to the subject matter covered. It is sold with the understanding that the publisher is not engaged in rendering legal, accounting, or other professional service. If legal advice or other expert assistance is required, the services of a competent professional person should be sought.

Library of Congress Cataloging-in-Publication Data

Names: Leo, David I., author. | Cmiel, Craig, author.
Title: The financial advisor's success manual : how to structure and grow your financial services practice / David Leo, Founder, Street Smart Research Group LLC, Craig Cmiel, Co-Founder, Great Lakes & Atlantic Wealth Management & Advisory Partners LLC.
Description: New York : American Management Association, [2018] | Includes index.
Identifiers: LCCN 2017023379 (print) | LCCN 2017036947 (ebook) | ISBN 9780814439142 (ebook) | ISBN 9780814439135 (hardcover)
Subjects: LCSH: Financial planners. | Investment advisors. | Financial services industry.
Classification: LCC HG179.5 (ebook) | LCC HG179.5 .L46 2018 (print) | DDC 332.6--dc23
LC record available at https://lccn.loc.gov/2017023379

About AMA

American Management Association (www.amanet.org) is a world leader in talent development, advancing the skills of individuals to drive business success.
Our mission is to support the goals of individuals and organizations through a complete range of products and services, including classroom and virtual seminars, webcasts, webinars, podcasts, conferences, corporate and government solutions, business books, and research. AMA's approach to improving performance combines experiential learning—learning through doing—with opportunities for ongoing professional growth at every step of one's career journey.

10 9 8 7 6 5 4 3 2 1

This book is dedicated to my wife and family for all of the love they have given me regardless (of my faults).

David Leo

To my amazing wife, Joyce, who has been a great partner on this wonderful journey.

Craig Cmiel

Acknowledgments

I was proud and inspired to have received a wonderful mention from Mitch Anthony. Mitch's comments made me believe it was my responsibility not to lose what I have learned over a lifetime if it could be of value to others. This was my motivation for this book. A *Forbes* article that I read stated, "But for all the good intentions, only a tiny fraction of us keep our resolutions; University of Scranton research suggests that just 8 percent of people achieve their New Year's goals."[1] In their book *Following Through: A Revolutionary New Model for Finishing Whatever You Start*, Steve Levinson and Pete Greider say, "According to some estimates, 90 percent of the books purchased in bookstores never get read past the first chapter," and that "nearly three out of four new [health club] members stop going within just three months of signing up."[2] I hope that many who read this book will find some ideas that can be of value to advisors, and to coaches of advisors, and ultimately to the clients of those advisors, and follow through by trying them.

David Leo

Contents

Executive Summary

Financial advisors must structure and organize their financial advisory practices so that they can put themselves in a position to grow their businesses. To structure and organize your business for efficiency and effectiveness, you need to:

- Formally segment your book and analyze the results in depth. You may have already placed clients into A, B, and C service tiers. This segmentation should be reviewed and modified as needed annually. It should also be based on more than assets and/or revenues. Likability, willingness to heed your advice, and whether clients are a source of introductions and their future potential all impact their value to the business and therefore their tier.
- Segmentation will also help you answer the question, "How many clients can I effectively and efficiently manage?"
- Detail your Client Service Model or Promise for each of the client tiers you choose to service. In this book you will learn exactly how to approach detailing these promises using a structure that provides consistency and completeness for both the client and advisor.
- Define and implement your six core client-facing processes:
    - *Intake Process*—putting your best foot forward at the onset of your relationship
    - *Financial Planning Process*—providing a comprehensive set of wealth management solutions
    - *Risk Management Process*—accounting for life's risk above and beyond investment risks
    - *Investment Planning Process*—delivered in a highly consultative manner

- *Client Service Process*—yielding a set of deliverables that is highly satisfactory to the client
- *Client Planning and Review Meeting Process*—designed to make your client communications highly effective and keep you and your clients aware of their satisfaction

Commit that every client you are willing to accept into your practice will receive a version of these processes based on their needs, the deliverables they deserve, their value to your business, and the fees you charge in compensation for the value you deliver.

- Understand the value you deliver but also the cost of your deliverables. Value is determined by the client; cost is determined by you. Don't deliver items that clients don't value, because they almost always have a cost.
- Develop a *real* business plan. This plan is much more than a set of goals. Goals are the "What" and the "How Many." What do I want my 20XX assets under management (AUM) to be? What do I want my 20XX production to be? How many new clients do I want to acquire?
- A business plan lays out the "How," the "When," and the "Who." In addition to outlining where I am and where I want to be, the plan defines the strategies and tactics for how to get there, by when, and who has responsibility.
- Develop a *quantitative* metrics plan. Quality actions lead to quality results. While you need to hit your numbers, it's the action you take that will drive the numbers. This book addresses how to create an action plan and convert those actions to results.
- Develop your marketing and sales approaches. Your business plan will call out the three to five marketing and sales approaches you plan to use as part of your client acquisition strategy. This book outlines the primary approaches available to you to acquire new clients and their assets. You need to detail which approaches you will use and how you will use them.
- Develop your differentiation strategy. Before this can be done, you need to understand the processes you must implement and what

they will deliver to your clients in terms of benefits to them. After that, you can define your differentiation (see Chapter 1).

These are the elements you need to implement to have a successful financial advisory practice. With the exception of the marketing and sales approaches you will choose to implement as part of your client acquisition strategy, this is not a pick and choose menu of options but is much more like a surgical process. From the time a patient arrives at a hospital for his or her procedure until the patient leaves the hospital as a healthy individual, there are no optional steps. They are all required for an optimal outcome. I haven't outlined all the other processes that a financial advisory team must execute (e.g., administrative processes, compliance requirements, continuing education requirements, and reporting). This book focuses on the processes and functions necessary for growing your business by bringing organization and structure to your practice.

Introduction

There is nothing more difficult to take in hand, more perilous to conduct, or more uncertain in its success, than to take the lead in the introduction of a new order of things. **—Niccolo Machiavelli**

This book is designed for financial advisors (FAs) who want to grow their business by bringing organization and structure to their practices. We will discuss tools and techniques that can be used by advisors to service and expand their books of business. These tools and techniques are ones that have been used in coaching practice since 2001 to help advisors gather necessary data, interpret the meaning of findings, draw conclusions, and take the proper actions for improving client service and driving business growth. It is through continuing contact and holding FAs accountable for using the tools and implementing the processes that we bring about the benefits of a new model for doing business.

Coaching includes:

- Discussing and explaining how each tool and technique applies to financial advisors and their practice
- Interpreting the data and helping advisors actually apply the tools and techniques to improve their business
- Holding advisors accountable for implementing the tools, techniques, and approaches

Each coaching engagement is specific to each FA and her or his book of business. Advisors must take on these roles themselves or with a partner, whether a coach or another advisor, who serves as an accountability partner. There are costs and benefits to both approaches.

The first goal of this book is to help advisors define and implement a set of processes that will save them time and energy while "ensuring" their clients are very well serviced, so little if anything falls through the cracks throughout the life of the client-advisor relationship. With a structured and organized set of processes the advisor can have the time to devote to the second goal of this book, which is helping to grow their advisory practice in terms of AUM and/or production. The top methods to acquire new clients will be discussed so that advisors can be successful in fulfilling their growth objectives.

There is much written about the mental aspects of improving an advisory practice. Little of that material will be addressed in these pages. Discussions of philosophy, psychology, the mental game, visualization, affirmations, mantras, motivation, and leadership principles will be limited. This book is about the tools and techniques you need to structure, organize, and grow your business. As Stephen Covey has said, "Motivation is a fire from within. If someone else tries to light that fire under you, chances are it will burn very briefly." Rather, we will describe a pragmatic approach to practice management.

This approach to practice management is described as "coachulting," a combination of coaching and consulting. The structure and methodologies of coaching are numerous but are predominantly facilitating. A coach mainly asks questions and challenges the coachee. Coaching also involves a teaching, training, and/or a development process so individuals and/or teams can achieve their desired results.

Consulting provides advice in a particular area of expertise. It helps organizations improve their performance primarily through the analysis of existing organizational issues and the development of plans for their improvement. Consultants provide external objective advice and access to the consultants' specialized expertise. Because of their exposure to and relationships with numerous organizations, consultants are also aware of "best practices."

Consulting is an *understand* (the situation), *tell*, and *do* methodology. Coaching is more of an *ask*, *guide*, and *monitor* methodology. Consulting is a more time-consuming process because of the need for data collection through interviews, data and interview analysis, information synthesis, development of conclusions and recommendations, and reporting. Consulting has end points such as "Here are the action recommendations or here is the process," or "We have completed system implementation or the users are trained."

Coaching may or may not have an end point. The end point can be a specific amount of time to get the coachees to a specific point or to a point where they believe they have enough knowledge and consistency to continue on by themselves. In some cases coaching engagements can go on indefinitely. In these cases, the coach may be constantly monitoring execution by the coachee and being an accountability coach and a "brainstorming" partner. The coachee may want a part-time "partner" with whom to check progress and continue to bounce off ideas. As some advisors and teams do not have anyone with whom they can regularly discuss their business, brainstorm with, and be accountable to, a coach can be a valuable resource. The right coach will care about your practice as much as you do.

It's important to decide what the engagement is: coaching or consulting or a combination of both. With financial advisors, a blended methodology is best (i.e., "coachulting"). The coach understands the business issues, provides advice, shares best practices, questions decisions, offers alternatives, and partners with the financial advisor, in this case, to help develop the structure and organization that their practices need to grow their businesses.

The tools and techniques discussed in this book tend toward consulting because they tend toward advice. The coaching part of an engagement helps financial advisors define those areas they and the coach believe can best serve the advisor, and the coach then works with them on how best to approach implementation. While many of the areas addressed in coaching engagements with advisors are included here, engagements are uniquely designed for each FA based on the advisor's current situation, their wants and needs, and where they want to be at some future point in time. There are additional areas for coaching (e.g., team development) that are not discussed in this book.

While we will not focus on the mental discipline that is an important aspect of being a financial advisor, there is a story from the 2016 Olympic Games that is instructive. Like many, we were incredibly impressed with one of the world's best athletes in her sport, Katie Ledecky. The following is from a profile of Ledecky at ESPN.com:

> "What I've done over the past couple years has been pretty great, but even that doesn't define my swimming," she said. "Working hard and doing everything I can to be successful should be my identity."
>
> That self-portrait captures much of the big picture of a now 19-year-old who can blend intellectual curiosity with the tunnel vision to train in an unchanging environment that has little visual or aural stimulation. Pools are different, but in all of them a swimmer sees gallons of water divided by lane lines. Strength, stroke efficiency, and aerobic capacity all help make champions, but none of those is what separates Ledecky from her rivals.
>
> "It's not physical, it's between the ears," said her coach, Bruce Gemmell. "It's the absolute, burning desire to get better, and the not being afraid of failure."[1]

You can hear these themes in other amazing Olympic athletes, too. It's how you must be an Olympic-level financial advisor.

Chapter One

Develop Your Differentiation Strategy

Progress is measured by the degree of differentiation within a society. **—Herbert Read**

This chapter outlines reasons why a client or prospect should do business with you (instead of anyone else). It will help you define your Unique Value Proposition. You have read about and been asked about your differentiation. You have thought about it, perhaps even written something down intending to define it, and perhaps awkwardly discussed it with clients, saying something to try to distinguish yourself and your services. The fact is, it is not easy to truly develop a clear and concise answer to the question, "Why should I do business with you instead of anyone else?" Perhaps only some clients or prospects have actually asked this question directly, but you need to work on the assumption that 100 percent of your clients and prospects have thought about this question and would love you to answer it without having to ask—just like many advisors want clients to know why they are different and better than anyone else, without having to state it.

Knowing, understanding and being able to crisply and clearly state your Unique Value Proposition (UVP) or Unique Selling Proposition (USP) will be of significant value for you as it will also bolster your own

---

Sections of Chapter 1 are based on "A Hierarchy of the Value a Financial Advisor Provides," *Nerd's Eye View* (blog), March 8, 2016, https://www.kitces.com/blog/hierarachy-of-financial-advisor-value/, with permission from Bob Seawright.

belief system and allow you to answer the question before it is asked. It's better to be proactive in discussing your UVP before you are asked what it is. Get it out of the way early, so your clients or prospects can focus on the rest of what you want to address without them concentrating on the "Why you?" question.

In this chapter we will discuss five key points that, if you master them, will help you deliver as effective a UVP as we believe exists in the financial advisory business today. We will:

1. Explain that a Unique Value Proposition has two distinct parts, value and uniqueness, and we will define both parts.
2. Define the elements of your deliverables and their value.
3. Explain the Law of Fractional Advantage and its applicability to you.
4. Discuss the need for effective and persistent execution in the six core client-facing processes.
5. Detail 16 elements that in aggregate will define your differentiation.

Key point one is to recognize that your UVP has two distinct parts: value and uniqueness. Every advisor has the ability to deliver each of the values we will discuss. The depth and breadth of the values you deliver start to contribute to your uniqueness.

Value is in the eyes of the client, so you need to answer the basic question: "What's in it for me?" (the client or prospect) or "What do you have to say that will improve my life?" It's important that your client or prospect understands that your deliverables have an inherent value in terms of time and effort saved and wealth made and/or protected, as well as in the reduction of various toxic emotions like worry, stress, and anxiety.

The value of reducing toxic emotions is difficult to measure monetarily but important to consider. The value of time and effort saved and wealth made and/or protected can be subjective but is quantifiable.

Value should be discussed in context of our present-day industry. It may therefore be helpful to review where we have come from, and how client expectations have changed over the past decades. The landscape has changed significantly, triggered by product development, technological advances, new regulatory oversight, industry consolidation and the growth of fee-based businesses. Decades ago, clients separated banking from investing. Then brokerage firms began offering cash management services, then came the Glass-Steagall Act. Now many advisors working for large firms are connected with a bank (e.g., Merrill Lynch, Wells Fargo, UBS, and others). Clients might view their relationship with an advisor much more holistically today than they did decades ago when the advisor was a "broker" who helped identify investments and execute transactions. As the industry has become less transaction-based we have seen the growth of advice-based relationships, fee-based wrap pricing, and the use of technology to help manage and model portfolios as well as relationships.

The new administration may halt the implementation of Department of Labor (DOL) Fiduciary Standard regulations. The effect could be less mandated compliance work; however, it will not stem the tide of movement toward fee-based relationships (and perhaps continuing movement toward fiduciary relationships). Clients and advisors are continuing to grow more comfortable with these fee-based relationships. During one of the sessions on technology at a recent industry conference, the speaker asked the crowd of about 200, "How many of you would say that investment selection and performance is the primary driver of adding value to your clients?" Only two hands went up. While this was not a scientific survey, it appears to us that advisors do not see performance as their primary value to clients in today's financial world. The point of the question was to challenge the audience to focus on what clients really want and value, as it relates to the investment of capital and personnel, and aligning the advisor's value accordingly. Data points us in the general direction of Planning, Trust, Guidance, Communication, Education, and Personalization. It is in the absence of these and other client-driven value criteria that the business becomes commoditized and focused on trading, execution, costs, and performance.

Another trend we have witnessed over the past decades is the maturing of the discount, robo, and do-it yourself investing businesses. Charles Schwab has grown dramatically since the 1990s because clients could not see value and decided to take matters into their own hands. This is akin to patients who don't like their dentist deciding to do their own dental work. It may be cheaper, but it will likely be more painful.

This movement has spawned and grown many other discount models where the client can save money without a dedicated professional. Large Wall Street firms have also created their own "call centers" for smaller relationships. These centers essentially remove dedicated advisors and replace them with a group of people who can field incoming calls. The primary driver in this model is efficiency and profits. A call center can generate profits of over 50 percent, compared to an advisor-centric model that can generate profit margins of 5–20 percent. These two developments led to the creation of the robo industry. Essentially robo advice is geared to clients who do not see the value of the advisor as being critical. Add robust technology to the initial Schwab model and the call center model and some clients can do their own planning and investing electronically. Schwab of course has also evolved and now provides "full service" through Schwab Private Client service and the Schwab Advisor Network. In fact, Betterment, which offers a robo model, is planning on adding "Human Touch" offerings with Betterment Plus and Betterment Premium with access to a team of Certified Financial Planners (CFPs) and licensed financial experts who monitor accounts and give financial planning advice throughout the year.

There are silos in the wealth management business. One is an advisor-based relationship; the other is a discounted, self-reliant silo, but even those silos are broadening. Advisors may realize that investment choices, fees, and performance are components of client satisfaction, but not the key drivers. In order to get a personal, dynamic, value-based offering, you must get answers to two key questions. The first is, "What do you do?" and the second is, "Who do you do it for?" The answers to these questions will create a "clarity of value." As you think more about these questions, consider two other industries: automobiles and hotels. Within the auto industry it is interesting to compare Mercedes-Benz to Kia. There are stark differences in price, warranties, service, image, and custom options. These companies target different consumers and provide different levels of service. They have different "What you do" and different "Who you do it for" value propositions, and this is reflected in their pricing.

Similarly, the hotel industry has many providers who define their "What" and "Who" very differently. For comparison's sake, consider the difference between the Ritz-Carlton and Holiday Inn. At a Ritz hotel you would find more staff, better dining options, larger fitness centers, well-appointed lobbies, personalization, and so on. At a Holiday Inn, a traveler would find the basics covered: a warm bed, hot shower, and free breakfast. These two companies are successful because they can articulate their "What" and "Who" and attract the consumer who fits their model best.

When examining and developing your own differentiation and value proposition, you can determine your pricing and the overall "feel" and culture and services you choose to provide. It is then critical to align your definition of what you offer with the people you are delivering your services to. If your team decides to provide disciplined research, investment due diligence, financial planning coordinated with tax professionals, regular meetings and communication including in-depth quarterly reviews along with a holistic set of other services, this will lead to one type of client. This practice may decide to have fewer, larger clients and price its business more like a premium brand such as Mercedes or Ritz. Another team may choose to let technology help them create models, have more clients with somewhat lower assets, have fewer meetings with clients, and provide more basic planning work and fewer services; these decisions would lead to another type of client.

It's critical to clearly identify your "What" and "Who" to find the best clients for you to service with the model you choose and to run your business effectively and efficiently. Before you can define your value, you must decide on "Who" your client is, and your target market, and "What" you do based on the wants and needs of your clients. Value can also be delivered by helping your clients change their behaviors to better meet their life and financial goals. Your value proposition can be enhanced by your team's ability to help change or "correct" client behavior by developing traits, habits, and approaches that generally lead to better outcomes: better savings and spending habits, better planning, less emotional investing, longer-term focus, and being better organized.[1] If you believe in these traits, habits, and approaches or others and are convinced they are in your client's best interest, it is important to also talk about them during your discussion of expectations, service, and pricing.

At your annual checkup, your doctor may suggest you exercise more, eat healthier, use less salt, drink more water, and get more sleep. Who can argue with any of those recommendations? If we do all of these things we will be healthier and feel better and have a life outcome that will be better than if we had no advice. Doctors try to change our behavior, entirely for our own benefit, just like you are finding behaviors in your clients that will lead them to the possibility of better outcomes. Unfortunately, doctors do not usually have the time or business model to follow up, but you have that opportunity at least for your best clients.

It's also critical to know that while clients and prospects may understand your value, yours may not be unique. Some advisors may be more empathic than others, some may be better able to communicate their value, and some may sell their deliverables and themselves better than others. Most advisors will state they are focused on the client and have the expertise, experience, education, integrity, professionalism, and performance standards to help their clients succeed. These traits are not unique; they are barely the price of admission for a quality advisor or wealth manager. Who would say less? Many FAs live up to this promise, some better than others. The point is, you have to make the sale (i.e., acquire the prospect) before you have a chance to prove it. Talking the talk is easier than walking the talk.

The more value you deliver contrasted to your competitors, the more distinctive you will be. Value, as stated, is in the eyes of the client, so start by asking:

- What are *your* client deliverables? Are you offering a holistic financial plan? Not all financial plans are equal:
    - What elements are included in your financial plans? Are you offering primarily a future cash flow projection, or do you also address savings and spending habits and projections?
    - How deeply do you address client wants versus needs?
    - What breadth of wealth management solutions do you address?
    - Why do you include or not include certain elements in your financial plans?
    - Do your deliverables vary by client, depending on their wants and needs and their value to the business?
    - Who do you deliver financial plans to and who does not receive a plan?
- What elements of your financial plans do your clients value or not value, and why?

- Have you explained the value you intend to deliver with each element of your financial plan? Does the client buy into your intent?

What Is *Your* Value?

Key point two is defining the components of your deliverables and their value. Most of your clients and prospects will question, vocally or in their minds, what value you provide for the 1 percent to 1.5 percent you charge. There are myriad responses to a simple Google search of "What is the value of a financial advisor?" or "Is it worth hiring a financial advisor?" Given the many, many thousands of articles and discussions revolving around the value that FAs deliver to their clients, one can conclude that firms and clients are concerned about their value and fees.

This has been a constant source of discourse in the media and within virtually all financial services firms offering investment solutions. It is a reasonable hypothesis that costs/fees and value have been an industry concern for at least forty years, ever since the rise of the discount brokerage in the 1970s[2] and 1980s. And, with the rise of robo-advisors, this discourse continues.

So, one goal of this chapter is to discuss the value that "full service" financial advisors or wealth managers can, and should, provide to their clients to earn their fees. After discussing value in general, we will discuss differentiating yourself based on the value you bring to your clients.

Few other professions are as focused on or concerned with the value they deliver to their clients. One can take a positive perspective by saying wealth management is a caring profession that wants to be sure the fees are warranted for the services delivered. One can also take a negative view by saying alternatives are needed because the cost of human-based financial advice is too high. These negative views have resulted in investors seeking the alternatives we discussed for investing and growing their assets using less costly do-it-yourself approaches, with or without "robo-advisors." An interesting and relevant statement can be found in a white paper on "Pricing Integrity," where it says that "at the core of pricing inconsistency *we find that advisors are not fundamentally convinced that they provide significant value to their clients*" (emphasis added).[3] This is an aha statement. We had better be clear and convinced of the value "full service" financial advisors and wealth managers deliver to their clients.

If there is any question or concern on the part of advisors about the value of their deliverables to the client, it is an imperative to overcome it. A couple of the most important rules in sales are to believe in your offerings and never sell yourself short! You must deeply believe in the value of your full-service offerings and advice. Let's discuss the value you can deliver to clients.

William Bernstein, the financial theorist and neurologist, was asked, "What essential services can and does a good FA provide?" He responded, "The three most important things are, in order, discipline, discipline, and discipline: the ability to maintain a strategy no matter what CNBC and *USA Today* are blathering about."[4] Bernstein's comments are supported by research into an individual's ability, or lack thereof, to "follow through." In the book *Following Through: A Revolutionary New Model for Finishing Whatever You Start*, the authors state that "we don't have a problem knowing what we should do. The problem is that we just don't do it!"[5] Our observations find this to be true. Even more critical is that David Rock and Jeffrey Schwartz, in "The Neuroscience of Leadership," state this is so "even when new habits can mean the difference between life and death."[6] Discipline is about consistent actions and follow through. Consistent action and follow through is of value and what wealth managers need to provide to their clients. We'll see more specifically what we mean by the discipline of consistent actions and follow through when we discuss service plans.

Bernstein also stated that after discipline, a good FA needs to provide "the humility to know that you cannot predict market movements and the historical awareness to know that economic forecasts are usually contrary indicators,"[7] and that "wealth is not a dollar amount, but rather a ratio measured in years."[8] In other words, it depends on how many years' living expenses you have saved. It is of significant value for advisors to put markets and wealth into a life perspective. We know clients have a tendency to look at their portfolio at different points in time and select its value at a peak and measure increases and decreases, which are your successes and failures, from that point until they establish a new peak and use that as a benchmark.

Figure 1-1 | Sample five-day S&P market change.

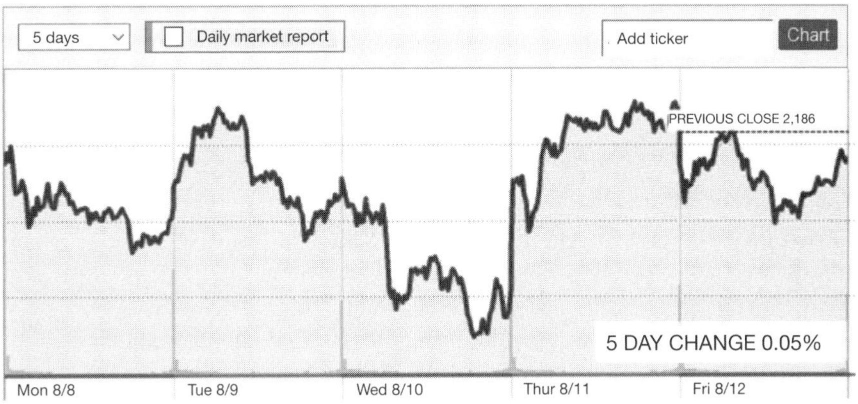

Figure 1-2 | Sample five-year S&P market change.

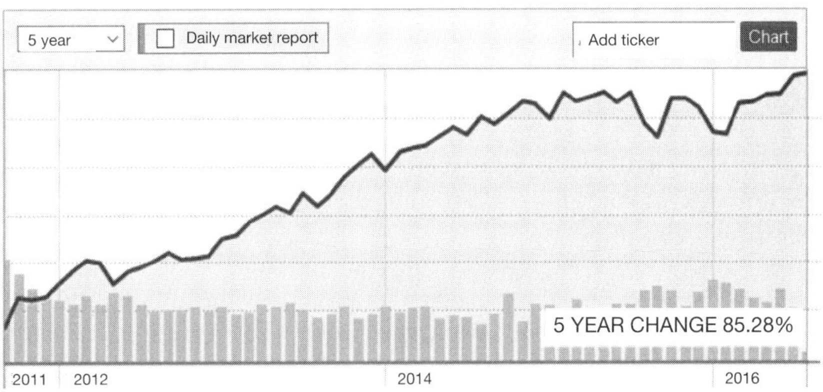

One of the jobs of a financial advisor in goal-based wealth management is to share perspective (i.e., discipline and focus on "how many years' living expenses" your wealth will support you going forward, whether in retirement or for other life goals). Your portfolio's value and growth since inception can be a good point if you have had the clients for a number of years. A Standard and Poor's (S&P) chart for five days doesn't show perspective nearly as well as a chart over 5, 10, or 20 years. See Figures 1-1 and 1-2.

William Bernstein is a realist whose philosophy fits the needs of most of your clients. He goes on to say that "if you think that your happiness is tied up in the things you own, then you are both sadly misinformed about human neuropsychology and doomed to be unhappy."[9]

Convincing your client about the realities of markets, portfolios, and even life alphas and portfolio betas in the context of life goals is incredibly meaningful and valuable. Your clients may not think in these ways themselves and consider these values. That's part of what you can bring to the table. You need in part to be a money psychologist. As an aside, it's interesting to note there is even a Financial Therapy Association (www.financialtherapyassociation.org) and a *Journal of Financial Therapy*. An article at IWillTeachYoutoBeRich.com[10] says:

> Your friends are idiots. Their personal finances are a mess, they're delusional about their spending, and most of them don't even max out their 401(k). The problem is: you're probably just like them.

The author goes on to explain that our makeup as humans often gives us "reasons" to delay doing things that are likely good for us like modifying our diet or exercising. This human behavior also causes us to wait to plan our finances, our wills, our large purchases, etc., at times with dire consequences.

It's clear clients need your help on many financial issues, technical and nontechnical, and you need to be aware of both the right and left sides of their brains.

Another area where we need to be more specific about addressing is what we deliver to clients for the fees we charge. There is an excellent article on Michael Kitces's site, authored by Bob Seawright, in which he discusses a hierarchy of advisor value.

Bob Seawright's Hierarchy of Advisor Value[11]

The four values at the base of the hierarchy are:

1. Encouraging Consistent and Increased Savings
2. Encouraging Consistent Investment
3. Financial Planning
4. Managing Expectations and Behavior

These are values that quality advisors can and must provide to clients. They relate primarily to financial decisions about how the client and the client's advisor manage their financial lives over and above investment management.

The other four values are:

1. Asset Allocation
2. Managing Costs and Fees
3. Portfolio Rebalancing
4. Security Selection

These values are the more technical aspects of investing. They are core capabilities every advisor can handle. While these elements add value to clients, they will not likely differentiate you because all or the vast majority of advisors provide these values. If everyone provides these values they are by definition not differentiators.

Seawright states:

> One's savings rate is far more important than his or her rate of return in determining how bright the future is likely to be. However, we are far more likely to obsess over squeaking out a bit more performance out of our investments or tweaking our asset allocation to increase our expected return rather than thinking about ways to save more. Good planning starts with putting the client's financial house in order and making sure that a good savings plan is in place with the proceeds invested into a solid, diversified portfolio.[12]

We don't have to tell you how many DIY friends talk about fees and how few talk about the time, effort, and angst they spend to save those fees. They also don't talk about 2008 or how well they performed since 2009 or how a rising tide lifts all boats. Yes, some people may do well or even very well, but you know that even the vast majority of fund managers do not beat their benchmarks with all the time, talent, access, and horsepower they have to manage investments. We have already spoken about values beyond performance and will talk more about those values.

Encouraging consistent and increased savings is about establishing discipline within your client base and their families. When we discuss wealth management, especially for your higher net worth clients, we reiterate that being the client's CFO should include not only investment management but tax planning, retirement planning, cash flow analysis, budgeting, and your client's multiple banking needs, commercial and personal, including the credit side of their needs. Offering these elements and encouraging consistent and increased savings are valuable services consistent with the client's goals. Your discipline is of value because most clients will not likely hold themselves as accountable as you can. They generally do not have the time or tools or education and knowledge, in addition to the follow through you can provide.

Seawright's model for encouraging consistent investment is another critical value you can deliver as your client's CFO because "out of our general fear, even if and when we invest, we often don't stay invested." He further points out that "volatility—drawdown risk, really—is the price we pay for the higher expected returns provided by equities."[13] It's only your discipline over time and your professional conviction that will keep the client moving forward toward their goals. It's easy to share charts, like in Figure 1-3, that show the time value of compounding and consistency in savings and investing.

Figure 1-3 | Sample compound value chart.

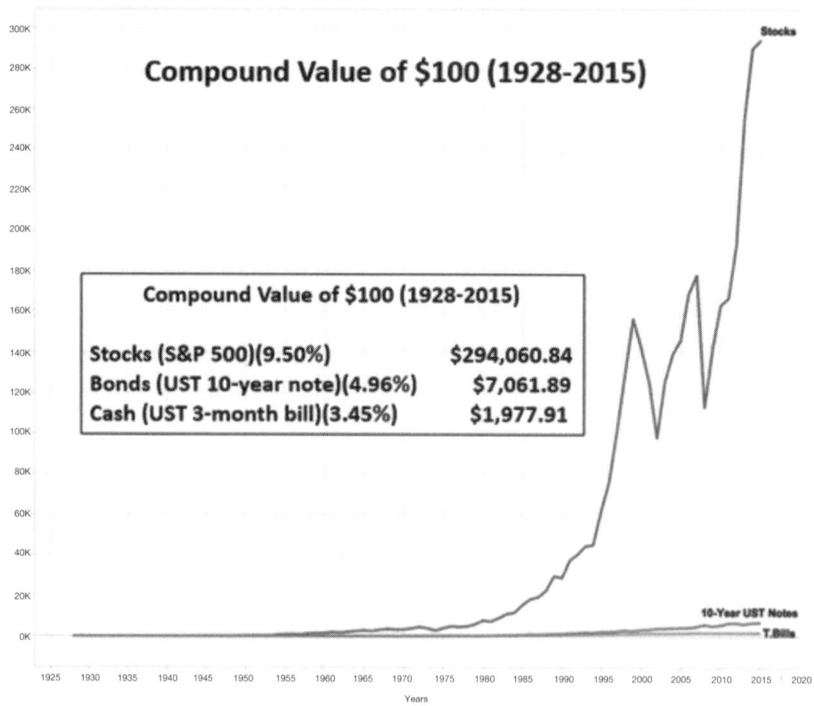

Source: Federal Reserve database in St. Louis (FRED).

We know that volatility is the price paid for higher long-term returns and that "if we have the wherewithal to keep our composure during difficult markets, we will almost surely be rewarded for it." Having said that, Seawright further says to be aware that "more recent efforts to deal with volatility differently haven't fared very well. For the period of 1998–2015 (the longest period available), alternative investments (represented by the HFRX Global Hedge Fund Index) have provided an average return of just 5.11 percent, with most of the better returns early in that period."[14] The question is, how well can you encourage consistent and increased savings and investments in the face of the natural behaviors of many clients?

Financial planning is a solid, high value deliverable. As Wade Pfau puts it, "Financial advisors who only focus on selecting investments will really struggle to add value." On the other hand, "there is immense value in comprehensive financial planning and good financial decision making. It's important to remember and easy to forget that the end goal of comprehensive financial planning goes beyond choosing investments."[15] There is good news, however, according to economist Tim Duy, who states, "As long as people have babies, capital depreciates, technology evolves, and tastes and preferences change, there is a powerful underlying impetus for growth that is almost certain to reveal itself in any reasonably well-managed economy."[16]

Seawright suggests one of the interesting values of providing comprehensive financial planning when he says, "In my experience, individual investors have a great deal of trouble establishing appropriate, realistic and manageable goals. Often they don't even know what they should be concerned with or what they should include as part of a list outlining what they want or need to accomplish. A good advisor will."[17] Michael Kitces offers this valuable guidance:

> Creating a financial plan starts with gathering the client data, which many advisors request by providing clients with a "data gathering form," typically structured in a manner that makes it easy to input the data into their financial planning software.
>
> The caveat, however, is that in practice clients often don't fill out the data gathering form. For some, they feel it's too much work. For most, the problem is simply that they aren't organized enough to provide all the requisite information. And may even feel guilty or embar-

> rassed about the fact that they're "failing" in the very first step of the financial planning process. So what's the alternative? Ditch the data gathering meeting, and have a "Get Organized" meeting instead. In other words, make the first meeting with the client about getting them financially organized in the first place.[18]

Prospects and clients rarely have all the data they need for you to put together a comprehensive financial plan. They often do not have a good set of ideas on what their goals are, probably for both the medium and longer term. Two points of value are important here. Helping clients establish their goals is of significant value. Another value is that since goals and situations change constantly over time, the value of financial planning is in the continuous process of planning[19] rather than in the plan itself, which is *merely* a "point in time" picture that becomes more and more irrelevant over time. In fact, many plans become dusty reports that sit on shelves rarely if ever to be looked at again, whereas an annual or biannual process of planning is a living, breathing way of being and keeping financially sound and secure over the next year or two and beyond.

For a final point of value in financial planning, Seawright says:

> Another crucial thing a good financial planner can do is to help to protect aging clients from the impact of inevitable cognitive decline. Research confirms what most of us have seen among our families and friends. The ability to make effective financial decisions declines with age. Thus, those age 60 and older unnecessarily lose nearly $3 billion to fraud annually. To put it starkly, research shows that financial literacy declines by about 2 percent each year after age 60. Despite that decline, our self-confidence in our financial abilities remains undiminished (or even increases) as we age. That's a scary combination that a good advisor can guard against.
>
> Ultimately, a good advisor can and will influence and even change client behavior. In a world where personal financial issues have become increasingly and often unnecessarily complex, a good advisor can help clients figure out what is true and what isn't, what works, what matters, what is useful, and what can go wrong. There are few . . . people with the expertise sufficient to begin to do that for themselves. Nobody can do it objectively. That's why good advisors are an absolute necessity.

Seawright's thoughts on managing expectations and behavior include, "We are all prone to behavioral and cognitive biases that impede our progress and inhibit our success. We are prone to flitting hither and yon chasing after the next new thing, idea, strategy, or shiny object." He goes on to say, "A good advisor can mitigate these tendencies. Doing so is vital, not the least of all because we tend to disbelieve that we are susceptible to them." This is a particularly interesting point. "While most people do well at assessing others, they are wildly positive about their own abilities. ... For instance, in a classic 1977 study, 94 percent of professors rated themselves above average relative to their peers. In another study, 32 percent of the employees of a software company said they performed better than 19 out of 20 of their colleagues."[20] Another article said, "About 93 percent of people consider themselves 'above average' drivers."[21] These thoughts come from the principle of *illusory superiority*. "Illusory superiority is a cognitive bias that causes us to overestimate our positive qualities and underestimate our negative qualities. People tend to think their memories are better than they are, that they're more popular than they are, or that they're healthier than they really are."[22] This bias can extend to one's perception of their performance, intelligence, personality, etc.

Seawright comments:

> There is a clear "behavior gap" between the average investor (money-weighted) return and the average investment (time-weighted) return that shows up consistently in the data, albeit in varying amounts. Thus there is some debate over whether the size of this performance gap could be overstated in certain studies due to the return calculation methods used or the pattern of returns over the time period analyzed. But irrespective of the particulars, it remains clear that the behavior gap is significant and the result of self-destructive investor behavior—most prominently panicking during market downturns and performance chasing.

Once again, there is value in managing the expectations and behaviors of clients.

The next four points of the "Hierarchy of Advisor Value" relate to portfolios and portfolio construction. In his point on *asset allocation*, Seawright tells us significant research has shown that figures we have heard about the impact of asset allocation on portfolio returns are likely overstated. Nevertheless, he goes on to say that:

> Good asset allocation is crucial to matching one's portfolio with one's goals, needs, situations, and risk parameters, all of which are subject to change. The exercise of allocating funds among various investment vehicles and asset classes is at the heart of investment management. Asset classes exhibit different market dynamics, and different interaction effects. Thus the allocation of money among asset classes and among investment vehicles within asset classes will have an enormous effect on the performance of an investment portfolio. A good advisor is vital to good asset allocation.

Sometimes we take for granted those things that bring value to clients. Do not assume clients understand the critical nature of a personalized asset allocation strategy. In fact, it's best not to "assume" that your clients understand any of these values you bring to the table as their CFO or "money coach." Don't just look at company charts and tell your clients what the chart says. Take into account their spending and savings habits, sources of income, personal desires for a legacy, "real" risk tolerance, projected income and expense needs based on age, and perhaps several other factors. Be a "money coach," not only a financial advisor. Your client may rather write that book they always wanted to write than study things you have studied and learned over the last 10, 15, 20, or 25 years. There is apparently an old saying that "if you don't blow your own horn . . . somebody else is going to use it as a spittoon." By no means are we suggesting that you be a braggart or vain, but have pride in the importance of your work and, in a respectful way, let the client know about the value you deliver to them; that's what they are paying for.

There is a need to fully understand the client in depth through a highly effective discovery process we will describe later. The advisor can then more effectively discuss the rationale for recommendations in the context of the client and the efficient frontier, making sure the client knows and understands the potential impact on long-term portfolio performance with the recommended asset allocation. It is critical that the client understands and accepts the potential performance implications of an investment portfolio as a result of these recommendations. We want to set rational expectations, and one of the ways to do that is by also providing each client with a personalized *investment policy statement* that incorporates the client's personalized asset allocation strategy.

The advisor also needs to manage costs, fees, and incentives as best as possible. By this, Seawright points to the need for advisors to research funds looking for cost-effective funds (and exchange-traded funds, or ETFs) and even funds in which the manager is also invested. There is certainly value in managing costs and understanding where you sit in terms of competition, especially in a marketplace where many clients are fee-sensitive. Again, do not "assume" clients understand what you do to manage their costs.

Good advisors also continue to rebalance portfolios periodically as required throughout the year, keeping an eye on the client's investment policy statement and costs as a function of trading in non-fee-based accounts and any tax implications. It's important not to overlook any value you as an advisor provide, whether or not it is a differentiator. You do not get credit for what you deliver that the client doesn't necessarily know about. What does your competition take credit for?

Finally, with respect to value is *security selection*. Data makes it clear that it is not likely that any particular financial advisor will be in the group that consistently outperforms markets, indices, or benchmarks. Security selection has value because you are a knowledgeable, studied, educated professional who does this for a living and you do save client time and effort and, hopefully, add a level of comfort by providing this service. Yet the facts are that only a small percentage of professional investors have beaten the market consistently over the past ten years and index funds generally outperform actively managed funds, though active managers may have lower risk. It's a difficult case to sell security selection as a differentiator, which also means you are constantly on the hook to be right and you are discounting the value provided in the rest of your deliverables. Seawright does state that "stock-picking may be dead, but various studies demonstrate that certain investment characteristics can and do outperform with persistence over time (even though they can and do underperform for significant periods)." He also states "a good advisor will stay on top of . . . trends and make sure that client portfolios continue to comport with the best research as well as client needs, goals and situations." Many or even most investors prefer not to spend time developing the expertise and experience that financial advisors and wealth managers have already acquired. Reinventing the wheel makes no sense.

Seawright makes another excellent point, or shares an opinion, from Dr. David Baltimore, winner of the Nobel Prize in Physiology or Medicine in 1975 for his work on the genetic mechanisms of viruses, who noted that "good science is a collaborative, community effort; on the other hand, crackpots work alone." While this is not a comment you will share verbatim with "do-it-yourselfers," Baltimore's insights include that we all tend to work better with help, advice, support, correction, criticism, and accountability. These are additional parts of the value you bring to your clients. Even when we readily spot the problems of others, we rarely see our own because most people are wildly positive about their own abilities (remember "illusory superiority").

Wade Pfau, in his 2015 *Forbes* article, "The Value of Financial Advice," makes great sense when he writes:

> Can an advisor charging a one percent fee provide enough value to justify the fee? It depends on the answers to two questions:
>
> *a.* Do you have the time, energy, interest, knowledge, emotional discipline, and desire to implement all of these decisions on your own?
>
> *b.* Are you working with a comprehensive financial planner who does more than just manage investment portfolios and is capable of implementing good financial planning decisions?

If you have the time, interest, energy, knowledge, emotional discipline, and desire to do this on your own, then you would make an excellent advisor. If your advisor is less than capable, you might be better off saving yourself the 1 percent or taking your business elsewhere.

If the answer to (a) is no, and to (b) is yes, then it is worth considering that both of these studies [Vanguard's Advisor Alpha and Morningstar's Gamma] demonstrate how working with a financial advisor can lead to net gains. It doesn't take much to improve your standard of living through better decision making, even after accounting for any fee related to planning advice. [23]

In summary, at this point we suggest you consider the following questions:

- Which of the values discussed in these previous pages do you deliver to your clients?
- How does each of these values pertain to your clients, especially your best clients?
- When and how have you discussed your value statement with your clients?
- How was your value statement received by your clients?
- Have you asked your clients if they value those deliverables—that is, what are their perspectives? Do they believe, based on their experiences, your deliverables are unique?

It should be clear by now that you and your competitors can deliver great value to your clients. In fact, most advisors are capable of delivering a similar set of these values. The question then becomes, how can you be unique in the values you deliver?

Uniqueness embodies the question, "How am I different from other FAs doing what I do?" It says that something or someone is unlike anything or anyone else or very special or unusual. While there are differing estimates of the number of practicing financial advisors in the United States, a Reuters article says there are about 285,000 financial advisors.[24] The Bureau of Labor Statistics estimated the number of "personal financial advisors" in 2014 at 249,400 (and growing by 73,900 through 2024.) [25]

One can reasonably conclude that being totally unique (i.e., "unlike anything or anyone else") would be extremely unlikely. Yet there is always a possibility to be a Katie Ledecky or a Michael Phelps, although even they take a Silver or Bronze at times. Being "very special or unusual" is a great goal, but it's important to remember you are not competing against 285,000 other advisors. You have a niche or a geographic area that significantly limits the number of your direct competitors. Furthermore, you need only 100 or 150 clients at the right quality to be a successful advisor.

Key point three is to remember what has been called the Law of Fractional Advantage.[26] This law says that "all you need to do to win at anything is to be slightly better than your competition." Sam Silverstein, looking at 2008 data in the world of golf, noted that Tiger Woods's "scoring average . . . [was] 67.91." He went on to say that "the second rated golfer on the top scorer list, Mike Weir, had a scoring average of 68.56. As good as Tiger [was], and as dominant as he [was], the only difference between [Tiger] and the number two player on the scoring list is 65 hundredths of a point." As said, "a small advantage can make a large difference in results." [27]

Your job is to gain a sustainable edge (real or perceived) over your competition. Differentiation or uniqueness does not have to be in absolute terms but in performance relative to competitors. Kenichi Ohmae states, "If you are fighting with a competitor who has equal qualifications, effective and persistent execution in critical functional areas may be the only differentiating factor." [28]

The intent of this book is to describe how to create both value and differentiation that is better than your competition. Key point four is that if you provide effective and persistent execution in the critical functional areas to be discussed—the "six core client-facing processes"—we believe you will be differentiated. These six core processes are the:

1. Intake Process
2. Financial Planning Process
3. Risk Management Process
4. Investment Planning Process
5. Client Service Process
6. Planning and Review Process

These processes will be discussed in Chapters 3, 5, and 6 and can deliver your value. The value of your deliverables in aggregate from these six processes can provide differentiation.

What Is *Your* Differentiation?

The goal of differentiating yourself (and your team, virtual and real) is to answer that question and to make it obvious that you are the only advisor who can fulfill all your client's or prospect's wants, needs, dreams, hopes, and visions for a "perfect" financial future. This could be an overstatement of investors' expectations—but maybe it's their real hope.

Key point five suggests 16 elements or deliverables to which you can commit to define your differentiation. If you do them ALL and work hard, consistently, and if you implement and provide effective and persistent execution, you will be in excellent shape on value and differentiation.

1. *It's always about the prospects or clients.* Your first meeting with any prospect is all about the prospect. It's not about you, your company, or your investment approaches. It's all about learning about the prospects and what makes them tick. Get to know them personally and then professionally. As Katherine Vessenes says, "Identify the land mines in their current strategies. Most clients are completely unaware of the problems lurking in their finances before they come to us—and the devastating consequences of not taking action now to help protect their future." [29]

   Prospects make up their mind about you within the first seven seconds of meeting you and spend the rest of their time justifying their initial belief.[30] A series of experiments by Princeton psychologists found that "all it takes is a tenth of a second to form an impression of a stranger from their face, and longer exposures don't significantly alter those impressions."[31] Make sure your first second is your best second in how you and your office look, how you speak, how you greet, how you listen, and how prepared you are. Note that it's natural to be nervous before meeting someone for the first time. That's actually a good thing; it means the meeting is important to you—and it is. This process is detailed in Chapter 5, Your Intake Process.

2. *You offer service commitments.* Have a *written* service level agreement (SLA) or service promise with your clients (which we will detail in Chapter 3, The Client Loyalty Process). The purpose of the agreement is to ensure that the proper deliverables, commitments, and reminders are in place to provide consistent communications, service, support, and delivery to the client by the FA and her team. The agreement provides accountability and responsibilities of the team and presents a clear, concise, and measurable description of your service provisions to the client. The agreement provides the client and FA with matched perceptions of expected service with actual service support and delivery. Most clients don't know the extent of services you provide on their behalf. The SLA is a written reminder

and addresses all the elements a "wealth manager" delivers and offers to deliver including financial plans, estate plans, education plans, communications plans, charitable giving, and the 30 to 40 or more deliverables outlined in your service model or promise. The SLA is customized with or by each FA by client or tier. Service level agreements need to be approved by compliance.

This is the place where you define and discuss the values you deliver with your clients. This is the place you ask your clients if they value those deliverables and gather their perspectives. This and the next point are also your opportunity to manage expectations and behavior.

3. *Your service commitments are a two-way agreement.* The client knows exactly what to expect and can measure you on living up to the promises you make. This is a unique experience in many cases. This is about DWYSYAGTD—Do what you say you are going to do.

4. *You send summary letters.* After each portfolio review meeting, whether in person or by telephone, send a summary letter to the client. The letter should include:
   - A thank-you for being your client
   - Meeting summary, which would follow the agenda you used
   - Any follow-up responsibilities of both your team and the client
   - A summary of the service feedback you received and comments on what actions you are planning to take
   - When your next meeting will be

   There is a sample letter later in this book. In my experience most advisors do not deliver this "summary letter." If they do, it's often an email. I realize it may be old school, but physical letters are in themselves different. These letters also serve as the summary you would include in your client relationship management (CRM) system.

5. *You are a financial planning–based practice.* In addition to developing a plan with the client, you are holding them accountable to the plan for their actions (e.g., spending, saving, investing) to make sure they stay on track for their goals. We discussed this previously as a value and this process is further discussed in Chapter 3 on client loyalty. In many cases it is a differentiator if complete. Figure 1-4 is an ex-

Figure 1-4 | Sample set of deliverables for a financial plan.

Financial Planning					
Cash Flow & Financial Positions	**Protection Planning**	**Investment Planning**	**Tax Planning**	**Retirement Planning**	**Estate Planning**
Cash reserve level	Live insurance review	Review current accounts	Tax reduction strategies	Savings strategies	Transfer assets
Cash reserve strategies	Life insurance needs	Risk tolerance	Tax deferrals	401ks review	Asset/ Ownership titling
Income expenses management	Disability insurance review	Asset allocation proposed	Future taxes withholding	IRA review	Trusts
Discretionary income	Disability insurance needs	Diversification strategies	Tax diversification	Roth conversion	Wills
Net worth	Long-term care options	Education planning	Effects of liquidation	Social Security maximization analysis	Advanced directives
Expect large inflow/outflow	Property & casualty review/needs	Options/ Restricted Stock	Filing status	Medicare/ Medigap	Succession planning
Debt management	Beneficiary designations	Annuity review	Business ownership	Pre-591/2 strategies	Minor children
Buying real estate	Special needs situations	Tax management portfolio	Same-sex couples	Minimum distributions	Special needs dependents
Line of credit/ mortgage		Cost basis		Withdrawal strategies	Longevity planning
					Estate tax planning

ample of a set of deliverables of a financial plan from a planner client. Note that not all clients need all deliverables and some of these deliverables may be created and delivered by strategic Center of Influence (COI) relationships.

This is your opportunity to encourage consistent and increased savings, encourage consistent investment, and develop a financial plan that meets the complete wants and needs of your client.

6. *Your work ethic can be a differentiator.* One nationally recognized FA we interviewed summarized it this way:
   - You don't come into the office at 8:15 a.m. and leave at 4:15 p.m. every day except Friday when you take off.

- You don't send out portfolio management reports by email with a note saying "if you have any questions, call me."
- You care about your client's wealth more than your own and you care about who they and their family really are.

This speaks to availability, personalization, and integrity, which are all parts of differentiation. Regardless of what you offer as solutions that you think are different from your competitors, as stated you must work hard and execute well. It's how in part you gain a sustainable edge (real or perceived) over your competition.

7. *Your certifications are important—especially external ones from the College for Financial Planning and/or Investment Management Consultants Association.* It's good to be able to say you have the Certified Financial Planner (CFP) designation, which is a professional certification mark for financial planners conferred by the Certified Financial Planner Board of Standards. Consider other designations such as the CPWA, CIMA, and CDFA.

   In his article "Can Becoming a CFP Boost Income?" Michael Kitces says "it appears that obtaining the CFP marks is becoming a key step to climbing up the adviser ladder." He also quotes an Aite study[32] whose "authors also find that while CFP certification is associated with higher income, it's not simply because consumers seek to hire advisers with the CFP marks. Instead, the positive impact derives primarily from enhanced overall credibility, improved technical expertise and knowledge—which also leads to higher self-confidence—and greater client satisfaction with the adviser's more comprehensive financial planning acumen." [33] If you are not already a CFP, you are behind the approximately 25 percent of your competitors who have a CFP designation.

8. *You offer a customized, personalized portfolio.* You must have enough money management expertise to know the markets and prepare asset allocations that are not solely in context of corporate models but in context of individual clients, their wants, needs, temperament, risk tolerance, family, etc. Some FAs farm out all money management, and while that works for some it may not allow them to be as involved in customizing portfolios as some high net worth (HNW) and ultra-high net worth (UHNW) clients think they want and some FAs prefer. You need to know how to address that as well

while not growing an inordinate number of different investments or positions across your book. (This process is further discussed in Chapter 3.)

This value is where you deliver the second part of the Seawright model: asset allocation, manage costs and fees, rebalance portfolios, and select securities.

9. *You are a team of professionals (real and virtual) who all "know" the client.* Your team consists of investment specialists, business people who understand markets and solutions, and operations who service clients. The *team* has a sole focus on the client and brings the resources of many heads to each client's wants and needs. If two heads are better than one, perhaps tens or hundreds or thousands of heads are many, many times better than that. There is not only the wisdom of many, but the service and support and continuity of the many who work as a team.

   It would be a very positive addition to your team's understanding of your client to have a written biography of your clients and their spouses at least for your A book. These biographies can be developed from your knowledge, client interviews, client resumes, LinkedIn and Facebook and other online data, as well as photographs of the family. How natural would it be to interview clients and gather information about their families to get to know them better while seeking others in their family you may be able to help? Most people like to talk about themselves, and implementing such an approach will be easy to incorporate into discovery meetings or check-in calls. If for any reason you need to have your clients meet a specialist, or you want to brief new people or your manager on the client, it would be most helpful to them as well to get to "know" the client better.

10. *Your interests, facilities, knowledge, and discipline—and time—can be a differentiator.* According to William Bernstein, you need four faculties in order to invest competently:
    - An interest in investing
    - The horsepower to do the math
    - The knowledge base
    - The emotional discipline to execute faithfully [34] (i.e., take the emotion out of investing)

These in fact are your and your firm's or Broker/Dealer's (B/D's) faculties, whether or not you use robo tools. While robo-advisors have some of these characteristics, there is no substitute for human interaction. Single individuals cannot yet replicate all the required faculties and will not likely ever be a substitute for social contact.

11. *You have a consultative process.* Bernstein also said that success is dependent on:
    - Defining goals and executing and adhering to a long-term investment plan
    - An ability to properly allocate and diversify the client's assets
    - Developing an investment strategy and selecting appropriate investment managers
    - An ability to monitor and make adjustments as necessary

    These factors are similar to the values mentioned previously. They are part of your differentiation as you conduct your business using a consultative process, have a buy-and-sell discipline that takes the emotion out of the process, and continually manage your client's assets, interests, wants, and needs and communicate consistently and proactively with them. Ensure that your clients understand your consultative process.

    Use the "pencil selling" technique to make your point and when explaining any concept or approach, such as your consultative process. Take paper and pencil and sketch a diagram of the concept or idea you want to explain. Using your version of the wealth management consultative process, create it as an example in front of the client. Most firms have a diagram of that process, which you can find online; it typically includes steps for discover, diagnostics, plan development, plan review, commitment, follow up, etc. Your sketch will help the client focus on the concept much better than a PowerPoint slide or image that is often shown in a single view. Pencil selling creates interaction and illustrates your competence. Think of using this technique for showing charts like the efficient frontier or any other basic chart or graph where you'd like to get more client involvement than a presentation or brochure typically allows.

12. *You can explain what makes you you, and your firm your firm.* When everything else is the same, you can be the difference. This is quality advice. Let the client know who you are, your values and belief system and that of your firm. Put your views, values, and beliefs in context of their values and beliefs and their wants and needs. This is part of your value and your humanity. You know yourself, are proud of what you do and why and how you do it, and you care about yourself, your family, your firm, and mostly about your client—and that needs to come across. People ultimately choose to do business with people they like, know, and trust, and everyone likes someone who appreciates them.

13. *You have a giving approach to clients.* Look for opportunities to be giving and make sure you recognize them. Be cognizant of your clients' lives, the events in their lives, their occasions, and their need for help, and react to each and every situation.

14. *You are the lead, the quarterback, the CFO, the "money coach" in your clients' lives.* We liken that value to a health advisor. If you are in your 60s and beyond, you have probably encountered gastroenterologists, pulmonologists, dermatologists, podiatrists, cardiologists, ophthalmologists, proctologists, urologists, nephrologists, and internists, among other specialists. What would it be worth to have a health coordinator who understands each of these specialties and could coordinate the delivery of health services to you? Your primary care physician refers and helps but doesn't provide this depth of coordination, though concierge doctors may provide improved coordination.

    And that's what you can do, and where you can provide tremendous value and differentiation. As a financial services provider, you are the equivalent of a concierge provider by being a single source for investment advice, insurance, mortgage, banking, financial planning, estate planning, accounting and taxes, and other services. It's called "wealth management." We call it a "personal CFO." You may not actually execute all these services but you can coordinate them, understand them, and integrate them as the client's CFO, based on their needs. What is it worth to have a financial services coordinator who understands each of these areas and the language spoken by all of them? This is a service that today's robo-advisors do not provide but you can, at least for your best clients.

15. *You are a human expert.* What is it worth to give your client's peace of mind, constant vigil, and a deep knowledge of their financial being and humanity? Your clients want human contact because they seek collaboration, congruency, clarity, and communications. These are elements not provided by robo-advisors or discount brokers. At the end of the day, the reason they hire YOU is YOU—your humanity, the trust they have in you, and the comfort you provide especially when markets get sketchy. Your differentiation really comes from becoming an expert in human beings, human behaviors, human psychology, and human fears.

16. *You document your value.* Finally, and you can add to the list, implement what we call a CAPS letter—a Client Annual Progress Summary letter. Clients don't always remember what you delivered throughout the year to service them. It's differentiating to recap the value-based deliverables you provided to them throughout the last 12 months or "what I have done for you lately." For a sample letter, see Figure 1-5. A well-managed CRM system with a complete set of notes will be central to delivering this.

    Again, we prefer a physical letter rather than an email.

These 16 points are not about doing the right thing today; they are about doing the right thing every day, day after day, with consistency and constancy. It's not about which of the recommendations you will execute. You need to do them all. This is an AND situation, not an OR situation.

You now know "What you do" and "Who you do it for." You also have the 16 points of value—and any more you may want to add—to develop your differentiation plan and prepare a UVP and a statement of differentiation. The prospects and clients who appreciate the deliverables that you consistently provide will understand your value.

We know you have many clients. We know time and affordability are concerns. However, these things are mandatory for the clients you want to retain—your A clients and perhaps many of your B clients—as well as the family, friends, and colleagues of those clients who would like to become your clients. Dentists say you only have to floss the teeth you want to keep. It's the same with clients you want to keep and grow with. If your team is large enough and of the right design you can have

Figure 1-5 | Sample Client Annual Progress Summary (CAPS) letter.

Street Smart Research Group, LLC
Practice Optimization for FAs

Dear Dr. Smith,

I wanted to drop you a line to thank you for your business throughout the last year and provide a service summary.

As you know, our relationship is based on a broad range of wealth management services that go beyond buying and selling investments.

For example, in 20XX, we:

- Prepared an updated financial plan that showed. . .
- Discussed an education funding plan for your son, NAME, and daughter, NAME. . .
- Met by telephone XX times, including a minimum of a call a month to discuss status. We also chatted on a number of occasions to discuss specific actions that we thought were appropriate for your portfolio.
- We conducted X portfolio reviews via telephone to discuss the performance of your portfolio and make any needed changes to rebalance your asset allocation.
- We met on MONTH, DAY, to review your portfolio and performance, discuss your asset allocation in context of the current market conditions, validate our investment policy, discuss, and validate your goals, and detail our go forward plans.
- We vetted your entire portolio by revalidating the quality of the money managers in whom we have entrusted your assets. In fact, of the industry's X,XXX money managers, the firm pre-vets the entire group and we further vet individual managers by style to make appropriate investment recommendations to you for the coming quarter.
- Etc. re: Wealth management services such as meetings with estate attorneys, CPAs.
- Etc. re: Wealth management services, Alternative investments, Business valuation, Deferred compensation plans, Education planning, Employee stock-option plans, Equity/Fixed income research, Estate-planning assistance, Hedging, Diversifying concentrated postions, IRAs, Insurance and annuities and so on.
- Etc. re: Other investment planning and management
- Etc. re: Liability services
- Etc. re: Review and recommendations with regard to your company 401(k) plan

(See your Client Service Model and CRM notes to flesh out your deliverables.)

(Include a summary statement and an expression of looking forward to another year of clientship. You can also reinforce your desire for feedback.)

Sincerely yours,

multiple delivery models—that is, you can have more than one "Who you do it for" and "What you do" models with different pricing based on client wants and needs and services delivered. In Chapter 3, in the section "Your Client Loyalty or Client Service Process," we will discuss multiple service models.

Author and consultant Julie Littlechild[35] has said: "We need to ensure that our value is expressed in every corner of our business. Value (differentiation) is more than a statement; it's an experience."[36] She suggests you review your business to make sure what you say is not only compelling but that it completely illustrates your value. Make sure what you say is what clients and prospects hear and see, that is, DWYSYAGTD, Do what you say you are going to do.

Despite your high-value deliverables, there are investors who are highly fee-sensitive, who may not see the value of these deliverables, who may prefer to be self-directed and believe they can invest and service their own financial well-being without an advisor. These are "do-it-yourselfers." We don't mean to disregard these investors. Over time, with consistent, periodic contact, some of these prospects could conceivably have a change of heart or mind as their wealth and family grows and their available time decreases.

Some prospects and clients believe they can defy the Dalbar data, which says:

- In 2014, the average equity mutual fund investor underperformed the S&P 500 by a wide margin of 8.19 percent. The broader market return was more than double the average equity mutual fund investor's return (13.69 percent versus 5.50 percent).
- In 2014, the average fixed income mutual fund investor underperformed the Barclays Aggregate Bond Index by a margin of 4.81 percent. The broader bond market returned over five times that of the average fixed income mutual fund investor (5.97 percent versus 1.16 percent).[37]

Some of these people may be right, even in the face of Dalbar data that reports similar results for many years.[38] See Figure 1-6.

Averages are just averages. By definition, there are some individuals who will perform better than the average. However, and as previously

Figure 1-6 | Dalbar analysis of past returns.

	Investor Returns (1)						
	Equity Funds	**Asset Allocation Funds**	**Fixed Income Funds**	**Composite Funds Investor**	**Inflation**	**S&P 500**	**Barclays Aggregate Bond Index**
30-year	3.79	1.76	0.72	2.47	2.70	11.06	7.36
20-year	5.19	2.47	0.80	3.34	2.28	9.85	6.20
5-year	10.19	5.09	1.21	6.84	1.69	15.45	4.45
3-year	14.82	7.15	0.72	9.57	1.34	20.41	2.66
12-months	5.50	2.24	1.16	3.98	0.75	13.69	

(1) Note that returns are for the period ending 12/31/14.

Data from Dalbar 2015 quantitative analysis of investor behavior

Explanation of data used at http://www.bellmontsecurities.com.au/wp-content/uploads/2015/04/2015-DALBAR-QAIB-study.pdf (page 4)

mentioned, "while most people do well at assessing others, they are wildly positive about their own abilities."[39]

If what we have written is not what your prospects want, they are not your best prospects. Quoting Bernstein one more time, "No one in his right mind would walk into the cockpit of an airplane and try to fly it, or into an operating theater and open a belly. And yet they think nothing of managing their retirement assets. I've done all three, and I'm here to tell you that managing money is, in its most critical elements (the quota of emotional discipline and quantitative ability required) even more demanding than the first two."[40] While robo-advisors may have much of the quantitative ability required, they still can't talk you off the ledge.

Action Summary | Develop Your Differentiation Strategy

Your value and differentiation is a matter of becoming expert in five key areas:

1. Understand that a Unique Value Proposition has two distinct parts, value and uniqueness, and you must detail both parts.
2. Define the elements of your deliverables and their value.
3. Understand the Law of Fractional Advantage[41] and deliver on enough of those elements to make you unique.

4. Provide effective and persistent execution in the six core client-facing processes to be described.
5. Deliver the 16 elements that will, in aggregate, define your differentiation. This includes:
    - Being your client's CFO and focusing well beyond investments
    - Helping your clients understand money, including how to build their assets through their saving, their investing, truly comprehensive financial planning, and setting their expectations and behaviors
    - Providing your technical skills to properly and continuously allocating their assets, managing the costs of their investments, rebalancing their portfolios as needed, and selecting appropriate investments

Sample Unique Value Proposition

Our team, OWN Financial Advisors LLC (Owens, Wynn, and Nickel), brings over 65 years of experience to our mission of providing objective financial advice and wealth management services to affluent individuals, families, businesses, endowments, and foundations. Part of our differentiation comes from having created an open learning and sharing environment with our team of special professionals and our clients in order to benefit all whom we are privileged to serve. The wisdom, knowledge, and experience within all our partners and clients creates a unique brand of service to all.

At OWN, we use a highly client-centric planning approach, looking beyond the surface and taking a deep, personal interest in helping to improve the quality of life for all our clients and their families. Whether their focus is on wealth accumulation, preservation, or distribution, we combine extensive due diligence and portfolio management experience to develop financial strategies and portfolios that address each client's special and unique circumstances.

Ongoing and honest communication is the hallmark of our approach. Clients deeply value our candor and willingness to be practical and direct, providing the necessary advice over the convenient message. It's this same forthright approach that makes us adept at working in tandem with our clients' other advisors, such as attorneys, accountants, and insurance representatives, so we can coordinate their wealth and estate management strategies whenever appropriate.

OWN Financial Advisors offers:

- A small boutique within a major financial institution. The team combines the true intimacy and personal attention of a boutique with the resources of a major financial services firm.
- Our word is our bond, which we will prove over a short period of time so we can demonstrate our proactive service and contact plan and the skills and experience we bring to the protection of your assets and the reaching of your goals.
- A team with multiple specialized skills and professional designations to deliver high-value services to clients with proven trust and integrity. Our work ethic, passion for the business, and desire to help clients is what drives these self-made successful professionals to always want to give more to their clients. These professionals know what it takes to be successful in everything they do for every client.
- Personalized strategic solutions, which we developed to address the complex needs of successful individuals. These solutions include discretionary portfolio management: stock option analysis, retirement and estate planning, hedging and monetization of concentrated equity positions, life insurance, and wealth preservation and transfer strategies.
- A team that meets regularly with clients wherever it's convenient for face-to-face meetings. Our family orientation allows us to take a proactive and personal interest in the well-being of each client and their families. At the heart of our philosophy is our passion to build honest and enduring client relationships by consistently providing objective and insightful guidance as well as outstanding service. As a result of our efforts and holistic family approach, much of our work leads to "multigenerational" client relationships.
- Services for business owners, for-profit and nonprofit, to provide strategies for cash management, short- and long-term financing, as well as retirement plans.

- "Follow through" and client satisfaction, which are of primary importance. We are sharply attuned to new situations and changing market conditions; our passion to be proactive is a key ingredient in our approach.
- Successful track records with over 65 years of successful experience.
- Strategies designed to help you reach your unique goals.
- An understanding that you are extremely busy, with too much work to do and not enough time to do it.
- An understanding that the process we will use together has to be understandable, focusing on areas in which you need help to make your life easier, better, and more enjoyable and rewarding.
- Personal service to help you through a rigorous process focused on what you need and on which you want to focus.

How Will Working with OWN Benefit You? What Value Do We Bring to the Table and How Will It Improve Your Life?

With our team you will:

1. Set far better goals that motivate you in a healthy way.
2. Accomplish goals more quickly if you stay on track.
3. Make fewer mistakes.
4. Move up to the next level of your financial life.
5. Reduce the number of problems you deal with and better resolve the problems that are left.
6. Be a lot happier—and that happiness will last.
7. Be much more effective in having time for your family, business, and personal relationships.
8. Have a better life, not just a better lifestyle.
9. Receive unlimited support to prevent you from reverting to old, unwanted habits and behaviors.

10. Master the secrets of the most successful people in the world.
11. Have an experienced professional to hold you accountable for the action steps necessary to get results.
12. Get help determining which action steps to take.
13. Identify the unconscious fears and negative beliefs about money that may be holding you back.
14. Clarify what you want in your life.
15. Get the results you want, with the help of a personal team of advisors who are all about you and helping you get those results.

Chapter Two

Formal Book Segmentation

Segmenting is the crucial first step in the strategic marketing process. All customers are not the same. . . .

—Joanne Scheff Bernstein

This chapter outlines how you can conduct a detailed assessment of your book and your clients so that you will know who contributes to your profitability and who does not and what strategies you can implement to improve that profitability. We describe exactly how to formally segment your book, analyze the results, and develop a structured client contact plan.

Why Analyze Your Book of Business?

Businesses do not grow by happenstance. You need a plan to grow it. However, before that growth plan can be put in place, you *must* understand your current book of business in detail. Most financial advisors know their top clients and those clients' assets under management, but many have not formally evaluated other factors that detail the value of those clients. Advisors need to answer these questions:

- Which clients require/deserve the most retention efforts?
- Which clients provide growth opportunities for assets under management (AUM), trailing 12-months revenue (T12), and return on assets (ROA)?

- Which clients may be candidates to be transformed or transferred to increase their value or reduce their costs to the business?
- Where should you focus introduction/referral efforts?
- Where should you focus marketing efforts?
- What specific communications protocols should be followed?
- What do you really know about your top clients?

You believe you know who your A clients are, your B clients, your C clients, and the rest. You may have segmented your book at some point, so you know who you need to pay the most attention to and who to deliver your best services to. You may have segmented your book by AUM or production or both. You may or may not have considered various subjective factors in your segmentation process.

This chapter explains a method to segment your clients that has worked for thousands of financial advisors and should work well for you, too. While the process is modifiable, we have not found that necessary to do in the vast majority of cases. Using a customized Microsoft Excel spreadsheet, readers will be able to prepare and evaluate their client base by the client's assets, revenues, and subjective "value characteristics." An initial assessment will define:

- The 20 percent of your book that is responsible for 80 percent of your assets
- The 20 percent of your book that delivers 80 percent of your trailing 12-months revenue
- The distribution of clients by value to the business
- The service levels that should be applied to each client tier
- The communications plan that should be applied to each client tier

We will then develop a sample book assessment and discuss the results. We will examine the rating criteria for the example and the options for what can be done with and for the top 20 percent of your book. You will understand the options for the "underperforming" 80 percent of your clients that contribute only 20 percent of your revenues.

The Value of Determining Your 80/20

The Pareto principle, also known as the 80/20 rule, states that approximately 80 percent of effects come from 20 percent of the causes.

While it is a common rule of thumb in business (e.g., "80 percent of your sales come from 20 percent of your clients"), I have rarely seen the 80/20 come out exactly that way. The point is that a small percentage of your clients account for a large percentage of your assets under management and/or a large percentage of your production. Similarly, a small percentage of your clients likely account for a large percentage of your problems. You know exactly who they are because when their name comes up on your caller ID, you cringe and ask your associate to please take the call or you simply get busy.

We are going to present an example where you will see that 20 percent of clients represent about 63 percent of assets and 65 percent of production. In the same example you will see that about 45 percent of clients represent about 89 percent of assets and 92 percent of production. To state this another way, the advisor in our example could "fire" 55 percent of her clients and production would drop only 8 percent. One of the other conclusions we will draw from this analysis is that those "extra" 25 percent of clients (45 percent versus 20 percent) are very important to the advisor's financial well-being because they represent 27 percent of her income. They are, however, obviously not as important as the 65 percent of her production. What does this mean?

It means that it is critically important to match your services to your clients' needs and their value to your business in order to continue to retain and develop your most profitable relationships and to replicate those relationships through introductions/referrals, while also providing enough value to retain the other 25 percent of your clients that represent 27 percent of your income. Pictorially this is shown in Figure 2-1.

While it might be "nice" to deliver the same high-quality services to all clients, time is your most precious and limited commodity and must be distributed rationally based on the needs of your clients, the firm, yourself, and the reality of the limits of time and other resources. (More on this later.) It is also important to recognize that clients with more limited assets likely have more limited needs and/or can be serviced by personnel with less experience and perhaps more time than the team leader.

Figure 2-1 | The higher the value of the client, the more value you must provide to retain that client.

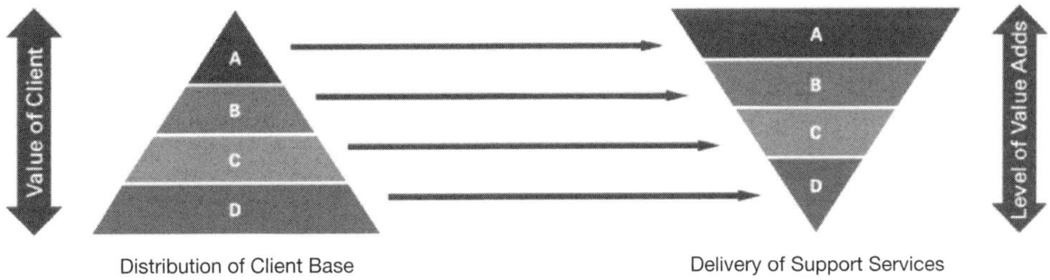

We will deliver support services to our clients in inverse proportion to the value of those clients to the business as well as considering their needs.

How Segmentation Is Done

Figure 2-2 shows the data the spreadsheet requires to calculate a proposed client tier. The spreadsheet is similar to that used by others and has evolved over time. Some of our colleagues use a similar sheet, though we have made modifications over the years of using this tool. Let's look at each part of the sheet and discuss its use.

Figure 2-2 | Sample client segmentation worksheet data.

CLIENT SEGMENTATION WORKSHEET																	
				Segmentation Criteria							Profitability Indicators				Service Matrix		
Proposed Tier	Current Tier	Seq. Number	Client Name	TOTAL SCORE	Assset Score	Revenue Score	Enjoys Rel.	Takes Advice	Referral Source	Potential	Assets	Revenue	ROA		Client Reviews	Check-In Calls	Lead FA
System Calc.	FA Defined	Seq.	From Firm Data	System Calc.	System Calc.	System Calc.	Yes = 1 No = 0	Yes = 1 No = 0	Yes = 1 No = 0	Yes = 1 No = 0	From Firm Data	From Firm Data	System Calc.		System Calc.	System Calc.	FA Defined
C	1			6	1	1	1	1	1	1			#DIV/0!		1	3	
C	2			6	1	1	1	1	1	1			#DIV/0!		1	3	
C	3			6	1	1	1	1	1	1			#DIV/0!		1	3	
C	4			6	1	1	1	1	1	1			#DIV/0!		1	3	
C	5			6	1	1	1	1	1	1			#DIV/0!		1	3	

There are three types of data used to calculate tiers and segment the book of business. Let's get into more depth on each data type:

1. System Data:
   a. Household name
   b. Assets under management (AUM)
   c. Trailing 12-months revenue (T12)
2. Subjective Data:
   a. The quality of the relationship between the financial advisor (FA) and client
   b. Whether or not the client listens to the FA's advice

   c. Whether the client is capable of introducing the FA to potential clients

   d. The client's potential to maintain or grow their value to the business

3. Spreadsheet Calculated Data:

   a. The tier the "system" proposes

   b. AUM score

   c. T12 Score

   d. Return on assets (ROA)

   e. Recommended contact frequency

Step 1 in the Segmentation Process

The initial data comes from the firm that stores that data in a central repository and consists of only three mandatory elements. These data are normally downloaded in a format that can be copied and pasted into the worksheet. See Figure 2-3.

Figure 2-3 | Initial data inputs.

CLIENT SEGMENTATION WORKSHEET																
				Segmentation Criteria							Profitability Indicators			Service Matrix		
Proposed Tier	Current Tier	Seq. Number	Client Name	TOTAL SCORE	Assset Score	Revenue Score	Enjoys Rel.	Takes Advice	Referral Source	Potential	Assets	Revenue	ROA	Client Reviews	Check-In Calls	Lead FA
System Calc.	FA Defined	Seq.	From Firm Data	System Calc.	System Calc.	System Calc.	Yes = 1 No = 0	Yes = 1 No = 0	Yes = 1 No = 0	Yes = 1 No = 0	From Firm Data	From Firm Data	System Calc.	System Calc.	System Calc.	FA Defined
C	1			6	1	1	1	1	1	1				#DIV/0!	1	3
C				6	1	1	1	1	1	1				#DIV/0!	1	3
C				6	1	1	1	1	1	1				#DIV/0!	1	3
C				6	1	1	1	1	1	1				#DIV/0!	1	3
C				6	1	1	1	1	1	1				#DIV/0!	1	3

- *Household name.* It is important to use "households," not accounts, because we want to treat households based on their total value to your business. Households are defined in the standard manner of common address and Social Security number.

  Households can also be thought of as "marketing units." We define marketing units as those people we have to market to or sell to and satisfy with our service levels. For example, if each spouse in the household has his or her own assets and makes his or her own decisions, they need to be addressed as separate marketing units, even if they are technically in the same household. If there are adult children either living in their parents' home or in their own domicile, we need to treat them as separate marketing units. If parents of a client are also clients but the adult children make all their parents' portfolio decisions, this is one marketing unit, even though they are technically different households.

At the same time we service individual "marketing units," it's also important to recognize the aggregate value of the household, which may include any number of marketing units. If any single marketing unit becomes dissatisfied for any reason, it may affect the satisfaction and relationship of one or more or all marketing units in the broader household. Therefore we treat households in two manners: by "marketing unit" and by "total logical household."

- *Assets under management (AUM).* As indicated, these are the assets under your management only. Total AUM, including assets not actively managed by you or your financial business but held elsewhere, that is, "assets away," may affect the tier but are not part of this phase of the analysis.
- *Trailing 12-months revenue (T12)* or other measure of the amount of income or production the client has generated to you and the firm, as opposed to the net revenue or gross paid to you, the advisor. Some advisors have used averages of the past 24 or 36 months, but that's not necessary because the tier the system assigns based on this data is essentially an estimate and the process provides for advisor input later in the tier determination process. We prefer using current data rather than historical data because it is likely more relevant to estimates or projections for the future.

  Note that T12 may include one-time revenue or revenue that may be "over reported"—for example, one-time revenue may include initial annuity revenue, or revenue from a new client whose portfolio is transitioned from current to new holdings. Revenue can be "under reported" when there is a new fee-based client and only a subset of her/his revenue is recorded up to the point when you are conducting the segmentation. There are two ways anomalies can be handled. One way is to estimate the annual anticipated revenue. We do not recommend this approach but would rather keep the data in concert with the system data at this point in time. Keep the raw data sheet as-is. During the last stage of the segmentation process the advisor can include her or his input in the final tier determination.

There is a potential fourth piece of data you can see on the spreadsheet in Figure 2-3 indicated by the left-most arrow. If the advisor has defined the client's tier in a previous segmentation, this can be indicated in the Current Tier column shown. We'll see how that tier compares to a system-calculated tier. It's another piece of guidance to consider.

Step 2 in the Segmentation Process

Step 2 asks you to consider four subjective factors in your client relationship (see Figure 2-4):

Figure 2-4 | Four subjective factors.

CLIENT SEGMENTATION WORKSHEET																
				Segmentation Criteria							Profitability Indicators			Service Matrix		
Proposed Tier	Current Tier	Seq. Number	Client Name	TOTAL SCORE	Assset Score	Revenue Score	Enjoys Rel.	Takes Advice	Referral Source	Potential	Assets	Revenue	ROA	Client Reviews	Check-In Calls	Lead FA
System Calc.	FA Defined	Seq.	From Firm Data	System Calc.	System Calc.	System Calc.	Yes = 1 No = 0	Yes = 1 No = 0	Yes = 1 No = 0	Yes = 1 No = 0	From Firm Data	From Firm Data	System Calc.	System Calc.	System Calc.	FA Defined
C	1			6	1	1	1	1	1	1			#DIV/0!	1	3	
C	2			6	1	1							#DIV/0!	1	3	
C	3			6	1								#DIV/0!	1	3	
C	4			6	1	1							#DIV/0!	1	3	
C	5			6	1	1							#DIV/0!	1	3	

1. Do you enjoy working with this client?
2. Does the client trust (and follow) your advice?
3. Does or can the client introduce you to quality prospects?
4. Will the client's revenue be maintained or grow?

For this subjective data we suggest a binary choice—either the client is or is not enjoyable to work with. Code the cell with a 1 for YES or a 0 for NO. Some approaches and some advisors attempt to get more finite in their coding. We recommend against that for several reasons:

- It makes the process more complex and granular than needed. We are only trying to segment clients into four tiers—A, B, C, or D—for purposes of applying a Client Service Model. Coding more finitely will not generate any additional useful information for segmentation.
- It takes too much time trying to distinguish between a 1 and a 2, a 2 and a 3, etc., in terms of enjoyableness or trust. Every advisor will

likely make different choices and later on may not remember why a particular choice was made at the time it was made. We suggest spending no more than 30 seconds per client to make all four subjective decisions.

- If you use a scale of more than 0 and 1, these four subjective criteria take on more weight or importance than either of the two objective criteria (i.e., assets and revenue).
- In the end there is an opportunity to change the system-developed tier considering what the FA knows or believes.

Do not overthink these four subjective criteria at this point.

If you are happy to hear from a client, they are a 1. If you cringe when they are on the phone it's a 0. If the client takes your advice most of the time they are a 1, because your advice is what they are willing to pay you for. If the client rejects your advice a great deal of the time the trust they are placing in you is questionable, so that's a 0. This particular client may be a problem client if they consistently tend not to follow your advice. At this point they are perhaps questioning your value to them, and you need to dig into the reasons.

As far as whether a client has referred others to you, you have a rating choice. If the client has introduced you to other prospects, they are a 1. If the client has not introduced you, it may be because you haven't asked or may not have asked the "right" way, or you may need to do more to provide value the client appreciates. If you believe this client knows referable investors and you would like to get introductions/referrals, we suggest coding this client a 1. If you have asked the client in any manner and the client has specifically said they do not or will not introduce you, even after you have had a rational discussion about their decision, code this a 0. By "rational discussion" we mean that if the client rejects your request, it is appropriate to ask why the client is against introducing or referring you. Perhaps the client had a bad experience or believes that confidentiality was not adhered to, or it just may be that the client is uncomfortable for any number of reasons. It pays to explore the concern and attempt to overcome it if your relationship is excellent and you have reason to believe an introduction might be important. This is a situational analysis.

Finally, in considering whether the client has significant future potential, if the client provides what you would consider good revenue and that revenue stream will likely stay the same or close to the same or increase next year, code this client a 1. If the client is providing good revenue but you expect that revenue stream will likely drop significantly next year (e.g., they are buying a vacation home with a significant portion of their assets), code this person a 0. If the client is providing low revenue and you expect that revenue stream will likely increase next year, code this person a 1. If the client is providing low revenue and you expect that revenue stream will likely continue to be low, code the client a 0.

Step 3 in the Segmentation Process

This step requires you to review the segmentation calculations approach used in the spreadsheet. Let's look at how the spreadsheet calculates asset score.

Figure 2-5 | Asset score.

CLIENT SEGMENTATION WORKSHEET

				Segmentation Criteria							Profitability Indicators			Service Matrix		
Proposed Tier	Current Tier	Seq. Number	Client Name	TOTAL SCORE	Assset Score	Revenue Score	Enjoys Rel.	Takes Advice	Referral Source	Potential	Assets	Revenue	ROA	Client Reviews	Check-In Calls	Lead FA
System Calc.	FA Defined	Seq.	From Firm Data	System Calc.	System Calc.	System Calc.	Yes = 1 No = 0	Yes = 1 No = 0	Yes = 1 No = 0	Yes = 1 No = 0	From Firm Data	From Firm Data	System Calc.	System Calc.	System Calc.	FA Defined
C	1			6	1	1	1	1	1	1			#DIV/0!	1	3	
C	2			6		1	1	1	1	1			#DIV/0!	1	3	
C	3			6		1	1	1	1	1			#DIV/0!	1	3	
C	4			6		1	1	1	1	1			#DIV/0!	1	3	
C	5			6		1	1	1	1	1			#DIV/0!	1	3	

Asset Score	
$ -	1
$ 250,000	2
$ 500,000	3
$ 1,000,000	4

Here's how the spreadsheet scores assets (see Figure 2-5). The client gets:

4 points if assets are $1,000,000 or more

3 points if assets are between $500,000 and $999,999

2 points if assets are between $250,000 and $499,999

1 point if assets are less than $250,000

Calculating Revenue Score

Revenue is scored in a similar manner (see Figure 2-6). The client gets:

Figure 2-6 | Revenue score.

CLIENT SEGMENTATION WORKSHEET																
				Segmentation Criteria							Profitability Indicators			Service Matrix		
Proposed Tier	Current Tier	Seq. Number	Client Name	TOTAL SCORE	Assset Score	Revenue Score	Enjoys Rel.	Takes Advice	Referral Source	Potential	Assets	Revenue	ROA	Client Reviews	Check-In Calls	Lead FA
System Calc.	FA Defined	Seq.	From Firm Data	System Calc.	System Calc.	System Calc.	Yes = 1 No = 0	Yes = 1 No = 0	Yes = 1 No = 0	Yes = 1 No = 0	From Firm Data	From Firm Data	System Calc.	System Calc.	System Calc.	FA Defined
C	1			6	1	1	1	1	1	1			#DIV/0!	1	3	
C	2			6	1		1	1	1	1			#DIV/0!	1	3	
C	3			6	1		1	1	1	1			#DIV/0!	1	3	
C	4			6	1		1	1	1	1			#DIV/0!	1	3	
C	5			6	1		1	1	1	1			#DIV/0!	1	3	

Revenue Score		
$	-	1
$	2,500	2
$	5,000	3
$	10,000	4

4 points if revenue (T12) is $10,000 or more

3 points if revenue is between $5,000 and $9,999

2 points if revenue is between $2,500 and $4,999

1 point if revenue is less than $2,500

Calculating Proposed Client Tier

The spreadsheet will calculate the client tier based on the number of total points when adding Asset Score + Revenue Score + 1 point each for "FA enjoys relationship," "client takes FA's advice," "client willing to introduce prospects," and "client has potential." See Figure 2-7.

The number of points a client can score is from 2 to 12, and clients are then segmented into "proposed" tiers, which the advisor can then upgrade or downgrade (which comes later, in Step 4 in the Segmentation Process).

If the Total Score is:

10 or more points, proposed tier is A

9 points, proposed tier is B

6 to 8 points, proposed tier is C

Less than 6 points, proposed tier is D

Return on Assets

Return on assets (ROA) is a simple calculation the spreadsheet provides by dividing revenue (T12) by assets under management (AUM). This

Figure 2-7 | Client tier score.

CLIENT SEGMENTATION WORKSHEET																
				Segmentation Criteria							Profitability Indicators			Service Matrix		
Proposed Tier	Current Tier	Seq. Number	Client Name	TOTAL SCORE	Assset Score	Revenue Score	Enjoys Rel.	Takes Advice	Referral Source	Potential	Assets	Revenue	ROA	Client Reviews	Check-In Calls	Lead FA
System Calc.	FA Defined	Seq.	From Firm Data	System Calc.	System Calc.	System Calc.	Yes = 1 No = 0	Yes = 1 No = 0	Yes = 1 No = 0	Yes = 1 No = 0	From Firm Data	From Firm Data	System Calc.	System Calc.	System Calc.	FA Defined
C	1			6	1	1	1	1	1	1			#DIV/0!	1	3	
	2			6	1	1	1	1	1	1			#DIV/0!	1	3	
	3			6	1	1	1	1	1	1			#DIV/0!	1	3	
	4			6	1	1	1	1	1	1			#DIV/0!	1	3	
	5			6	1	1	1	1	1	1			#DIV/0!	1	3	

Points	Segment
3	D
5	C
9	B
10	A

is another "profitability indicator" because it determines (and is determined by) the revenue as a function of assets. The higher the ROA the more revenue there is as a percent of assets. ROA is also known as *basis points* or *beeps* (financial industry jargon for basis points) or *velocity* in some cases. Advisors need to be competitive with their fees and on average generally charge between 100 and 150 basis points on their fee-based accounts. Remember that if ROA is too high, in addition to not being competitively priced, it may be an indication of overcharging or overtrading in a non-fee-based account. This can be of concern when it comes to compliance, as well as the client. See Figure 2-8.

Figure 2-8 | Return on assets.

CLIENT SEGMENTATION WORKSHEET																
				Segmentation Criteria							Profitability Indicators			Service Matrix		
Proposed Tier	Current Tier	Seq. Number	Client Name	TOTAL SCORE	Assset Score	Revenue Score	Enjoys Rel.	Takes Advice	Referral Source	Potential	Assets	Revenue	ROA	Client Reviews	Check-In Calls	Lead FA
System Calc.	FA Defined	Seq.	From Firm Data	System Calc.	System Calc.	System Calc.	Yes = 1 No = 0	Yes = 1 No = 0	Yes = 1 No = 0	Yes = 1 No = 0	From Firm Data	From Firm Data	System Calc.	System Calc.	System Calc.	FA Defined
C	1			6	1	1	1	1	1	1			#DIV/0!	1	3	
C	2			6	1	1	1	1	1	1				1	3	
C	3			6	1	1	1	1	1	1				1	3	
C	4			6	1	1	1	1	1	1				1	3	
C	5			6	1	1	1	1	1	1				1	3	

(Note that we won't get into pricing policies as pricing is also a function of the client, the financial advisor's range of deliverables, firm policy, the type of firm, type of securities within the portfolio, type of account, and frequency of trading in certain account types, etc.)

However, one article has noted that (for full-service advisors) "most clients with more than $100,000 pay less than 1.25 percent of assets per year in account management fees, according to Cerulli Associates. But fees vary widely, exceeding 2 percent for some less-affluent investors.

Of those with just $100,000 in assets, a quarter pay more than 1.5 percent per year."[1] Furthermore, "of clients with more than $10 million in assets, Cerulli Associates estimates, two thirds pay less than 0.75 percent per year." [2]

From what we have seen, most books of business of full-service FAs have ROAs between 65 and 90 basis points, given their mix of clients, the length of time the client has been a client, and the types of securities in the portfolio.

In a 2012 white paper by Pusateri Consulting, entitled "Pricing Your Value Unapologetically,"[3] the charts indicate that in "typical fee accounts" of $250,000 to $500,000 in assets, balanced accounts only, the average fee-based ROA ranges from 81 basis points to 208 basis points, with an average of 127 basis points. They also report that in a "typical high-net worth account" of $5 million to $7.5 million in assets, balanced accounts only, the advisor average fee-based ROA ranges from 48 basis points to 142 basis points, with an average of 94 basis points. The data Pusateri cites is from PriceMetrix 2012.

Contacts

Our contact recommendation is based on the "Supernova" model and the Total Score (see the previous section on Calculating Proposed Client Tier). This contact model has been around for quite a while and was originally created at Merrill Lynch. The model relates to person-to-person interactions, whether by telephone or in-person contact. In general, emails do not substitute for personal or voice contact, though there are exceptions. See Figure 2-9.

Figure 2-9 | Contacts.

CLIENT SEGMENTATION WORKSHEET				Segmentation Criteria							Profitability Indicators			Service Matrix		
Proposed Tier	Current Tier	Seq. Number	Client Name	TOTAL SCORE	Assset Score	Revenue Score	Enjoys Rel.	Takes Advice	Referral Source	Potential	Assets	Revenue	ROA	Client Reviews	Check-In Calls	Lead FA
System Calc.	FA Defined	Seq.	From Firm Data	System Calc.	System Calc.	System Calc.	Yes = 1 No = 0	Yes = 1 No = 0	Yes = 1 No = 0	Yes = 1 No = 0	From Firm Data	From Firm Data	System Calc.	System Calc.	System Calc.	FA Defined
C	1			6	1	1	1	1	1	1			#DIV/0!	1	3	
C	2			6	1	1	1	1	1	1			#DIV/0!	1	3	
C	3			6	1	1	1	1	1	1			#DIV/0!	1		
C	4			6	1	1	1	1	1	1			#DIV/0!	1	3	
C	5			6	1	1	1	1	1	1			#DIV/0!	1	3	

The Supernova model calls for a standard contact plan by tier:

- A Tier Client Contact is a "12-4-2" plan. This means in monthly contact (12), 4 contacts are portfolio reviews of some length and 2 of those 4 contacts are recommended to be in person. We will discuss service time commitments later, but for now, we estimate or allocate an approximately 11- to 12-hour commitment for these proactive annual contacts, sans travel.
- B Tier Client Contact is a "6-2-1" plan. This means semi-monthly contact (6) in which 2 contacts are portfolio reviews of some length and at least 1 of those contacts is recommended to be in person. We estimate or allocate an approximately six-hour commitment for these proactive annual contacts, sans travel.
- C Tier Client Contact is a "4-1-1" plan. This means quarterly contact (4) in which 1 contact is a portfolio review that can be by telephone or in person, depending on the client, their value, and their geography. Relationships are generally built and grown through in-person contact rather than solely by telephone contact. Time availability and your business will help determine your decision. If you travel, C client proximity to other clients is a factor in determining if or whether to make in-person visits. If you want to keep and grow C clients, in-person meetings at least once every two years should be considered. We estimate or allocate an approximately three-hour commitment for these proactive annual contacts, sans travel.
- D Tier Client Contact calls for a "0-0-1 or 0-0-2" plan. This means annual or semi-annual contact all by telephone. This is purely a time availability and client value decision. D clients are often "courtesy clients"—that is, you service them out of courtesy perhaps because they became your clients early in the development of your practice, they may be relatives with few assets, or they may be people who have been with you a long time and have drawn down their assets significantly. We understand the compassion you may have for these clients, so it may be a difficult decision. Solely from a value perspective you probably don't have the resources to spend time with these clients unless they are related to A or B clients. Considering their needs you may want to offload many of these clients to a service unit or a new FA. You can also ask your client or sales assistant to make these contacts. If you choose to retain these clients, we estimate or allocate approximately a half hour to one-hour time commitment for these proactive contacts. There are advisors who

allocate perhaps 5 percent of their books and time to pro bono cases like these.

Figure 2-10 | "Supernova" annual contact plan.

Segment	Reviews	Check-Ins	Total Contacts
A	4	8	**12**
B	2	4	**6**
C	1	3	**4**
D	0	1 - 2	**1 - 2**

Travel time is not considered in these estimates. We will discuss the content of these meetings later on. See Figure 2-10.

The system-calculated tier will be posted to the spreadsheet automatically. See Figure 2-11.

Figure 2-11 | System-defined code.

CLIENT SEGMENTATION WORKSHEET																
				Segmentation Criteria							Profitability Indicators			Service Matrix		
Proposed Tier	Current Tier	Seq. Number	Client Name	TOTAL SCORE	Assset Score	Revenue Score	Enjoys Rel.	Takes Advice	Referral Source	Potential	Assets	Revenue	ROA	Client Reviews	Check-In Calls	Lead FA
System Calc.	FA Defined	Seq.	From Firm Data	System Calc.	System Calc.	System Calc.	Yes = 1 No = 0	Yes = 1 No = 0	Yes = 1 No = 0	Yes = 1 No = 0	From Firm Data	From Firm Data	System Calc.	System Calc.	System Calc.	FA Defined
C	1			6	1	1	1	1	1	1			#DIV/0!	1	3	
	2			6	1	1	1	1	1	1			#DIV/0!	1	3	
	3			6	1	1	1	1	1	1			#DIV/0!	1	3	
	4			6	1	1	1	1	1	1			#DIV/0!	1	3	
	5			6	1	1	1	1	1	1			#DIV/0!	1	3	

Step 4 in the Segmentation Process

In this step the advisor will use her/his personal knowledge of the client to "promote" or "demote" each of them. See Figure 2-12.

Figure 2-12 | FA-defined code.

CLIENT SEGMENTATION WORKSHEET																
				Segmentation Criteria							Profitability Indicators			Service Matrix		
Proposed Tier	Current Tier	Seq. Number	Client Name	TOTAL SCORE	Assset Score	Revenue Score	Enjoys Rel.	Takes Advice	Referral Source	Potential	Assets	Revenue	ROA	Client Reviews	Check-In Calls	Lead FA
System Calc.	FA Defined	Seq.	From Firm Data	System Calc.	System Calc.	System Calc.	Yes = 1 No = 0	Yes = 1 No = 0	Yes = 1 No = 0	Yes = 1 No = 0	From Firm Data	From Firm Data	System Calc.	System Calc.	System Calc.	FA Defined
C	1			6	1	1	1	1	1	1			#DIV/0!	1	3	
C				6	1	1	1	1	1	1			#DIV/0!	1	3	
C				6	1	1	1	1	1	1			#DIV/0!	1	3	
C				6	1	1	1	1	1	1			#DIV/0!	1	3	
C				6	1	1	1	1	1	1			#DIV/0!	1	3	

Having worked with hundreds of FAs, we understand that there are so many more things they know about their clients than can be found in the pure numbers. One of the things that you as a financial advisor need to do is *treat clients in the tier in which you want them to be.* In a job, it's common to expect employees to show that they are capable of performing at the next level up. When you have clients that you believe are capable of moving to the next level up, it's important to show them that belief by servicing them at that level before they reach it.

Consider "promoting" clients to the next tier up (or more) if:

- They are related to key clients, whether family or friends. It can be touchy if you treat one client with A-level service and a related client with C- or even D-level service. We usually suggest increasing service levels by only one level, in part because lower-level clients probably don't need as much service as an A-level client. You may have to have a discussion with your higher-level clients about some of the reasons you are not in as much contact with their related client. When we discuss Client Service Models, we will discuss reviewing those models with clients so that you can set level expectations.
- The client has an impending liquidity event such as selling a business or coming into a significant inheritance. You need to show the client that you can service their higher-level needs in advance. Once we had a coaching client who had a lottery winner as his client, and it was a nominal amount, considerably less than $1 million. Obviously you can't predict lottery winners or windfall inheritances, but some advisors don't want to offload lower-end clients because of the possibility. However, if a client has a wealthy family and may inherit money, treating a C client as a B client or higher may make sense.
- You have clients with limited assets who are, or have the potential to be, high-income earners. These clients may be millennial clients, though they can be older (perhaps up to age 45); they are probably college graduates, employed in a job paying $100,000 or more, or are self-employed, possibly as attorneys, managers, high-profile C-suite executives, physicians, software developers, or entrepreneurs in the tech sector. They are ambitious, they are savers, and they are potentially entrepreneurial and/or have social or philanthropic interests.
- Your client is a potential Center of Influence (COI) such as a CPA or attorney or has a large network for any number of reasons.

Consider "demoting" clients to a lower tier if:

- They have limited potential and are withdrawing assets at a significant rate for their current lifestyle and you have not been able to get across their risk of running out of money in retirement. If a

> As financial planning firms grow more efficient, especially with the use of technology, it becomes possible for planners to manage an increasingly large number of clients. The only limitation, it would seem, is the time it takes to service them. However, research in psychology and anthropology suggests that there may be another limit to the maximum number of clients—the physiological limit of our brain's neocortex that constrains the number of social relationships that can be actively maintained. This threshold—called "Dunbar's number"—is estimated to be about 150 people on average, and corresponds not just to the average size of many ancient tribes and villages, but also the military unit size of the Roman army, and even the average number of Facebook friends or engaged Twitter followers! The implication of the research is that even as firms continue to become more efficient, there's still a physiological brain-based limit to how many clients we'll ever be able to manage, which allowing for some personal relationships as well may never be much higher than 75–125 for any planner regardless of the new tools and technologies we create in the future! [5]

- Does this advisor have too many low-end clients? Yes! Almost 55 percent (172 clients) in this sample book of business in Figure 2-15 are low-revenue, low-asset clients. In this case, there were extenuating circumstance for this having occurred, but nevertheless it is an untenable situation if the advisor wishes to grow the book. These 172 clients are taking time away from servicing clients with higher value and greatly restricting the amount of time the FA has for acquiring new higher-asset, higher-revenue clients. Also note that the ROA for D tier clients is below the average of the other three tiers. This could indicate that the advisor doesn't even have time to optimize the relationships with those D clients. This may not be relevant as these D clients have limited assets and it would likely take a lot of work to move these clients to a fee-based platform, assuming it was even appropriate.

  However, you can see that the 80 clients who are C tier are producing 30 basis points less than B tier clients. Perhaps this is an opportunity within this book. Note that the A tier clients also have a lower-than-average ROA. This is not unusual. The portfolios of high-net-worth clients tend to have higher fixed-income content than lower-net-worth clients, yielding lower revenues and ROAs. In addition, high-net-worth clients, may be given lower fee charges than lower-net-worth clients. The level of effort and time for servicing high-net-worth clients is not always proportionately higher than many somewhat lower-net-worth clients.

One other point to discuss at the book level is the distribution of ROA. See Figure 2-16. The hypotheses we have in this view are that:

Figure 2-16 | Sample distribution of ROA.*

ROA Range	#	Assets	Revenue	ROA	Average Revenue
75 + BPS	172	$35,326,021	$414,010	1.17	$2,407
50 - 74 BPS	32	$13,812,681	$84,914	61	$2,653
25 - 49 BPS	32	$10,902,055	$41,779	38	$1,306
< 25 BPS	77	$9,306,246	$13,340	114	$173
	313	$69,347,003	$554,043	80	

*One account had no revenue therefore no ROA, so we have 313 clients in this view instead of 314.

- Fifty-five percent of book (172 clients) have "acceptable" ROAs at 75 basis points and higher.
- The 32 clients yielding between 50 and 74 basis points (average 61 basis points) is probably okay for a variety of reasons, such as makeup of the book, low cost basis securities, and other considerations. Of course, the advisor can look at each individual client and determine if there are opportunities. With 32 clients in this group and assets of $13.8 million, an increase of 20 or 30 basis points overall might not have a large impact on total revenue, though it could mean $25,000 to $40,000. The advisor has to consider whether the time and effort spent on improving ROA is better than time spent on service and/or new client and asset acquisition. An analysis of individual clients is required, including the type of account and the context of the new Department of Labor (DOL) rule.
- The 109 remaining clients with less than 50 basis points are likely too many low ROA clients. At an average of about 27 basis points on about $20 million in AUM, there is likely some potential in low

ROA clients. However, as stated already, the advisor has to consider whether the time and effort is better spent on service and/or new and "better" client and asset acquisition. The advisor may have already looked at each individual client, and if she determined there are opportunities, she would make individual decisions on actions to take.

There may be other points to discuss at the client level, but these are some of the main questions to be considered at the book level.

Sample Client Contact Plan

Once we are satisfied with our client segmentation and analysis, the next step is to develop a client contact plan. A quick method is simply posting the client's tier and name and perhaps their telephone number in those columns to the left of your spreadsheet. You can also post the client's assets and revenues in columns on the right. The spreadsheet will calculate the ROA.

For A tier clients, we posted an M for meeting and a C for check-in call in a simple diagonal pattern to spread out calls and meetings relatively evenly throughout the year (see Figure 2-17). We used the Supernova contact plan previously discussed (see Figure 2-10). For B, C, and D tier clients we follow the same approach. You would add the number of rows you need to address your entire book.

You can color-code tiers to make it easier to see the tier breaks. Some advisors use this spreadsheet directly. They would print out the annual contact sheet, using legal-size paper to make the spreadsheet one sheet wide and as long as needed.

Some advisors ask their assistants to put together a monthly contact plan showing the month and who gets a check-in call that month, who gets a meeting that month, and perhaps how the last meeting took place (over the telephone or in person) using their CRM system. For meetings, one of the duties of the assistant would be to schedule the meetings for the advisor.

Some advisors or assistants post the calls and meetings to the advisor's CRM system. The FA or assistant would typically divide the number of calls and meetings by four and spread a quarter of the calls and meetings out throughout the month. Most often calls are posted on the Monday of each week. Meetings should be scheduled at one or two a day, for three or four days a week at most. We recommend that the advisor blocks out time during the week for meetings and the assistant offers those blocks to clients; this way the advisor generally knows that meetings with clients are between 2 p.m. and 3:30 p.m. on Tuesdays and Thursdays, for example. (More on this later.) Naturally, clients don't always want to stick to the advisor's available openings, so there are usually exceptions and rescheduling, a common challenge.

Figure 2-17 | Sample contact plan.

															Profitability Indicators		
Proposed Tier	Client Name	Telephone	Jan.	Feb.	March	Apr.	May	June	July	Aug.	Sept.	Oct.	Nov.	Dec.	Assets	Revenue	ROA
A			M	C	C	M	C	C	M	C	C	M	C	C			#DIV/0!
A			C	M	C	C	M	C	C	M	C	C	M	C			#DIV/0!
A			C	C	M	C	C	M	C	C	M	C	C	M			#DIV/0!
B			C		M		C		C		M		C				#DIV/0!
B				C		M		C		C		M		C			#DIV/0!
B					C		M		C		C		M				#DIV/0!
C			C			C			M			C					#DIV/0!
C				C			C			M			C				#DIV/0!
C					C			C			M			C			#DIV/0!
D				C						C							#DIV/0!
D					C						C						#DIV/0!
D						C						C					#DIV/0!

Action Summary | Formal Book Segmentation

Part of structuring and organizing your business is to formally segment your book and analyze the results in more depth than you may have previously done. This is a mandatory step to determine:

- Which clients are critical to your financial success
- What service levels each of your clients should receive
- Where opportunities may exist to improve the value of clients to your business

While you may have segmented your book in the past, this approach will add value to your analysis. The process should be reviewed annually. Segmentation needs to be based on more than assets and/or revenues. As outlined previously, you need to be able to quickly recall which of your A and B clients take your advice, provide introductions, and have additional potential. You need to know this and think about it in every client contact.

Segmentation and analysis will help you get started in answering the questions:

- What does my contact plan look like and how do I establish it?
- How many clients, by tier, can I effectively and efficiently manage?

  You have 2,000 to 2,500 working hours per year and many tasks beyond client contact. Our experience and analysis suggests that you should be spending about 50 percent of your time in client contact, or 1,000 to 1,250 hours/year.

  You can effectively serve and retain 80 to 100 A-level clients depending on how you define them. If you have an evenly distributed set of clients in three tiers, you may be able to effectively manage and retain up to 150 clients. This is part of the analysis you need to do. Chapter 4 will answer this question based on your segmentation.
- How many and which clients do I want to manage and retain?

  If you need to reduce your client load, then you need to understand and consider your options as well as your personal and professional philosophies. Does it serve you or your unprofitable clients well to service them just in case? Are you doing the right thing by either servicing those clients the way they deserve to be serviced or by ignoring them? Should you bring support to them in a different manner than your current approach?

Chapter Three

The Client Loyalty Process

If you work just for money, you'll never make it, but if you love what you're doing and you always put the customer first, success will be yours.—**Ray Kroc**

The client experience refers to defining how you work with your clients. There are two ways to grow advisory practices:

1. Retain and deepen relationships with existing clients to acquire assets away, cross-sell, and earn access to their networks (e.g., the client's other professional providers and centers of influence) for introductions.

2. Consistently acquire new relationships and their assets, fulfill their other financial needs, and also earn access to their networks for introductions.

However, business growth can be limited by a lack of organization and structure in financial advisor (FA) practices such that there is little if any time for new client acquisition. What separates top FAs from the pack is an efficient and effective structure and organization that allows

---

Sections of Chapter 3 are based on *The Behavior Gap: Simple Ways to Stop Doing Dumb Things with Money* by Carl Richards (New York: Portfolio, 2012) and Michael Kitces's *Nerd's Eye View* blog, with permission from Carl Richards and Michael Kitces.

time for both servicing their existing client base and acquiring new clients, managing their assets, and fulfilling their other financial needs.

The key points in this chapter are that:

- Client retention and advocacy are functions of high-quality client service deliverables and are mandatory to earn growth from existing clients and the acquisition of new clients.
- You must manage your quality and proactive client service system tightly to ensure that you:
    - Deliver the right levels of services to the right clients.
    - Leave enough time to grow your business through new client acquisition.
    - Deliver service levels consistent with the value of clients, their needs, and your business and its profitability.

Asset Growth Starts with Client Retention

Client retention is the most important priority for an FA as it is the entry point for growing the business. An effective and proactive client service brings retention as well as loyalty and advocacy. *Retention* is keeping what you have today; *loyalty* is keeping what you have today "forever"; *advocacy* is keeping what you have today "forever" and receiving introductions to prospective clients. There are many components of a proactive Client Service process that can deliver retention, then loyalty, then advocacy.

The second most important priority is getting new business, but the first priority is client retention because if you are not servicing your current clients' wants and needs and keeping what you have, it's not likely you will be able to get introductions to prospective clients from either current clients or Centers of Influence (COIs). Introductions to prospective clients from either current clients or COIs will represent about two-thirds of your business growth opportunities. Being able to talk about how you service your existing base needs to be fact-based.

High-quality client service leads to growth through introductions from high-quality clients and COIs. It's high-quality client service that avoids having to spend the time, cost, and effort to replace clients. Effective client service must also be proactive, not reactive. Service leads to retention, but retention is not enough for growth. Growth requires advocacy. Advocacy requires approaches that go beyond mere satisfaction. Just satisfied is not enough to allow FAs to reach their growth goals. Loyalty and advocacy are a function of clients being extremely satisfied. This is defined as being rated a 4.7 on a scale of 1 to 5, what has been called a WOW!

The April 2016 J. D. Power study[1] supports the need to improve service deliverables in the financial services industry:

> The full service investment advisory industry is undergoing a historic shift, driven by an actively engaged investor population that is demanding a more hands-on approach from their advisors. According to the J. D. Power 2016 U.S. Full Service Investor Satisfaction Study . . . a steadily increasing number of investment advisory customers have disrupted conventional thinking about full service and self-directed advisory services, favoring a hybrid approach in which advisors become validators, or sounding boards, but not final decision makers. . . . Validators (36 percent of full service investors) want to make their own decisions, but still have access to an advisor for support and as a sounding board.

The study also says that "full service firms will need to adapt to these changes by providing more value and transparency to investors, making a clear case for the value they provide vs. lower-cost alternatives." It is this search for value that drives the need for a more effective client service experience than ever before. As the study reports, "Nearly 4 in 10 investors (38 percent) indicate their advisor did not help them set goals or discuss risk tolerance, and only 42 percent indicate their advisor met key performance indicators (KPIs) related to setting goals, implementing strategy and ongoing tracking." These are "after the sale" service needs.

The Value of High-Quality Client Service

Part of the value of high-quality client service is that it's a baseline to earn introductions to prospective clients. In addition:

- A satisfied customer is a loyal customer. "Customers who rate you 5 on a scale from 1 to 5 are six times more likely to buy from you again, compared to 'only' giving you a score of 4.8."[2]
- Client retention is less costly than client acquisition and more profitable. It's apparent that FAs have spent countless hours, significant energy, and many dollars to acquire new clients and their assets. With all the investment in acquisition, client retention via client loyalty is your best bet for a profitable and growing business.

  According to Bain & Company,[3] it costs six to seven times more to acquire a new customer than retain an existing one. Marketing Metrics[4] also says, "The probability of selling to an existing customer is 60–70 percent." The probability of selling to a new prospect is 5–20 percent.

Even if you deliver quality service, satisfied customers may defect. The *Harvard Business Review* (*HBR*) article "Why Satisfied Customers Defect" points out that "except in a few rare instances, *complete* customer satisfaction is the key to securing customer loyalty and generating superior long-term financial performance . . . the more competitive the market, the more important the level of customer satisfaction." The article further states that "there is a tremendous difference between the loyalty of merely satisfied and completely satisfied customers."[5]

It is clear that client satisfaction drives client loyalty, but there is a question as to how much satisfaction and how much loyalty. In the *HBR* article, "Putting the Service-Profit Chain to Work," the authors show that if clients are highly or very satisfied, their loyalty is also very high. Clearly, "very satisfied" is not specific but may suggest a loyalty of over 80 percent and perhaps approaching 100 percent. There are two points to be made:

1. To succeed with client retention and growth, clients and centers of influence must be completely satisfied. It is primarily those who are completely satisfied with you and your exceptional service who will be pleased to advocate for you and be a potential source of introductions. These are what we have also referred to as engaged clients.
2. The second point may be reiterative of the first—that is, it is not enough for clients to be merely satisfied. The VIP Forum of The

> Executive Board once showed that very satisfied investment clients, those in the zone of affection, are three times more likely to use their primary provider for their next financial action as compared with somewhat satisfied clients and twice as likely to refer their primary institution. The VIP Forum defined the zone of affection as a rating of 4.7 or better on a 1 to 5 scale, with 5 being high.[6]

Note that the best way to understand client satisfaction in detail is through an independent formal survey, a topic for another time.

The same *HBR* article also states that a Xerox survey some years ago showed that "customers giving Xerox 5s (5 = very satisfied) were six times more likely to repurchase Xerox equipment than those giving 4s (4 = satisfied)."[7] The article further suggests that clients fall into three zones:

1. The *zone of affection* is where clients are very or close to very satisfied and whose loyalty is highest. The higher the satisfaction, the higher the loyalty and the closer to advocacy.
2. The *zone of indifference* is where clients are generally satisfied and perhaps on occasion slightly dissatisfied. Loyalty and retention ranges widely, and clients are susceptible to defecting depending on a number of factors. These clients are not advocates.
3. The *zone of defection* is where clients are extremely dissatisfied, somewhat dissatisfied, or often at least slightly dissatisfied. Loyalty and retention ranges. Clients are highly susceptible to defecting depending on a number of factors. Some of the most extremely dissatisfied and angry clients are dangerous and could do harm to your practice (e.g., bad mouthing).

To produce very loyal clients who are advocates, advisors need to create a pool of highly satisfied clients in the zone of affection. This is where the magic can happen.

The *HBR* article, "Why Satisfied Customers Defect," states that "where competition is intense, we found a tremendous difference between the loyalty of satisfied and completely satisfied customers." It goes on to say, "Occasionally, the match is so good that even a 5 on a 1-to-5 satisfaction scale doesn't fully capture the strength of the relationship." There are "individuals who are so satisfied, whose experience so far exceeds their expectations, that they share their strong feelings with others. They are apostles." [8]

Here are a few more findings on the rewards of client loyalty:[9]

- Over the previous 12 months loyal clients gave an average of $376,000 each to their primary financial advisors—an amount more than *16 times* greater than that given by satisfied clients to their primary financial advisors.
- In the coming 12 months, 94.4 percent of loyal clients were extremely or very likely to give their primary FAs more assets.
- Just 33.5 percent of the satisfied clients planned to give their primary financial advisors more assets to invest.
- Just 13.4 percent of the moderately satisfied clients planned to give their primary financial advisors more assets to invest.

Getting Your Client to "Completely Satisfied"

Vince Lombardi said, "Perfection is not attainable. But if we chase perfection, we can catch excellence." Perfection in client service needs to be a target so we can catch excellence. It has also been said that "the most difficult part of attaining perfection is finding something to do for an encore." Be assured that there is always more to do.

Delivering satisfaction and therefore gaining loyalty requires a process and a strategy. It is not a one-time event. All client-facing processes and service MUST BE EXCEPTIONAL. The six core client-facing processes and their high-level components are shown in Figure 3-1.

We will discuss each of these processes from a service and value perspective. These core client-facing processes all provide value to the client and are part of the services value you deliver for the fees you charge. We will develop your Client Service Model or Promise to summarize your deliverables in a form you can share with clients, prospects, and centers of influence. Your structured processes and deliverables will differentiate you, and the formality of a written service model will also distinguish you.

Figure 3-1 | Six core client-facing processes.

Intake	Financial Planning	Risk Management	Investment Planning	Client Services	Planning & Review
About you and your family About your finances and financial experiences A strategy and plan for you and your family	Goals-based plan Cash flow analysis Net worth statements Excesses and gaps Liability needs	Family lifestyle protection Estate planning Gifting A strategy and plan for you and your family	Highly structured Investment policy Risk tolerance Income needs Solutions plan	Contact plans Planning needs Administrative needs Research Education Financial organizer Quarterback	Scheduled calls and reviews Portfolio performance diligently tracked Goals and family changes Portfolio changes

- *Structured processes deepen relationships.* Deepening relationships happen because we are delivering completeness and consistency. Every process and each step in its execution is intended to ensure that nothing falls through the cracks. Processes, executed well, provide consistency. The intent is a consistent client experience that signals what you do and how you do it. Explaining the steps you are taking a prospect or client through prepares them to understand what you are delivering and makes them better able to explain to others how well you work. These "others" are your prospects.
- *Deepened relationships lead to asset growth through account consolidation.* This is a primary goal of financial advisors. Using outside data sources, most firms project that most clients have about the same amount of assets away as assets held by that firm. At the same time, most FAs claim they have all their clients' assets. A holistic financial planning approach and a trusted advisor can uncover assets held away.

  Financial advisors know the important rationale for their investment recommendations. Those recommendations and decisions to be made must be in context of the complete financial picture of the client. At times, however, securities and other liquid assets are held with the advisor and elsewhere, whether with other advisors or in tax-deferred accounts at their workplaces. It may also be important to making effective investment recommendations to include less liquid assets, whether real or personal property and anything else of value that can be converted into cash. There are cases where retirement plans may include converting various less liquid assets into liquid assets. Better decisions with respect to asset allocation are made when all assets are under single management or, at a minimum, are known to any advisor making those investment recommendations.

These reasons then become opportunities to identify and acquire assets away. There are points within each process to discover those assets. They should be identified in the initial intake process and uncovered when developing a financial plan, putting together a legacy plan, making investment recommendations, or reviewing a client's portfolio. Conversations are opportunities to gather assets away.

- *Deepened relationships lead to asset growth via introductions based on outstanding service.* This is one of two primary goals of outstanding client service, client retention, and client acquisition. We will discuss introductions and/or referrals in Chapter 9. One of the keys to "earning" introductions is delivering such high-quality service that clients would like their family and best friends to also have the benefits of working with the advisor who does such great work.

- *These relationships reduce costs of acquiring "replacement clients."* As retention rates approach 100 percent, the need for replacement clients does not exist. Instead, time and effort can be directed toward new client acquisition.

- *You increase cross-sell from knowing your client well.* The more you know about your clients and their families, the better able you are to identify needs beyond investments, whether it's insurance, lending or other banking solutions, or legal or accounting services. You may not provide legal or accounting services but if the need generates an introduction to a CPA or Trust and Estate attorney, this becomes an opportunity to attract a quid pro quo, because you are a problem solver.

- *By being a problem solver you increase trust and confidence and show your value.* Delivering your services in a consistent and complete manner, understanding your client or prospect in depth, being clear about what you do and how you do it, and constantly being a helpful and considerate problem solver builds trust and confidence while you are delivering solutions that are always to the benefit of the client.

To set your client service strategy, let's look at each of the six core nt-facing processes. We will separately address the "Client Planning Review Process" in Chapter 6.

Your Intake Process

The intake process is about working with a prospect in the sales process to convert that prospect into a client. There is additional material in Chapter 5 to detail the intake process conversations.

The intake process is a three-phase meeting construct that gives you the opportunity to demonstrate your strengths and capabilities at the initiation of your relationship. The organization and structure of this approach provides service and value to the client because it provides completeness and consistency that results in high-quality client plans.

- *Meeting 1* is about the prospects and their family. In this meeting the prospects should be speaking 80 percent of the time; you are listening and taking notes. All you have with you is paper and pencil—no charts, no iPad, no visual aids. This is NOT a presentation meeting. The talking you do is focused on asking and answering questions. You have no prescriptions, recommendations, or opinions until you fully understand the prospects.
- *Meeting 2* is about the client's finances and financial experiences. Assuming you have a meeting of the minds in Meeting 1 and you get along, have built an initial level of trust and likability, and both believe you can help the prospects, then you schedule Meeting 2. You will ask the prospects for the material you need to get an in-depth understanding of their financial situation and experiences.
- *Meeting 3* is about discussing your strategy and plan for the prospects and their family. Assuming Meeting 2 and the material you have meets your needs for a professional analysis, you are ready to discuss a plan for their future financial well-being. This is NOT a "proposal"—it is a *plan*, which is more assumptive and personal. A plan assumes the sale as a prelude to the question, "Are they ready to agree to work together?" Your plan is general enough so the prospects cannot implement it themselves but specific enough to define the actions they need to take with you. The on-boarding process is also designed to ensure completeness and consistency so

that new clients feel part of the firm and your practice and receive all the components they need to feel comfortable that they made a good decision.

You need to show your strengths, capabilities, values, integrity, and character in each meeting. Again, your grooming, your welcome, your demeanor, your teammates, and your opening comments, as well as the physical environment in which you meet, needs to approach perfection. There is no point in striving for less. Consider the following:

- *Meet with both parties when there is a couple relationship.* If your prospect is part of a couple, you must meet with both parties. From a pragmatic perspective, it is imperative to develop in-depth and personal client relationships with both people from the beginning and throughout your relationship. When one client of a couple dies, there are often outside pressures from other family members on top of grief to deal with during this highly challenging time. Many articles report the loss of client assets when the male spouse of a couple passes away. For example:
  - "While few women seek a new FA before the death of their spouse, over 70 percent do so in the aftermath of the funeral—though they may wait to take action for several months, or even several years."[10]
  - "While their husbands are still alive, few women plan to leave their FA. Yet in the months and years after they become widows, up to 70 percent do just that, according to some estimates."[11]

  If you don't meet with both spouses in the first meeting, you are the advisor of the person with whom you first met. You need to keep the relationship with both parties equal throughout the relationship or you will likely be part of the 70 percent who lose the assets upon the death of the spouse. You know that men's life spans are shorter than women's. In addition, adult children and others can hold sway on a surviving partner if they have an advisor they like and trust.

  From a service and value viewpoint, traditionally, women haven't taken an active role in their investments and financial planning. While this is a changing paradigm, it is likely changing more slowly than necessary and changing more with millennials than with boomers. Some brokerages and advisors don't treat women with equal respect. Because Wall Street has historically been largely male-dominated, some of the language used when talking about money is ego-based, and women may relate differently to investments and financial planning than men do.[12] It is critical, respectful, and appropriate, as well as of value and service, to treat couples in any relationship as equals in all ways—from what you say and how you say it, to the amount and the type of professional attention you pay to each partner. You need to understand each partner's wants, needs, goals, risk attitudes, time frames, etc. They may well differ, and two perspectives are required if you want to appeal to the household as a unit. This is a big topic and outside the scope of this book, so let's just say that we strongly suggest that you always treat partners in relationships with equal respect and focus.

- *Listen for your client's message.* Have you really listened to the message the client is sending? Can you subjugate your ego to listen, hear, and understand your prospects?

  This is not a lesson in listening. There are myriad media, courses, and articles to learn listening skills. One website[13] simply says:

  > Listening is the ability to accurately receive and interpret messages in the communication process. Listening is key to all effective communication. Without the ability to listen effectively messages are easily misunderstood . . . communication breaks down and the sender of the message can easily become frustrated or irritated.
  >
  > If there is one communication skill you should aim to master then listening is it. Listening is so important that many top employers provide listening skills training for their employees. This is not surprising when you consider that good listening skills can lead to better customer satisfaction, greater productivity with fewer mistakes, and increased sharing of information that in turn can lead to more creative and innovative work.
  >
  > Many successful leaders and entrepreneurs credit their success to effective listening skills. Richard Branson frequently quotes listening as one of the main factors behind the success of Virgin.

> Effective listening is a skill that underpins all positive human relationships. Spend some time thinking about and developing your listening skills—they are the building blocks of success.

Listening results in better discovery, better recommendations and decisions, better plans, more respect for you, and uncovering opportunities based on the prospects' true wants and needs. These results all benefit your prospects and clients. This is service and value.

Your job in this first meeting, then, is primarily focused on listening in order to learn about your prospects: who they are, their family, their wants, their needs, their goals and situation. Where are they today, where do they want to be at some future point in time, and when is that time?

Your Financial Planning Process

We do not have a separate chapter on the financial planning process because:

- Financial advisors and financial planners should be well aware of this process and capable of delivering financial plans to their clients.
- Many firms already provide financial planning tools and support to their advisors. It is a must to use them.
- There is already a plethora of resources available on this subject, so we limit our discussion to some current thoughts and experiences that can add value to your process.

Carl Richards is a financial planner and blogger for the *New York Times*. His first book, *The Behavior Gap*, makes outstanding points about financial planning and its value to the client that advisors can effectively deliver. These points go beyond software and tools by discussing the role of financial planning in the client's financial life.

Many Americans do not have their financial lives in order because they don't have their life plans in order. If we don't know what will make us "happy," then it's difficult to make financial decisions that support those goals. Life decisions have to be made before financial decisions can be made. While financial planning is about knowing where you are today, where you want to be at some later point in time, and how you will (or have to) behave to get there, Richards points out that financial plans themselves are worthless unless goals are established first. If goals change, plans have to change, so the *process* of financial planning is what is vital. Essentially, if you put together a plan and it becomes "shelfware" while your life and goals move on, it's of little value. However, if the plan is re-created on a regular basis—annually or as needed, based on changes—that plan can keep current with the client. Therefore the value is ongoing and continuous. At least two things are true: Financial planning is not a one-time event, and the "tool" itself is not as important as the process. You bring great value to the process by helping your clients establish their life goals as well as their financial goals and by delivering your process on a continuing basis.

Richards brings reality to the process and delivers verbiage that can help advisors help clients in understanding these realities. *The Behavior Gap* is a worthwhile and easy read. He says, "No plan will cover every situation—and that's okay. You don't have to choose the perfect investment or save exactly the right amount or predict your rate of return or spend hours watching television shows about the stock market or surfing the Internet or stock picks. You don't need a plan for every contingency." He asks, "If planning isn't the solution to our money problems, what is? More simply, what can we do to get what we really want?" He gives us his answers, which are the points advisors need to get across to their clients:

- "We can stop chasing fantasies. We are not going to get what we want by beating the market or picking the perfect investment or designing the perfect bulletproof financial plan. In fact, when we try to do these things we get into big trouble."
- "We can protect ourselves—to a point. Risk is what's left when you think you've thought of everything. Our assumptions about the future are almost always wrong. We can never think of everything—but we can take sensible steps to protect ourselves from life's inevitable surprises."
- "We can embrace uncertainty. If we aren't locked down into a rigid plan, we can recognize and seize opportunities when they come up."

- "We can decide what we really want. When someone asks you what you really want out of life, you're probably not going to say you want an investment that delivers good returns. Like the rest of us, we want to be happy and fulfilled. Your financial decisions should align with what you know about yourself and the world. The more you know about yourself, the more successful your investments will be—that is, the more they will align with your true goals as a human being. Deciding what you really want takes an awful lot of work, but once you know what you (and your family) really want, you will know what to do—how much insurance to buy, where to invest your money, whether to quit your job and start a new venture."
- "We can make decisions that make sense. We can't control the markets or the economy, but our behavior is up to us. Sensible, reality-based choices are our best shot at reaching our goals."
- "We can trust our luck. . . . Most financial planners (and advisors) don't like to talk about luck". . . but "one of the lessons is that you aren't in charge of everything. Do what you can, and then relax."
- "We can trust ourselves. In the end, financial decisions aren't about getting rich. They're about getting what you want—getting happy. And if there is a secret to getting happy, it is this: be true to yourself."

These are part of Carl Richards's belief system. Hopefully they make sense to you and your clients and prospects. They point to some of the things advisors can do to add value to their clients.

- Help the client focus on the reality of the markets.
- Put an investment policy statement in place that incorporates appropriate asset allocation and diversification approaches.
- Frequently validate with the client that their goals, family, or extended family situation, income, values, and financial situation have remained constant or have changed.
- Perhaps the most valuable deliverable you provide is managing client behavior when changes take place, especially in the markets. We know markets go up and down. We know the challenges of managing client behavior in changing markets. You don't have to go back

very far to recall the panic some clients, and advisors, experienced in 2008. Behavioral management is one of your biggest and most difficult challenges, but this is where value-add takes place.

Richards says, "I coined the term 'behavior gap' to label the gap between investor returns and investment returns. I've used the behavior gap to describe all kinds of situations where our behavior leads us to subpar results. Impulses to buy and sell are dangerous. Clients rely on me to help them get their impulses under control." That chapter in his book is titled, "We Don't Beat the Market, the Market Beats Us." One of the advisor's primary jobs is creating the discipline for clients so they stick with the plan instead of making irrational decisions. Serenity is inversely proportional to expectations.

This is true not only for market movements but things like savings and spending as well, all of which are part of good financial plans. Though you are responsible for your behavior, you can't control results.

Carl Richards delves into the area of "life planning" or "financial life planning," an approach that has a small number of excellent proponents including Carol Anderson of Money Quotient (http://moneyquotient.org/), Mitch Anthony of Financial Life Planning Institute (http://www.flpinc.com/), and George Kinder of The Kinder Institute of Life Planning (https://www.kinderinstitute.com/). Richards makes the point that the moral is "whatever you have to do to gain self-knowledge, do it. Find out who you are and what you want. Then you can stop wasting your life energy and your money on stuff that doesn't matter to you—start making financial decisions that will get you to your true goals."

As Mitch Anthony says, "If you want to survive and thrive, your value proposition must move from ROI to ROL (Return on Life)—which means helping your client get the best life they can from the money they have."

If you think ultra-high net worth (UHNW) individuals get over money concerns, see the article "Secret Fears of the Super-Rich."[14] A study by Boston College asked the question, "Does great wealth bring fulfillment?" The study addressed people with fortunes in excess of $25 million.

- "The result is a surprising litany of anxieties: their sense of isolation, their worries about work and love, and most of all, their fears for their children."
- "The respondents turn out to be a generally dissatisfied lot, whose money has contributed to deep anxieties involving love, work, and family. Indeed, they are frequently dissatisfied even with their sizable fortunes. Most of them still do not consider themselves financially secure. . . ."
- "One respondent, the heir to an enormous fortune, says that what matters most to him is his Christianity, and that his greatest aspiration is 'to love the Lord, my family, and my friends.' He also reports that he wouldn't feel financially secure until he had $1 billion in the bank."

The point is to understand that your HNW clients need your help to put money in context of life. Only humans can satisfy deep interpersonal needs. That's how close the best advisors get to their best clients. Read an outstanding article in *Fortune*, "Humans Are Underrated,"[15] which was adapted from a book by the same name by Geoff Colvin.

You can and should make these points a part of your services and value-added deliverables. You have enough information in this chapter and Chapter 1 to develop your very powerful Unique Value Proposition.

Carl Richards delivers an excellent summary of the financial planning process. Use these ideas in your UVP to stress your financial planning deliverables and the value they provide with continuing and ongoing service.

> There are a number of reasons why we're hesitant to spend time planning for our financial future. It's time-consuming; it makes us anxious; we're not sure how to do it. But I think the most important reason is a subtler one. I think we have confused the process of financial planning with its supposed end product: a financial plan.
>
> Financial plans are worthless, but the *process* of financial planning is vital. A plan assumes that you know what's going to happen—even though you don't. By contrast, *planning* in its truest sense is a reality-based process that allows for life's unpredictability.

> We don't know that inflation will average 3 percent annually, or that the stock market will go up 8 percent annually, or that we'll be able to save 10 percent of our pay (or what that pay will be), or when we'll retire (we might not get to choose), or how much retirement will cost, or even when we'll die (at age 61? 78? 92? 37?).
>
> Financial surprises are the rule—not the exception, which means that your plan, whatever it is, will be largely based on more or less plausible fiction—or even outright fantasy. Remember, however, good things happen as well. The process of planning may—in fact, probably will—require us to chart a course that's headed in the direction we hope to go. That may involve making some assumptions about the future. But reality-based planning acknowledges that some assumptions are mere guesses. We make the best guess we can. Then we can move on to the more productive business of investigating our current motives and circumstances, so that we can act from a place of understanding—not hope, not fear, but clarity.[16]

Richards does caution us that "once you have a general idea of your destination, the focus should shift to what you can do over the short term. Focus on the next three years" because . . . "financial planning based on reality tends to lead to better results."

Carl's concepts and words are excellent. Read and use them.

Advancing Your Financial Planning Process

There are several additional points that Michael Kitces brings to the discussion of financial planning as it is executed today in most cases. In his *Nerd's Eye View* blog, Kitces says, "Financial planning is . . . increasingly focusing around an approach of identifying and understanding client goals, and then crafting a plan to help the client succeed in achieving them."[17] Similar to Carl Richards's comment, Kitces says:

> The reality is that in practice the goals-based approach doesn't always go as smoothly as hoped. Some clients haven't crafted their goals yet in the first place, while others have goals that are wildly unrealistic and force planners to be the bearers of bad news. Often the goals-based planning process can get mired down in countless iterations of alternative 'what if' plans, culminating in a giant physical tome that clients aren't committed to and is never read again after being presented away.

> But perhaps the fundamental problem with goals-based planning is simply that it puts the cart before the horse; clients shouldn't be selecting the goals to pursue until they understand what the possibilities are in the first place![18]

Kitces suggests using "the software interactive with clients to explore the possibilities of multiple scenarios and understand the trade-offs just to arrive at what the goals should be in the first place. Once the possibilities have been selected, realistic goals can be chosen, and then a more productive series of financial planning recommendations can be delivered for implementation!" In addition to being an interesting idea for realistic goal setting, this approach would get the client deeply involved in the process and hopefully committed to an execution of the plan. This doesn't obviate the suggestion to continue the planning process on a regular basis. Having said that, we would want to limit the iterations of the plan because, given the number of variables in the plan and the uncertainties of the future, plans are only a temporary picture of today's estimates. The process of ongoing and continuing planning is what we want to focus on.

In another article Kitces says, "Creating a financial plan starts with gathering the client data, which many advisors request by providing clients with a 'data gathering form,' typically structured in a manner that makes it easy to input the data into their financial planning software." He goes on to say, "The caveat, however, is that in practice clients often don't fill out the data gathering form. For some, they feel it's too much work."[19] Regardless of the form or survey you mail to clients or prospects or advisors to fill out, the vast majority will not complete the task. If you want data and/or signatures from a prospect or client, it should be done in person and you should fill out forms with or for them. Filling out forms with prospects or clients enables you to gather much more and better data and dig deeper into responses. If the client or prospect is worth having, it's worth working the forms with them.

Perhaps more important, Kitces says:

> For most, the problem is simply that they aren't organized enough *to* provide all the requisite information. And may even feel guilty or embarrassed about the fact that they're "failing" in the very first step of

> the financial planning process. So what's the alternative? Ditch the data gathering meeting, and have a "Get Organized" meeting instead. In other words, make the first meeting with the client *about* getting them financially organized in the first place.[20]

He goes on to discuss how to execute that meeting. The "get organized" meeting is a very insightful idea and can be a great part of your service delivery model for top-tier clients, adding tremendous value. This is the opportunity to help your client establish rational life goals for the near term, mid-term, and long term and establish a lifelong relationship that has mid-term goals become near-term goals and long-term goals become mid-term goals, etc. Now you are becoming your client's CFO.

Finally, many of the plans that advisors prepare are often limited in scope when compared to those of a financial planner who may charge $2,500, $3,500, or significantly more. It depends on the complexity of the plan, including the assets of the client and how else the planner earns her or his income.

Figure 1-4 was an example of one planner's deliverables. As an advisor, this may be what you are competing with. Though the figure identifies 53 deliverables, it's important to note that not all clients require every deliverable; some deliverables may be high level and actually drawn up by strategic partners for a separate fee (e.g., wills and trusts), and many of the elements are likely part of your normal review plans (e.g., insurance reviews).

Your Risk Management Process

There are many other resources for advisors that provide additional details on the subject of risk management and the opportunity it provides. Most firms and advisors also have access to support for key risk management solutions. The importance of this process is the consideration of risk as it affects your client's financial plans.

The following are a few of the risks that advisors need to work on with their clients. Risk management is a critical part of the financial planning process. The intent is to protect one's goals, dreams, treasure, and personal well-being from those "what ifs" before they become "what nows."

There are four broad categories of risk to consider: Income risks, Expense risks, Assets and Investment risks, and Credit and Debt risks.

1. *Income risks.* The basic risks and reasons for investing in securities portfolios are well known to advisors and discussed as part of financial planning—namely, to fulfill the client's goals and dreams after their current income stream ceases. Goals and dreams include, but are not limited to, a comfortable retirement, college for children, caring for a spouse and others as needed, vacation homes, travel and toys, etc. Some people's goals and dreams are primarily about freedom, as least when work first ceases.
   a. Robert Laura, in his *Forbes* article "Three Retirement Goals People Never Achieve,"[21] says that "retirement doesn't come with a voucher that says you get 20, 30, or 40 years to do whatever you want, when you want. It can, and often does, change in a moment, making it important to eliminate excuses and maximize the opportunities you have today." Having said that, the risk here is clients not being able to afford their dreams. This is the risk they are counting on you to minimize.
   b. If income stops prematurely due to death, disability, long-term illness, or loss of job, the individual and family may be left to cope without enough income to pay debts and living expenses, no less dreams. Plans should be made to handle such calamities. These situations can be addressed through insurance of many kinds, and it's incumbent on the part of the advisor to ensure that appropriate discussions have taken place so these risks and others are considered. You will want to document these discussions and consider appropriate notation to the client on how the situation was addressed.

2. *Expense risks.* These are other risks that can seriously affect the financial plan. Spending via budget management should be tracked and kept in line with the plan, as should income and emergency spending. The latter needs to be part of the plan as well and can be monitored by the client and/or the advisory team.

3. *Assets and investment risks.* Savings like expenses also need to be tracked to plans. As Carl Richards says, "While making wise decisions about how you invest your money is important, it doesn't have nearly the impact of working hard and saving more—let alone start-

ing a business, going back to school, or reinventing yourself in any number of ways."[22] Of course you are tracking investments and return on investments as well as inflation and changes to real and personal property values if they are part of the plan.

4. *Credit and debt risks.* Debt and any other items that are part of the plan need to have attention focused on them as well.

You can see that annual to biannual plan reviews are likely necessary and there is significant work involved. All of these items are part of managing the plan that you developed with the client. Obviously the more effort, the more time and cost, and that is part of the value of your services, whether charged separately or as part of your asset fees. We are not suggesting the details of tracking and monitoring are done by the advisor, but rather by part of your team, real or virtual. These services can be separately billed if required and appropriate.

Your Investment Planning Process

Again, there are volumes of resources for advisors in this area and this is their primary area of expertise. Advisory firms provide significant resources and support in this area including, but not limited to, research, model portfolios, asset allocation models and guidelines, and support desks.

The investment planning process, a subset of the broader subject of wealth management, is a core capability of advisors who have gone through much training and experience. Our goal in this section is to show the value you add over and above portfolio construction, which is essentially a commodity and could be accomplished by technology. Today's competitive investment management/wealth management marketplace requires a consultative selling approach and has for almost 50 years. Before "consultative selling," selling investments tended to be about products. Advisors may have called clients or prospects to buy a "hot stock," offer a bond with a good interest rate and rating, or offer "penny stocks" or some high-performing fund, among other offerings.

The term "consultative selling" first appeared in the 1970s book *Consultative Selling* by Mack Hanan. It describes a selling technique in which the salesperson acts as an expert consultant for the prospect, asking questions to determine the prospect's needs and wants, then using that information to select the best product or service to match those needs.

Consultative selling also works with value-added selling. Properly done, the consultative process digs deeply into the prospect's wants and needs starting with the "intake process" and continuing through all six of your core client-facing processes. The intent is for you to be able to incorporate the prospect's wants and needs and match them with the wealth management solutions you offer. The consultative approach is also intended to discover your prospect's emotional as well as financial wants and needs, and, critically, to develop rapport as an expert who truly understands and will be an outstanding resource for your prospect. Building rapport will develop by sharing information that is both helpful and valuable while not pressing too soon for a commitment. By demonstrating your understanding, even compassion when appropriate, your expertise, and how you can meet your prospect's wants and needs, you will earn the right to establish a mutually beneficial relationship. Consultative professionals do not rush the process.

Consultative selling has advanced over the years and needs to be customized to the industry in which it is used. However, the tenets are the same; understanding the client as discussed in the intake process, building rapport as is done in every communication with the client or prospect whether business or social, understanding the value and benefits you offer in the context of the client's situation, being expert at what you do, and building confidence so that you can present a plan that delivers solutions to the client's needs and having them know you are acting as their trusted partner in a fiduciary manner.

Essentially, the steps in a wealth management consultative process include working with the investor interactively to:

- Define their attitudes toward investing, their experiences with investing, their personal and family situation, their work situation, their income, the level of investment risk they are willing to accept, their wants, needs, dreams, and goals as discussed.
- Articulate and prioritize the investor's financial needs and life goals to ensure a meeting of the minds.
- Assess the investor's financial situation and needs. The FA works with the client's current situation in terms of current and projected

income, all forms of assets including investments and real and personal property, their status with regard to insurance, even health, hobbies, and other interests, etc.

- Create a portfolio investment approach that is intended to help meet the investor's objectives, through an initial planning document.
- Develop and agree to an implementation strategy to enable the initial plan. Working together, the investor and advisor would then modify the plan as needed and/or desired.
- Review the progress of the investments to the plan and goals and, as needed, periodically adjust the portfolio. This is an ongoing and interactive process with the client and advisor incorporating any changes to the current situation of the client and/or markets as appropriate.

Your Client Loyalty or Client Service Process

The Client Service process represents a summary of many of the deliverables we have discussed to this point. The sum of your deliverables are intended to be presented formally to your clients as your "promise" to them of your services—hence, your "Client Service Promise." This promise is intended to be a key part of generating loyalty and advocacy from your client as well as differentiating you as a financial advisor. The set of deliverables is rarely put together in a formal, written manner. The written promise is also rarely presented formally to the client by FAs. The primary pushback has been a concern about putting the promise in writing. We agree that if the advisor does not intend to deliver some component of the promise it should not be included. However, if it is included, it needs to be delivered. Because clients would have some expectations for the fees they pay, some or all of what you promise may have been discussed in your sales process.

In the manufacturing industry, "service level agreements" (SLAs) are legally binding contracts and agreements between a customer and the service provider. Your Client Service Promise is essentially the same concept with different deliverables.

Figure 3-2 shows a sample Client Service Promise that we will detail further and discuss how it can be created. This particular Client

Service Promise is for an A-level or "Diamond" client. It is two pages in length. There are similar service promises for B, C, and D clients. We have chosen the four names Diamond, Platinum, Gold Plus, and Gold as the levels of client service. It may be a small point, but we suggest that each level client get a positive name. (Don't use names like Silver, Brass, Tin, or Lead. Noncomplimentary naming conventions are inappropriate and don't represent how advisors need to think of their clients.)

The process for building a customized Client Service Model or Promise begins with the "Client Service Matrix" spreadsheet. The spreadsheet is about two pages encompassing about 70 rows of deliverables. It lists the six structured client-facing processes we have been discussing and makes the point that we deliver these processes to every client. (Note that we have not yet discussed the Client Planning and Review Process, which is covered in Chapter 6.)

There are five functions listed on the Client Service Promise that address client deliverables:

1. Planning
2. Investing
3. Communications
4. Extended Services
5. For Internal Notation Only—services the advisor can deliver (e.g., sending a birthday or Thanksgiving card, dinner or lunch meetings, etc.) but are not shown as deliverables because they are relationship builders

Since this is a spreadsheet, additional rows representing additional deliverables can easily be added.

Each tier will or will not be provided particular deliverables based on the advisor's practice. If you wish to deliver that line item you merely annotate that cell with an X, as shown in the sample Client Service Matrix (see Figures 3-3 through 3-8).

Figure 3-2 | Sample Client Service Model.

Street Smart Research Group, LLC
Practice Optimization for FAs

James Advisor, Senior Vice President
Diamond Service Model

Certified Financial Planner®
Certified Private Wealth Advisor®

Deliverable	Frequency
Planning Services	
Lifestyle and Retirement Planning	Annual
Philanthropic Planning	Annual
Private Bankers—Cash and Liquidity Management	Annual
Liability Planning and Management	Annual
Estate and Insurance Analysis and Planning	Annual
Wealth Transfer Planning	Annual
Education Planning	Annual
External 401k Guidance	Annual
Intergenerational Family Planning	Annual
Investment Management	
Investment Policy Statement	Annual
Investment Process	On-Going
Integrate Multiple Accounts	On-Going
Investment Planning, Advice, and Management	On-Going
Portfolio Manager Reviews	Monthly
Communication Plan	
In-Person Performance Reviews and Progress Tracking	Semi-Annual
Telephone Portfolio Review	Semi-Annual
Check-In Call	Monthly
Mailings (TBD)	Monthly

Figure 3-2 | Sample Client Service Model (continued).

Street Smart Research Group, LLC
Practice Optimization for FAs

Statement Reviews	As Required
Visit Place of Business	Annual
Invitation to Firm Sponsored Events	As Available
Topical Events, Education Seminars, and Workshops	As Available
One on One Special Events	As Available
Extended Services	
CPA Package (1099)	Annual
Year-End Gain Loss	Annual
Online Access and Support	On-Going
Contact CPA	Semi-Annual
Update Missing Cost Basis Information	As Required
Banking Solutions	As Required
The Essential Organizer	Initial
Client Experience Survey Results	Annual
Private Briefing	As Required
The FIRM NAME Advantage	On-Going

James Advisor, Senior Vice President
Diamond Service Model

Certified Financial Planner®
Certified Private Wealth Advisor®

Note there are two additional columns for consideration:

- Time in Hours (required for this deliverable)
- Person Responsible (FA, Client Associate CA, or outsource to a third party if appropriate, designating the person responsible by initials)

The time in hours can be used to estimate workload. Essentially an X along with time and the person responsible can be used to estimate cost of service. This can be used to develop tier-based profitability. More discussion on this topic is needed but is not specifically addressed in this book except for the costs of contact in Chapter 4.

Once the Xs are filled in by tier, the service promises are completed by using the template for Tier A. Tiers B, C, and D are simply a matter of deleting rows that aren't part of that tier's deliverables. As needed, items unique to B, C, or D tiers can be added as the template is a Word table.

Figure 3-3 | Structured process section of the Client Service Matrix.

	A	B	C	E	E	F	G
1	**Client Service Matrix**	**Tier A**	**Tier B**	**Tier C**	**Tier D**	**Time**	**Person Responsible**
2		**Level 1**	**Level 2**	**Level 3**	**Level 4**	**Hours**	**FA/CA**
3	**Structured Processes**						
4	Intake Process	X	X	X	X		
5	Financial Planning Process	X	X	X	X		
6	Investment Planning Process	X	X	X	X		
7	Insurance Planning and Risk Management Process	X	X	X	x		
8	Client Service Process	X	X	X	X		
9	Planning and Review Process	X	X	X	X		

Figure 3-4 | Planning section of the Client Service Matrix.

	A	B	C	E	E	F	G
1	**Client Service Matrix**	**Tier A**	**Tier B**	**Tier C**	**Tier D**	**Time**	**Person Responsible**
2		**Level 1**	**Level 2**	**Level 3**	**Level 4**	**Hours**	**FA/CA**
10	**Planning**						
11	Integrated Advice and Planning Services						
12	Retirement Income Planning	X	X	X			
13	Lifestyle and Retirement Planning	X	X	Initial			
14	Philanthropic Planning/Charitable Gift Planning	X					
15	Integrated Tax Planning (or Tax Planning with CPA)	X	X	X			
16	Liability Planning and Management	X	X				
17	Cash and Liquidity Management	X	X				
18	Estate Insurance Analysis and Planning	X	X	X			
19	Estate Wealth Transfer Planning	X	X				
20	Education Planning	X	X				
21	External 401(k) Guidance	X	X				
22	Intergenerational Family Planning and Asset Transfers	X	X				
23	Other Corporate Executive Services as Desired						

Figure 3-5 | Investing section of the Client Service Matrix.

	A	B	C	E	E	F	G
1	**Client Service Matrix**	**Tier A**	**Tier B**	**Tier C**	**Tier D**	**Time**	**Person Responsible**
2		**Level 1**	**Level 2**	**Level 3**	**Level 4**	**Hours**	**FA/CA**
24	**Investing**						
25	Development and Review of Investment Policy Statement	X	X				
26	Investment Process	X	X	X	X		
27	Integrate Multiple Accounts	X	X				
28	Investment Management (Update for life changes, research, asset allocation changes, investment changes, rebalancing, etc.)	X	X	X	X		
29	Performance Monitoring	X	X	X	X		
30	Portfolio Manager Reviews	X	X	X	X		
31	Tax Loss Harvesting	X	X	X	X		
32	Stock Option Exercise and Concentrated Stock Management						

Figure 3-6 | Communications section of the Client Service Matrix.

	A	B	C	E	E	F	G
1	**Client Service Matrix**	**Tier A**	**Tier B**	**Tier C**	**Tier D**	**Time**	**Person Responsible**
2		**Level 1**	**Level 2**	**Level 3**	**Level 4**	**Hours**	**FA/CA**
33	**Communications**						
34	In-Person Portfolio Reviews and Progress Tracking	2	1			2.5	FA
35	Telephone Portfolio Review and Progress Tracking	2	1	1	1	1.5	FA
36	Check-In Call	8	4	3	1	0.25	TBD
37	Special Calling Plan	TBD					
38	Mailings of Corporate Publications, e.g.,						
39	• Monthly Research Report	X	X				
40	• Monthly Newsletter	X	X	X	X		
41	• Monthly Fixed Income Report						
42	• Weekly Market Monitor						
43	• Morning Markets						
44	• Other TBD	X	X	X	X		
45	Ad Hoc Articles of Personal Interest						
46	Special Mailings of Personal Interest						
47	Review Statements	X	X	X			
48	Visit to Client's Place of Business	X					
49	Invitation to Firm Sponsored Events	X	X				
50	Topical Events, Educational Seminars, and Workshops	X	X	X	X		
51	One-on-One Special Events	X	X				
52	Client Appreciation Events	X					

Figure 3-7 | Extended services section of the Client Service Matrix.

	A	B	C	E	E	F	G
1	**Client Service Matrix**	**Tier A**	**Tier B**	**Tier C**	**Tier D**	**Time**	**Person Responsible**
2		**Level 1**	**Level 2**	**Level 3**	**Level 4**	**Hours**	**FA/CA**
53	**Extended Services**						
54	Accountant Package (Dec. Statement, 1099, Realized Gain/Loss)	X					
55	Online Access (Paperless Statements)	X	X	X			
56	Contact CPA	2X	X				
57	Update Missing Cost Basis Information	X	X	X			
58	The Firm Advantage	X	X	X	X		
59	Banking Solutions	X	X	X	X		
60	Essential Organizer/Family Binder	X					
61	Private Briefing	X					
62	Client Experience Survey Results	X	X	X	X		

Figure 3-8 | Internal "notation only" section of the Client Service Matrix.

	A	B	C	E	E	F	G
1	**Client Service Matrix**	**Tier A**	**Tier B**	**Tier C**	**Tier D**	**Time**	**Person Responsible**
2		**Level 1**	**Level 2**	**Level 3**	**Level 4**	**Hours**	**FA/CA**
63	**For Internal Notation Duty**						
64	One-on-One Special Dinner	X					
65	One-on-One Special Lunch		X				
66	Magazine Birthday/Anniversary Gift	X					
67	Referral Thank-You Letter	X	X				
68	Holiday Gift	X	X	XAnni			
69	Mutual Fund Structured Accounts			X	X		
70	Welcome Letter	X	X	X	X		
71	Welcome Gift (TBD)	X	X	X	X		
72	Birthday Card or Other Occasion, e.g., Anniversary of Client-Ship	X					

Is It Enough?

Now that we have an extensive and formal Client Service Promise and a set of deliverables, we need to answer the question, "Is it enough?" Some advisors offer many or even most of the discussed deliverables. However, many FAs may not formally discuss their deliverables with or present them to their clients, and most clients couldn't list a majority of the deliverables that are delivered to them. It's impossible to understand the value of what is being delivered to you if you don't have a solid understanding of what those deliverables are and have agreed they are elements you want delivered.

It is important to understand which deliverables clients value and how much they value them. We recommend that advisors discuss the Client Service Model or Promise they develop for their clients and have a discussion about what they deliver and what the clients value. As well as determining what each client values, you learn what deliverables you should keep on delivering, enhancing, or even deleting for that client. You are also setting the client's expectations as well as your own. It's simply a meeting of the minds and is worth reviewing annually or as appropriate. You are now balancing client value and the cost of servicing that client. It's a good way to run a business. We agree that cost and profitability has many nuances and the process is more complex than discussed here, but this is a good start for our business.

There is, however, a progression of service expectations or a growth of service expectations over time. It's never enough because that which pleased, even delighted, a client yesterday becomes a basic expectation today. Client's requirements, wants, and needs change over time. In essence, "delighting" the client and solidifying his or her loyalty takes more and more effort over time. What may have been a unique service 10 years ago over time became a "normal" expectation and has now become "expected." Therefore, to delight and retain the loyal client takes more and more and continually growing levels of service over time. An example is the Central Asset Account. First announced 30 years ago, it was a source of excitement to attract significant new client assets. The creation of Central Asset Accounts has become so "normal," so expected, that its unavailability creates dissatisfaction and a competitive disadvantage in today's financial services world. Its original excitement quality has become a normal expectation and quite possibly a basic requirement for many of today's investors.

Value of Continuing Improvement in Client Loyalty

We have already stated that marketing to existing clients is significantly less expensive than marketing to potential clients. Cross-selling to current clients is also more likely to occur than cross-selling to new clients or prospects. Loyal clients can be defined as clients who conduct business with only you now and plan to conduct business with only you in the future. They are also interested in considering new strategies, services, and solutions you recommend while resisting the "pull" from your competition. They also provide solicited and unsolicited referrals.

We have established that client loyalty and retention are based on client satisfaction but that *"mere satisfaction" is likely not enough to allow FAs to reach lofty goals.* And we have also attempted to show that *delivering satisfaction and loyalty is a process and a strategy, not an event.*

The issue in financial services, as in other industries, is that this has to be displayed on a continuing, ongoing basis: contact after contact, opportunity after opportunity, and month, quarter, and year after month, quarter, and year. In terms of adding value, you have to go beyond the core value of the client's expectations. When performance coaching financial advisors you learn that every advisor works on their core values: rational investment planning and execution, 100 percent accuracy, timely and regular contact, etc. These are expected and no longer the base for client loyalty or retention. All advisors express their strengths of investment expertise, experience, education, integrity, performance standards, and caring. These capabilities are also expected and no longer the base for client loyalty or retention. Though we need to make sure solid deliverables are in place, these skills, capabilities, and values do not differentiate advisors from many of the other 285,000 or more financial professionals they compete with. All advisors at least claim all these characteristics.

The Kano Model

Dr. Noriaki Kano[23] developed a model that speaks to adding client value over time. This model of client satisfaction, and hence loyalty, predicts that the degree of client satisfaction is dependent on the degree of need fulfillment, but is different for different types of client expectations.

In short, Dr. Kano's model looks like Figure 3-9.

Figure 3-9 | The Kano model.

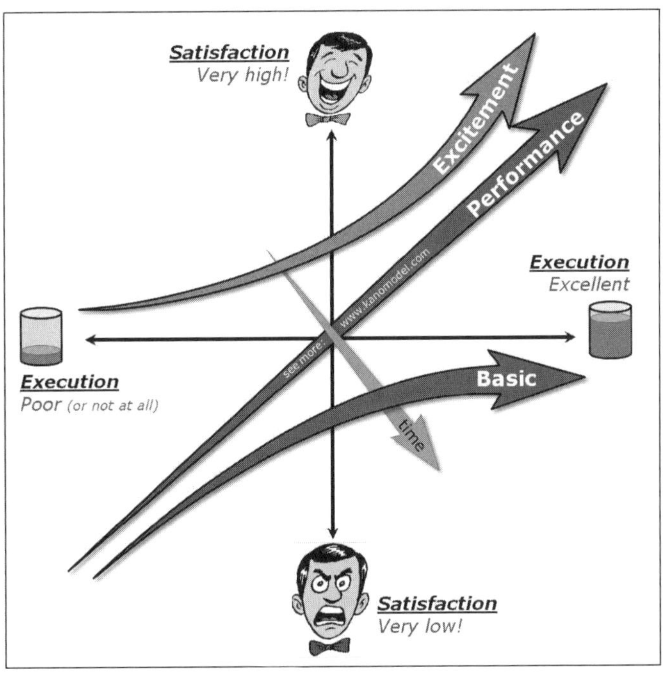

Kano's model of customer satisfaction is a function of need fulfillment. The model addresses three types of customer requirements.

Basic Expectations/Deliverables

Expected requirements are so obvious to the client they do not state them overtly as requirements. When these requirements are met, the client says nothing and probably doesn't even notice. When these features or services are not present, the client complains. Continually improving on meeting these kinds of needs will not elicit client loyalty or delight. Satisfying basic needs allows a company or individual to get into the market.

Examples: Telephone dial tone, brokerage statements

The following are Basic/Expected deliverables in a full-service brokerage:

- Investment planning and execution
- 100 percent accuracy
- Integrity
- Expertise
- Experience
- Education
- Timely and regular contact
- Portfolio reporting
- Caring/personal touch

Normal Performance Expectations/Deliverables

These are "fundamental" to quality delivery. Clients overtly state these needs and are very aware of them. When these needs are met, clients are satisfied; when they are not met, clients are dissatisfied. For many types of requirements in this category, it is possible to deliver more than client requirements and generate additional perceived benefit. Satisfying performance needs allows a company or individual to sustain and remain competitive.

Example: Performance reporting

It is important to note that deliverables such as estate planning, education planning, tax-advantaged strategies, financial/retirement planning, and Central Asset Accounts are at this point in time nondifferentiated services. Most FAs and virtually all significant advisory firms preach and teach these as standard deliverables.

The following lists Performance/Normal deliverables in a full-service brokerage:

- Estate planning
- Education planning
- Tax considerations
- Retirement planning
- Financial planning
- Asset allocation
- Performance reporting

Exciting Expectations/Deliverables

Clients have needs they are not aware of. These are referred to as "latent" needs. They are real, but not yet in most clients' awareness. If these needs are not met by a provider, there is no negative client response. They are not dissatisfied because the need is unknown to them. If a provider understands such a need and fulfills it, the client is rapidly delighted, as happened when Central Asset Accounts first emerged in the late 1970s. Satisfying excitement needs allows a company or individual to excel and be world-class.

Example: 3M Post-it Notes when first introduced

The Future of Delight

Sources of excitement, when they are first introduced, tend to become expected as the market becomes familiar and saturated with them. That which delighted the client yesterday becomes a basic expectation as competition makes it an undifferentiated service. "Delighting" the client and increasing their loyalty takes more and more effort, and cost, over time.

Service offerings that were seen as premium yesterday may be considered ho-hum today. To keep your clients loyal and attract new business, you need to continually create "delight" with strategic updates.

A question remains as to what are the latent client demands that will delight them and provide a differentiated solution. We see several possibilities. One is a function of poor execution on the part of some of today's industry participants. Two other opportunities relate to enhanced services—financial and nonfinancial.

"Walking the Talk"—Improved Execution

One possibility to delight the client comes from consistently and continuously "walking the talk" instead of just "talking the talk." An example we have detailed is to establish a Client Service Model or Promise for each client that varies based on the client's value to the advisor's business. That value considers more than assets and revenues and is established based on the quality of the relationship, whether the client provides introductions, future potential, and other factors. We outlined a minimum number of face-to-face meetings per client, a minimum number of telephone-based portfolio reviews per client, and a minimum number of check-in calls per client. Every meeting has an agenda and goal and every face-to-face meeting is intended to solicit feedback and introductions as appropriate. (This will be discussed in Chapter 6, Your Client Planning and Review Process.) Advisors are coached to prepare a summary for every meeting with top-tier clients. This is to be shared with the client with any follow-ups required by the advisor and client.

There is still a lot of "talking the talk" instead of "walking the talk" in service delivery. A new level of service delivery that will meet and exceed client expectations calls for a new delivery and cost paradigm. This leads us to a discussion of enhanced services, financial and nonfinancial.

Enhanced Financial Services

Given constantly growing client expectations and competition from many sources, one of the possibilities for delighting the client is a new set of financial services that are a "facsimile" of family office services for clients with perhaps $1 million to $5 million and even up to $10 mil and more in assets under management. Such services could include

- Higher levels of financial planning
- Legal guidance and/or paralegal services
- Tax advice and even preparation
- Accounting services such as record keeping, budgeting, bill paying
- Family governance
- Clinical social workers to help clients with true goal definition
- Family support partnerships for senior care facilities and geriatric planning

These are an exemplary subset of the types of services that family offices for the ultra-wealthy already often provide. Many of these services could be provided by affiliated strategic partnerships at separate fees.

Questions remain such as:

- Are these services implemented through regional centers at the firm or through affiliated strategic partnerships?
- Which clients receive which services?
- How are these services paid for?
- What happens to the referral-based relationships advisors have already established with Centers of Influence?
- Where do we find the time and expertise to offer these services?

Enhanced Nonfinancial Services

Such services could include:

- Assistance with identifying legitimate and relevant sources of health information and curating other lifestyle needs[24]
- Family education programs
- Business and personal security

- Concierge services such as travel planning
- Luxury acquisition services
- Property management

These are also an exemplary subset of the types of services that family offices for the ultra-wealthy may provide. Questions also remain such as:

- How are these services implemented?
- Is there enough demand to warrant organized lifestyle services?
- How are these services paid for?

The next step will be to determine which clients or prospects will value which services. This is one of the themes of *life planning*.

As Wayne Dyer said, "There is no scarcity of opportunity to make a living at what you love to do, there is only a scarcity of resolve to make it happen."

Execution is critical because small advantages in key areas or deliverables can make a large difference in results (recall the Law of Fractional Advantage, discussed in Chapter 1). Put another way: "All you need to do to win at anything is to be slightly better than your competition," and "We don't have a problem knowing what we should do. The problem is that we just don't do it!"[25]

Action Summary | The Client Loyalty Process

- Define and implement your six core client-facing processes:
  - Intake Process (Chapter 5)
  - Financial Planning Process (Chapter 3)
  - Risk Management Process (Chapter 3)
  - Investment Planning Process (Chapter 3)
  - Client Service Process (Chapter 3)
  - Client Planning and Review Meeting Process (Chapter 6)

- Commit that every client you are willing to accept to your practice will receive an appropriate version of these processes based on the needs of the client, the deliverables they deserve, their value to the business, and the fees you charge in compensation for the value you deliver.
- Client loyalty and retention based on "delighting" clients has significant value.
    - That which pleased and even delighted the client yesterday becomes a basic expectation today.
    - Delighting clients and solidifying their loyalty takes more and more effort and cost over time.
    - Opportunities to delight the client come from at least three sources:
        - Improved execution
        - Enhanced financial services
        - Enhanced nonfinancial services

A case in point. . .

- A recent WealthManagement.com article[26] quotes investors speaking about their new financial advisor.
    - Old firm
        - The place sounded awesome with celebrity sports people as clients. I was pretty star struck.
        - The office was designed to impress; lots of framed articles about their famous clients. The lobby in the building was really cool.
        - We met with one of the main guys whose name was on the door and two other people—someone more junior and an account manager who would take care of basic stuff like wire transfers.
        - They waved their arms and talked about the stock market and how they handle other clients. They were selling us; I wasn't paying attention.
        - We meet with them about once a year and in between we'd get statements and other things, like their investment committee's views.

    - I might as well have been getting notifications from a bank—that's how impersonal it was.
    - I came to realize we were just a little slice in their pie. They were doing the absolute minimum to keep our assets.
    - I never once felt they tried to understand us. They were only interested in a very narrow part of our life—literally just our investment account. This is how your money's doing. Nothing else. We never talked about our children, our interests. They had no desire to learn about anything to do with our lives. And they never tried to educate me.
    - I didn't have a grip on our relationship to money—that's their job. They're wealth managers.
- New firm
    - In the first year, they did some very basic work, getting our portfolio allocated the way they thought was best for us. That involved a lot of questions about our goals and needs.
    - They also have gone above and beyond the call of duty, like recommending some things that weren't even in their interest, but were right for us. For example, when we wanted to refinance our house, they suggested getting a shorter-term mortgage, which required taking out money from the account—money they would not be earning a fee on anymore, as a result.
    - We meet with them about once a quarter, but we don't see a partner like we did at the other firm. It doesn't bother me. That partner wasn't very helpful.
    - They ask us about our kids, their schools, real estate, our car, our lifestyle, etc. We've talked about those things over time and they're constantly updating our profile.
    - They have a monthly cocktail party at their office that's really nice. I've only gone once or twice, but I liked it. You get to meet other people at the firm and other clients. We feel we have a bond with them.

For any client with whom you want to develop a relationship, who would do less than this new firm? If you cannot deliver this as a basic set of services, you are not delivering value to the client. Robo-advisors don't do these things but they are inexpensive. While there are varying costs and ways to charge for robo-advisors, they often cost as low as 25 basis points. Any competitor in this industry that doesn't offer the services of the new firm should not accept the client in our view. What would your clients say about your firm?

We'll end with a favorite quote from Lewis Carroll in *Alice in Wonderland.*

> "Well, in OUR country," said Alice, still panting a little, "you'd generally get to somewhere else—if you ran very fast for a long time, as we've been doing."
>
> "A slow sort of country!" said the Queen. "Now, *HERE*, you see, it takes all the running YOU can do, to keep in the same place. If you want to get somewhere else, you must run at least twice as fast as that!"

Elite advisors run twice as fast.

Chapter **Four**

But What's the Cost of Loyalty?

What is a cynic? A man who knows the price of everything and the value of nothing. **—Oscar Wilde**

How do you balance the cost of the services to be delivered in support of client retention and loyalty with the value of the client?

Many FAs feel they are too busy keeping their clients happy and managing problems to grow their businesses. That could be true or untrue but for the most part, advisors have not had a way to "know" where they were spending their time and whether that time was being appropriately invested in the "right" clients. Instead of advisors guessing where bottlenecks to growth are, this chapter proposes a methodology for estimating the time and cost of delivering services to client tiers. The process can determine what is restricting growth. We will describe an approach to calculating advisor contact workload so advisors can then determine how to fix it.

Advisory practices have two ways to grow their businesses: Grow existing relationships and acquire new relationships. A desire to grow the business makes it an imperative for advisors to have the time to focus on both of these activities.

We have discussed the services and values advisors can deliver to retain and grow their books. We have detailed the Client Service Matrix and discussed how to develop your Client Service Model or Promise by tier. The question remains, "Do you have the time to both grow the business and effectively service your existing book?"

Managing Your High-Quality Proactive Client Service System . . . It's About Time and Money

Harvey Mackay said, "Time is free, but it's priceless. You can't own it, but you can use it. You can't keep it, but you can spend it. Once you've lost it you can never get it back."

The reality is there is really no way to "manage" time. An hour takes an hour, a minute takes a minute, and no matter what you do all of us have exactly the same 1,440 minutes a day to spend any way we like, but we can spend each minute only once. There is no managing this time. It takes exactly as long as it takes, never longer, never shorter. No matter what techniques or tools you use, that never changes. Since we all get the same amount of time, and it's a fixed amount, all we can do is know what we spend it on and possibly spend it, or invest it, differently than how we do today.

We need to manage ourselves and how we use that fixed amount of time. How can you best allocate those 1,440 minutes to activities in a way that effectively serves your wants, needs, and goals *and* meets the needs and wants of your clients? As suggested, time management is a misnomer; the real question is: How should we allocate time? From a business perspective for FAs, the how is a function of your business goals and priorities, and that's before taking into account your life's realities, like kids getting sick and needing to be taken home from school, or you getting sick and needing to eat and sleep, and maybe even taking a vacation.

Michael Kitces says, "The reality is that every financial advisor eventually hits some personal productivity wall—the point at which there just aren't any hours left in the day to serve more clients, even with the assistance of technology and a team of support."[1] While this is true, FAs need to be able to look ahead and see where that wall is before they hit it and plan what to do about it in advance.

Primary FA Business Activities

Some advisors view their client or prospect contact work in terms of making some arbitrary number of calls per day or week, among a host of other important business actions they need to address. *To add certainty to their workload FAs need to and can calculate their workload based on the facts of their books and their business goals.* At a high level, FAs have the following key activities that need to be addressed on a regular basis:

- Client and Book Asset and Portfolio Management
- Client Service/Relationship Management (including client planning and review meetings and contacts, among the host of other services and deliverables outlined in the Client Service Matrix)
- Marketing/Business Development (in a number of ways discussed in Chapter 9)
- Team Management
- Business Planning and Tracking

There are other tasks that need attention, but let's assume they are mostly handled by a client associate/sales assistant and perhaps a junior advisor. Each of the above-listed FA tasks also has subtasks that need to be addressed, but that's a separate discussion.

One of our first tasks is to determine how much time we have to spend with our existing book on our retention, loyalty, advocacy strategy. Part of this strategy is to decide how many clients we have in each tier of our book—our segments—based on the criteria you have chosen to use to rate those clients (as discussed in Chapter 2). In our example in this chapter, another hypothetical book of business, we started with four segments: A, B, C, and D. After more analysis, we divided the C segment into two groups because our analysis showed that C clients with less than $1,000 in revenue were providing an average of only 30 basis points (BPS) while C clients with over $1,000 in revenue were providing an average of 121 BPS. A conclusion we came to is that we should not service these two tiers the same because they are not the same in their value or profitability to our practice. Instead, we divided this group into two tiers—tier C1 and tier C2.

Figure 4-1 | Hypothetical book of business.

Tier	# Clients	% Clients	AUM	Revenue	ROA
A	29	13.2%	$37,703,163	$400,216	1.06%
B	41	18.6%	$24,108,817	$195,355	0.81%
C1	52	23.6%	$10,897,041	$131,334	1.21%
C2	77	35.0%	$15,784,099	$47,329	0.30%
D	21	9.5%	$3,387,296	$23,615	0.70%
	220	100.0%	$91,880,416	$797,849	0.87%

Here's our hypothetical book in Figure 4-1. This is a good book of business, though it has too many clients and too many "low end" clients.

Client Contact Plan

For this book we decided on the contact plan shown in Figure 4-2 in order to support retention, loyalty, and advocacy especially from the clients we want to replicate. We have discussed our service and contact plans with our A, B, and C1 clients to get their agreement that these plans will serve their wants and needs. (See Chapter 3.) As stated, this sets expectations for the client and the financial advisor.

Figure 4-2 | Contact plan for our hypothetical book of business.

Tier	# Clients	Face to Face Meetings per Year	Phone Portfolio Reviews per Year	Check In per Year	# Contacts by Tier per Year
A	29	2	2	6	10
B	41	1	1	4	6
C1	52	0.5	0.5	2	3
C2	77	0	1	1	2
D	21	0	0	1	1

Contact Workload in Volume

Using the spreadsheet shown in Figure 4-3, we can calculate the number of meetings and calls this FA would have to make to execute this

Figure 4-3 | Meeting and call volumes for our hypothetical book of business.

Tier	# Clients	Face to Face Meetings per Year	Phone Portfolio Reviews per Year	Check In per Year	# Contacts by Tier per Year	# Face to Face Client Meetings per Year	# Client Phone Portfolio Reviews per Year	# Client Check-In Calls per Year
A	29	2	2	6	10	58	58	174
B	41	1	1	4	6	41	41	164
C1	52	0.5	0.5	2	3	26	26	104
C2	77	0	1	1	2	0	77	77
D	21	0	0	1	1	0	0	21
Annual Totals	220					125	202	540
Weekly Totals						2.6	4.2	11.3

contact strategy. This FA would have to conduct approximately three face-to-face planning and portfolio review meetings a week (2.6), four telephone planning and/or portfolio review meetings a week (4.2), and 11 or 12 check-in calls a week.

We then estimate how long each meeting type and call takes. We have assumed average meetings and calls take the following amount of time:

- 2.5 hours for a face-to-face planning and portfolio review meeting including preparation and review after the client has left the office, which includes a follow-up letter or email to the client and recording notes into your CRM system. This breaks out as:
    - 1 hour of meeting preparation
    - 1 hour for the meeting
    - 0.5 hours for review after the meeting
- 1.5 hours for a telephone planning and/or portfolio review meeting including preparation and review after the client call ends. This breaks out as:
    - 0.5 hours of preparation
    - 0.75 hours for the meeting
    - 0.25 hours for review after the meeting
- 15 minutes for a check-in call

Figure 4-4 | Meeting and call time commitments for our hypothetical book of business.

Tier	# Clients	Face to Face Client Meetings per Year (Time)	Annual Client Phone Portfolio Reviews per Year (Time)	Annual Client Check In Calls per Year (Time)	Totals per Year (Time)	% of Total Contact Time	% of Revenue
A	29	145.00	87.00	43.50	275.50	38.69%	56.80%
B	41	102.50	61.50	41.00	205.00	28.79%	21.22%
C1	52	65.00	39.00	26.00	130.00	18.26%	14.27%
C2	77	0.00	77.00	19.25	96.25	13.52%	5.14%
D	21	0.00	0.00	5.25	5.25	0.74%	2.57%
Annual Totals	220	312.50	264.50	135.00	712.00		
Weekly Totals[1]		6.51 Hrs.	5.51 Hrs.	2.81 Hrs.	14.83 Hrs.		

(1) Weekly totals assume the FA works 48 weeks a year, taking vacation, classes, etc.

Contact Workload in Time

It's all in the spreadsheet! As is shown in Figure 4-4, the process as described defines the number of meetings the FA is committed to and the FA's time commitments. It also shows how the time commitment the FA is making relates to the revenues the clients provide. We know in many books that A clients tend to subsidize lower-revenue-producing clients. This is a way of showing it clearly and showing the gap so that we can take adjusting actions.

Additional Client Service Time Commitments

This plan requires approximately 15 hours a week (14.83) of the FA's time for client contacts. This may seem like an appropriate amount of time to spend on client contact. However, there are other necessary service commitments including the time it takes to prepare financial plans, liability planning and management, estate and insurance analysis and planning, wealth transfer planning, education planning, client CPA contact, and lunch and/or dinner meetings. This is only one step in the time allocation process. The design of the Client Service Matrix and Client Service Promise, along with the approach given here, provides the tools for that analysis.

There is a critical point to highlight: Looking at the two columns on the right in Figure 4-4, Percent of Total Contact Time and Percent of Revenue, you see that while A clients contribute almost 57 percent of this FA's revenue, the advisor is spending only about 39 percent of his/her contact time on these clients. In the case of the B, C1, and especially C2 clients, this FA is overspending his/her contact time when compared to their respective revenue contributions.

The FA can rebalance this distribution of time by either:

- Adding the time it takes to provide other services to A clients
- Reducing the time spent on lower revenue clients
- Increasing the revenue on current low revenue clients
- Reducing the number of current low revenue clients by shifting low revenue clients to other alternatives such as newer FAs, service centers, or "Pool FAs" (a group of younger in-branch advisors)

These are the realities of determining the profitability of your book. There are considerations other than profitability. That's another, separate decision. Some FAs feel obliged to service low revenue clients because of their belief system, their commitment to long-term clients, or their commitment to the community. There are beliefs other than money. The point in this chapter is to provide a structured basis for decision-making based on the numbers, not on belief systems.

Next Steps

The next steps would be to determine how much time you spend on the other tasks in your business: client and book asset and portfolio management, other client service/relationship management services, marketing/business development, team management, tracking, and assumedly other activities like problem resolution. In addition, there are emails and inbound phone calls. Similar techniques can be applied to each of these other FA business activities. The point here is to organize and structure your business as best you can based on the realities of your current book of business, your team, an effective and efficient set of roles and responsibilities, your business plan, and the goals your plan includes.

With these steps completed, use a simple formula:

Number of Servicing Hours per Service Deliverable × Hourly Rate for Service Provider = Cost of Service (for that deliverable)

The sum of the costs for all Service Deliverables for a tier is the Total Cost of Service for that tier. Client costs are a function of their tier and can be increased or decreased by the advisor for special cases (e.g., if the client consumes more time than usual in review meetings, or consumes less time because they want only two reviews a year instead of four). In most cases we suggest using the standard cost for that tier.

The Total Cost of Service is not the same as Total Client Cost because there are other costs not related to direct service but associated with non-service activities like research, administrative, management, and marketing and sales. These latter activities are for the benefit of *all clients or the practice* itself. They can be allocated to clients as a factor determined by dividing Total Work Hours (e.g., 50 hours a week on average) by Total Servicing Hours (e.g., 25 a week on average) to account for the cost of non-servicing hours spent doing the rest of the FA's or team's work. In this example, Total Service Cost is about 50 percent of Total Client Cost, or Total Client Cost is two times Total Service Cost, so you can allocate all hours. It can be more complex than this analysis. That would likely require a consulting engagement funded for a firm-wide program using tools like activity-based costing. However, it's not necessary to get more granular here since we are working with approximations and the relative costs of servicing by tier. The approach we present here will give an individual- or team-based practice guidance for determining general profitability by client. Comparing revenue by client with cost of servicing by tier will enable the financial advisor to estimate relative profitability so adjustments can be considered (e.g., reduce the number of meetings for a low profitability client). A more detailed analysis would not be efficient or effective for most practices.

Additional Guidance

You also need to develop a "Model Week" or "Model Calendar." Model calendars and time blocking are a couple of the tools and techniques that can help you allocate your time and will be discussed in Chapter

7. The most important tool in your tool bag, however, is commitment and discipline. You need to develop your plans and follow through with them rigorously for them to be effective.

Our suggestion is also that you never overschedule your time because of the many things that can arise during your normal (usually hectic) weeks. You can pretty quickly see that the reason you may always be too busy is that you probably underestimate the time it takes to really do your job. There are solutions. The solutions are often not complex but they do require analysis and much thought and they sometimes cost money. It is likely that with a "full book" and a desire to grow your business a 40-hour week would be quite a luxury.

As time is one of your most valuable assets, you need to think through the "four steps to freedom": eliminate, simplify, automate, and delegate. Once that is done, advisors need to deliver services using two key principles:

- *Proactive preparation.* We define this as having systematic processes, clarity in expectations, and defined roles for every team member. This principle will help your team manage issues dealing with effective use of your time in addition to loyalty.
- *Alignment of your target clients and business and service model.* If you go to a high-end retailer on a busy weekend with commissioned salespeople looking for buyers of larger-ticket items and you approach them looking to buy a pair of socks, they may see you as an ineffective use of time. If you go to the best restaurant in town for a cup of coffee or perhaps to share a dessert, the wait person may also see this as an ineffective use of time. In these cases, from the perspective of the service providers, they are being inefficiently and ineffectively used. These examples, and the example of the book of business in this chapter, show that it's challenging to build an organization that efficiently and effectively services a wide range of clientele, whether in terms of wealth management or clothing or food services. While there will be exceptions, you need to align your services and business model with your target clients.

Over the past several decades what we have witnessed has led us to several conclusions:

- High-performing advisors have systematic plans to manage their processes and make effective and efficient use of their time.
- High performers have set very clear expectations with their clients as to what each client can expect from the relationship.
- High-performing teams have well-defined roles and responsibilities for each team member.

If these key elements are in place, it makes it easier for high performers to make decisions about the services that result in strong relationships and loyalty. In fact, with effectively planned service models, the number and types of decisions are reduced because decisions are part of the process; they are predetermined courses of actions. Whether a team is dealing with the cost of loyalty or other issues, high-performing teams are excellent at "proactive preparation" and having a targeted set of clients.

Action Summary | What's the Cost of Loyalty?

- In addition to understanding the value you deliver to clients, you need to understand the costs of delivering that value. Each client loyalty process can bring value to the client. It also generates costs to you, mostly in terms of your time and that of your team. You need to be in balance for an efficient and effective financial advisory practice.
- Time is one of your most important assets and the one that is specifically limited. It's your most precious raw material because it's one thing that we can never get more of.
- Value is determined by the client and cost by you. Don't deliver items to the client they don't value because they almost always have a cost. Remember that your service model for a given tier may call for a certain deliverable (e.g., a financial plan). If a client doesn't value a financial plan, you either need to convince them of their need for that plan or it may not be of value to deliver it. Find that out in conversation by asking.
- This chapter asks you to specifically decide how much time you should spend with each client, at least by tier, and how much you

can afford to spend with each client. You are running a business, and there are practical aspects of that responsibility to your clients, your family, yourself, and your firm.

- You can choose to be altruistic and do some or even all your work at a loss, but that needs to be a conscious, fact-based decision.
- Your other important asset is your knowledge as a financial advisor, which should always grow over time.
- Costs are more effectively and efficiently managed in an environment that is process-based, establishes clear expectations for the client and team, has defined team member roles, and works with a definitive set of targeted clients.

Chapter Five

Your Intake Process

Customers love certainty, make sure you give it to them. **—Amit Kalantri**

This chapter discusses how to structure and execute meetings with prospects and convert them to clients. We recommend a three meeting approach to prospect meetings.[1]

Meeting one consists of building rapport and trust; showing you care; uncovering needs, wants, unfulfilled desires, and concerns; emotionally and economically qualifying the prospect; creating interest; and getting the prospect ready to change by selecting you as their financial advisor. This phase of the process involves a detailed creative discovery so that you know as much about the prospect as possible.

The second meeting will be a complete diagnostic of the prospect's current financial situation. The goal is to uncover technical needs, review their goals, and continue to increase their level of congruence so that when the time comes to take the action of committing to you, they will say yes.

The third meeting will be about your game plan. You will demonstrate how you are going to help prospects achieve their goals. You will shape your presentation around the prospect's communication and buying style and their personality. You will use emotional tie-ins and be prepared to handle objections so the prospect takes action with you.

It is critical to *never* meet with a prospect without that person's significant other. Until recent years, especially with baby boomers, more men than women have taken the lead in financial issues when couples are involved. However, while women are already a significant force in the financial world, they are projected to be more so as time moves on—by 2020, women will control half of the wealth in the United States.[2] There will also be a dramatic increase in their earning power, with 4 in 10 women outearning their husbands. This is an increase of more than 50 percent from 20 years ago.

The National Center for Women and Retirement estimates that 9 of 10 women will be solely responsible for their finances at some point in their lives.[3] While this is an opportunity for FAs, we know that 70 percent of women fire their FA within a year of the loss of their spouse. Attempting to start developing a relationship with a surviving spouse after the death of the other spouse is too late. Relationships with both spouses need to be built from day one. The same report that gives these statistics states that Fidelity research says that women aren't afraid to ask for the help of an advisor: Among women decision-makers without an advisor, 49 percent of those surveyed said they would like to find an FA to manage their assets compared to just 17 percent of their male counterparts. But they are also not afraid to take their business elsewhere if their advisor neglects to build a relationship with them.[4]

"Unfortunately, the advice industry has not received high marks on working with female investors," the report says, citing a study by The Boston Consulting Group (BCG) that found that "women were more dissatisfied with the financial services industry than any other industry" and that "women reported being treated with disrespect and condescension, and given poor advice specifically because of their gender," and despite this dissatisfaction, female investors present an opportunity for advisors.[5]

Fidelity's research suggests that women are:

- More interested in holistic financial planning
- Typically more risk averse than men
- Often better candidates for financial advice

While there will be special cases, all meetings with clients and prospects who are part of a couple should be conducted with both parties. Beyond meetings, establishing a relationship with both parties and with their adult children should be considered mandatory for long-term success.

Meeting One: Discovery

The first meeting with your prospects is about "discovery." The processes we discuss are for true wealth management/financial planning practices using the consultative approach. In that case, your objective for this meeting is to understand the prospects as people as well as their needs and wants. These are two separate perspectives of discovery. From the standpoint of understanding the prospects you want to know their thoughts about their lives; their values, beliefs, hopes, and how they got to where they are; what they care about and why; who they care about; and what's most important to them. In this meeting your questions will go beyond money and finances. You want to know about the prospect's family, their health, their leisure interests, what they are interested in learning, their inner growth goals, and their home, community, and work lives. You can certainly note that most if not all of these "other" parts of life also have financial implications, though the focus here is on wants and needs, not on funding.

Some prospects won't necessarily or easily want to get into the depths of their psyches on their first time meeting you. However, now and as time goes on, this is where you need to go with your "to be" best clients. This discovery process is done through your manner, your questions, and your reactions. Remember that prospects make up their mind about you in the first seven seconds of meeting you and spend the rest of their time justifying their initial belief. In those first seven seconds your prospects observe your grooming and your welcome, your demeanor, and your opening comments, as well as the physical environment. Ideally you are meeting in a nice meeting room (not your office) and appropriate beverages and perhaps light snacks are served, if appropriate. Your assistant should have previously discussed with the prospects their choice of beverages. Each of the seating places has a pen and paper awaiting the visitors and you. You and your assistant are present to greet your guests. You will not be using a PC or presentation. A round or square table is better than a rectangle because there is no head of the table. Have your guests sit where they prefer and after they are seated, you join them. Your assistant asks if you need anything else and assuming not, she leaves, telling both prospects, "It was nice meeting you."

There should be no further need to introduce yourself, your credentials, or your background. If that hasn't been previously done through collateral material, it can very briefly be mentioned at the end of the meeting or preferably, if necessary, in your follow-up email, letter, or a handwritten note, which is my preference.

The goal of this first meeting is to have the prospects become comfortable with you and commit to a second meeting. That implies the prospects and you will come to the conclusion that you should both continue to discuss working together based on the prospects' belief that you can be of service to them and your belief that you can provide the services and solutions that will meet the prospects' objectives. In the end, there must be a sense that the prospects and you have begun a good working relationship.

After you have a context, and it appears there is a general meeting of the minds, you can get more into the details of the prospects' financial picture and begin to put together a plan to meet the prospects' wants and needs, which takes place in the second and third meetings.

To recap, the first meeting consists of building rapport and trust with the prospect and showing you care, uncovering needs and wants and issues they deal with in their lives, while qualifying the prospect both emotionally and financially and, most critically, creating interest from the prospect and getting an understanding they are prepared to change—either moving from their current advisor or from managing their portfolio themselves.

In their book *Storyselling for Financial Advisors*, Scott West and Mitch Anthony state: "In selling, there is no denying that analysis, number crunching, logic, and organization play a necessary role. However, these left-brain functions constitute at best, about 10 to 20 percent of the critical mass necessary for sales success. The other 80 to 90 percent comes from right-brain functions, which play primary roles in the sales realm."[6] The point for the advisor is to understand the prospect's right-brain and the person's emotional drivers. When and where appropriate, without taking too much time, share some of your own relevant emotional drivers, especially if you can identify with the prospect.

West and Anthony also state, "The greatest mistake we make in selling is neglecting to learn more about our customers before making our presentation. We are so excited or passionate about telling our story that we fail to hear our clients' stories."[7] Do not do this! This meeting is all about them, not about you!

West and Anthony also discuss how the more time you spend learning about the experiences and views of your clients and prospects, the more weight they will give to your experience and views. If you don't ask before you tell, you have no assurance that what you are saying is what the client or prospect is asking for. How can you be sure you are on target with your thoughts if you have not taken the time to let the client define the target? Ask the right questions and people will talk. Critical emotions, experiences, values, and hopes are revealed when you ask the right questions. This is payoff. Once you ask you'll understand what makes your clients tick, what they can and can't tolerate, the highly charged emotional issues to avoid, and the principles you can use to forge a bond. Prospects and clients will appreciate your questioning, as it shows you are *interested in them as individuals*, not just as accounts.

This meeting is an 80/20 experience, with the advisor speaking 20 percent of the time, mostly asking questions and answering a few, but the prospects should be speaking 80 percent of the time, telling you about themselves. Be certain to concentrate equally on both spouses.

Before listing some questions for your consideration, we want to mention the "permission technique." Using the permission technique softens situations. Asking for permission to ask a question before asking the question is a wonderful way of getting someone to really think about their answer when your question comes their way. It's a heads-up that a response is desired and it allows your prospect to mentally get in position to answer whatever you are about to ask. It gets attention, and holds it. If you choose to ask for permission, make sure that you wait to receive it before proceeding. Because this is a question, it requires a response, thus involving your prospects. Once someone gives you permission, his or her consent becomes the green light for you to ask your question or present your proposition. Asking permission works, because anything you say with permission is bound to find a more receptive audience than anything you say without it. Permission gives your prospect something to say yes to, and a "yes" is almost always a good beginning to persuasion. In fact, asking permission is so powerful that you can continue to ask permission throughout the meeting.

The following are some of the questions to consider asking your prospects in your first "discovery" meeting. You can of course start by saying, "I'd like to ask you a number of questions. Do you mind if I work from my notes so we are sure to cover everything?" P...A...U...S...E... for answer. "Are you ready to get started?" P...A...U...S...E... for answer.

- What do you hope comes out of our meeting today? (Look for values, beliefs, priorities, and hopes.)
- I would like to get to know you both a little bit better because it will allow me to make sure I give you both the proper advice for your situation.
  - Could you take a few minutes and tell me about yourselves? (Note that each spouse should give a separate answer.)
  - Where are you from? (You can ask what it was like there growing up if appropriate.)
  - How did you two meet?
- Please tell me about your family.
  - Is there anyone besides yourself whose future hinges on your financial decisions? (Give examples such as parents, children, special needs, etc.)
- Tell me about your family when you were growing up. Were there any messages about money you received when growing up? What financial values of your folks continue to affect you today? What does money mean to you?
- What are your most important financial concerns? How do you hope we can address them?
- What are your most important nonfinancial concerns and objectives?
- What are some of the things in your life that you are most passionate about? People? Causes?

- What and who are more important in your life than money?
- What are your aspirations for the future?
- What would you do differently if you had no financial concerns?
- Tell me about your work (or the work you did).
- How did you gather the wealth you have?
- What are things that you want your money to do for you? What is your "wish list"? Everyone I meet always has dreams, goals, or some deep want that they don't believe they can attain. I can't promise you we can make it happen, but let's take a moment and put together our wish list. (Give examples such as travel, family, giving, and experiences.)
    - What have you done to date about these wishes? (An example is asking where have they traveled and what did they like there.)
- What is the best financial decision you have made in your life?
- What is the worst financial decision you have made in your life?
- Are there any current or anticipated factors or circumstances in your life that could affect your financial plans?
- May I ask about your experiences with other financial advisors?
    - How did you meet your current financial advisor?
    - What is most important to you about your relationship with a financial advisor?
    - What did the advisor do that you liked?
    - Was there anything the financial advisor did that wasn't valuable or helpful for you?
    - What are some things you want to avoid in any relationship with a financial advisor?
    - What didn't the advisor do that you'd like to see added?
- Do you understand your portfolio and why it's invested the way it is?
- On a scale of 1 to 10, with a 10 being exceptional, what would cause a 10 rating for your advisor?

- There are emotional issues and life-altering traumas in every person's life. Is there anything that affected your life that you'd like to bring up? (Examples might be a layoff, medical issue, loss, etc.)
- How are you feeling about the world these days?
- What have been your sources for learning about investing, and what principles do you follow with your money?
- What would you want of this relationship? What do you expect from a financial advisor?

As time allows, it's of value to understand where the prospect is today with respect to a host of issues and where they see themselves in perhaps five years or longer, depending on the issue.

- We discussed your *family*. Do you anticipate any major changes over the next five or so years? (Examples are parental dependency, college costs for children, wedding or other event costs.)
- How is your *health* and that of your family, and do you anticipate any major changes over the next five or so years?
- How is *business* doing, and do you anticipate any major changes over the next five or so years? (If they have a business of their own you might also ask for details about employment, growth plans, and succession plans.)
- What do you do outside of work, and will you be doing more or less of that over the next five years or so? (As an example, to meet their future desired *lifestyle* wants or needs, people may need to downsize and/or move geographically. To put your plan together you need to gather that knowledge so you can prepare alternative options.)
- Do you see any *threats* to your financial security?
- Would you be willing to give me a high-level *overview* of your financial status?
    - To get a *financial picture* you want an overview, no details! If they want to show you statements, you can say, "If you think we have a meeting of the minds, and it appears we can be of help, in our next meeting we will get into the details of your accounts and finances."

    - If they want to leave their financial materials, great—it's a sign of trust.

- Do you have a recent *estate plan* in place, including *business succession planning* (if appropriate)?
- How satisfied are you with the level and quality of *insurance protection* you currently have?
- How satisfied are you with your *current investment choices*?
- How satisfied are you with being on track to build a sufficient *retirement nest egg*?
- How satisfied are you with the feelings you have about your *money* life?
- I need to ask you about situations that you definitely *want to avoid* with your investments and finances. Tell me about all the situations we need to avoid.
- How satisfied are you with the *working relationships* you have with your other service providers (i.e., insurance agent, banker, broker, financial planner, accountant)?
- Are there any questions I haven't asked you that you would like to add to give me more background?
- What questions do you have for me?

There are too many questions here to ask in a single session. At most, these discovery sessions should be kept to 90 minutes and 60 minutes, if possible. After that attention wanes, on the part of both the prospects and the advisor. It's always courteous to ask your prospects (as well as clients) how much time they have allocated to the meeting.

Prepare a questionnaire in advance. It's quite okay to have it in front of you and use it to record answers, noting from whom the answers came (i.e., spouse 1 or spouse 2). Feel free to ask the prospects if they mind if you use the questionnaire so you make sure to cover everything. It is extremely rare that people would ever say they would mind. In fact, using the questionnaire is a way of showing your preparation and professionalism.

There are some questions you can ask that give you time to respond if you need a minute to think about a reply. You can essentially ask for further clarification with these questions:

- What's important about that to you? Why is it important? (Ask the other partner if they feel the same way.)
- Tell me why you say that. (For example, if a prospect suggests the cost of a full-service financial advisor is too high, you ask, "Why do you say that?" Understand what the prospect's experience may be before responding. You do have to answer this question in many cases, whether it's overtly asked or not.)
- Tell me more. (You can slow a conversation with these three words.)

By the end of this first meeting you should have qualified the prospect and gained an understanding of whether you are on the road to a good relationship and they are willing to consider you as their advisor.

The most telling moment here is whether they commit to a second meeting. At the appropriate point, you can say, "Thank you very much for sharing about yourself and your situation with me today. Is there anything else you want to address that I may not have asked you about? Your answers and comments have given us excellent background that we can integrate into your plan. Our next step will be a complete diagnostic of your current financial situation. I can't promise that we can fulfill all of the wants, needs, and goals we discussed, but if you are comfortable with me so far, we need to see your financial data in detail." Then provide a checklist, such as the one in Figure 5-1.

The second meeting should be within a week of the first meeting. You can say, "In our next meeting we'll discuss your financial situation in depth and your technical needs, go over your goals, and continue to gather the information we need to develop a financial plan. Let me suggest that we get together next Tuesday at 3 p.m., if that fits your schedule."

At this point you also want to review and validate your understanding of the current meeting. So you can say:

> I'd like to summarize today's discussion. This is my understanding:
>
> - Of the needs you have described
> - Of the concerns you have described

Figure 5-1 | Client meeting preparation checklist.

Client Meeting Preparation Checklist

Name ______________________________ Date ____________

Use the checklist below to help prepare prior to our meeting:

Key Life Events

Check	Event	Notes
❑	Births	
❑	Weddings	
❑	College	
❑	Retirement	
❑	Misc.	

Financials

Check	Event	Notes
❑	Pay Stubs -Spouse 1 -Spouse 2	
❑	Investment Statements	
❑	Other Inv. Accts (e.g., 529)	
❑	CDs	
❑	Cash Balances	
❑	Last Tax Return	
❑	Cash Balances	
❑	Wills and Other	
❑	Cash Balances	
❑	Trusts	
❑	Life Insurance Stmnts. or Policies	

Figure 5-1 | Client meeting preparation checklist (continued).

Check	Event	Notes
❑	Annuity Statements	
❑	Long-Term Care Insurance	
❑	Disability Insurance	
❑	Mortgage Infor. - Current Amt. - Interest Rate - Monthly Payment - Est. Mkt. Value	
❑	Other Assets (e.g., Real Estate, Art, etc.)	

Business

Check	Event	Notes
❑	Annual Est., Prescriptions, Medical, Charitable, Private Schools, Taxes, and Insurance	
❑	Est. Lg. One Time Exps. Next 3 Years	
❑	Est. Exp. Projection Next 12 Months	

- Of the wants you have described
- If our plan can address your needs, wants, and concerns you are prepared to work with us. You are ready for the next step—a meeting to get back together and review investments and start creating your plan.
- Are my understandings correct?

After your discovery meeting, also debrief yourself about the meeting to ensure that you understand the prospects' wants and needs, their personalities, and how they communicate, so that in your next meeting you can work even better with them. Medical professionals also record their notes; advisors can record the debrief using a transcription service and app like Copytalk (www.copytalk.com) or other technology. Send the prospect a summary of your meeting notes and post your notes to your CRM system.

Most important, send a thank-you note to your prospect and make it personal. We prefer handwritten thank-you cards without corporate logos. Hand-address the card and use a regular stamp. Do it the day of the meeting.

Meeting Two: Detailed Discussion of Financial and Related Status

It's always important in a set of meetings to review the previous meeting you had with the prospects. Assuming you have made headway in understanding the prospects and their status and concerns, you want to play back your conversation to validate the information and show the prospects you understand their situation. If you have elevated their concerns, you want to get the prospects back to the state they were in during your first meeting. You want the prospects to remain ready to work with you. Any negative or painful emotions prospects may have had over their current situation could have dissipated since the last meeting so they need to be restored. If any changes have taken place since your last meeting you will want to identify them.

This second meeting will be a complete diagnostic on the prospects' current financial and related situation. Your objective is to review their goals, continue to ensure they are on the path to work with you, and identify technical needs. You want to continue to build rapport and trust and show you care and have their interests first in mind as a fiduciary. Wherever possible, begin to link potential actions or tentative recommendations to getting the results they want. Continue to get the prospects ready to work with you.

You do this through the questions you ask, similar to the first meeting:

- What are your desired outcomes for our meeting today?
- How do you *both* feel about first meeting?
- Are you *both* ready to get started on our meeting today?
- Before beginning, let's recap our first meeting for a moment. Is that okay?

While you are gathering the financial data you need to put together your wealth management action plan, continue to validate that you are on course with the prospect. You will gather a full picture of their assets, liquid and illiquid, and whether you will manage them. If they have any concerns and fears relative to these assets, it will be of value to know them. You have already asked about the prospect's best and worst financial decisions, but as appropriate you can validate that they believe the assets identified were good or bad decisions and why. This is another opportunity to ask if there is anything you have discussed as part of their full picture that is disturbing about their current financial situation. You are searching for the prospect's motivations for taking actions and reaffirming they want and need your help.

Focus on the prospects' biggest concerns and fears so they feel the need to change. Ensure that you are accurately describing the expressed concerns. Understand their perspectives about their portfolios so that you understand their role in investment decision-making and how they feel about that role now and going forward and their rationale for their various holdings.

Where appropriate, be on the lookout for opportunities to test-close and identify objections so that you can figure out how to best present your plan and recommendations. For example, you can say, "If you like our plans, how soon would you want to get started on putting them in place?" As it fits the discussion bring up alternative strategies to get reactions and ideas. This can tell you something about the prospects' willingness to make changes. For example, you can use questions like, "How would you feel about investing part of the portfolio in well-known dividend-paying equities instead of bonds to get a better yield?" Or, "We might want to invest in ABC. It's a solid company with a fairly stable stock price and pays a dividend of X percent and has done so for *N* years. How would you feel about that?" Or, "I'm curious. Have you ever considered XYZ?" You are also testing the prospects' willingness to consider various alternatives. This can help when developing and presenting your plan.

By the end of this second meeting, you have qualified your prospects as being ready and willing to commit to an implementation plan if your plan meets their wants, needs, and goals. Explain that your next step is to prepare their personalized wealth management plan, including asset allocation and general portfolio recommendations. This plan will show the prospects how you are going to help reach their goals. Whether direct or indirect, it's important to let the prospects know that developing this customized game plan will take a significant amount of analysis and preparation and you want to make sure that if the plan is on target, there will be every reason to accept it and move forward with its implementation if the plan meets with their approval.

At the end of this second meeting, you again want to thank the prospects for sharing themselves and their financial details. Ask if there is anything else they want you to address you may not have answered. State that it will take a week for the team to put together their plan and then suggest you get together on such and such a date—for example, "next Tuesday at 3 p.m.," if that fits their schedule. Your primary goal is to have gotten positive receptions on all points until now and to get your prospect to the third meeting.

Meeting Three: Detailed Discussion of the Prospect's Game Plan

This third meeting in the process is about the personalized game plan your team prepared for the prospect. Your objective is to gain commitment to implement your plan.

You want to make sure your prospects are looking forward to the meeting, so 48 hours before the meeting the advisor should directly call the prospects to confirm the meeting and minimize any concerns or fears that could hold them back from taking action.

> Sid and Nancy, I'm very much looking forward to seeing you on _________ because I know you are going to be really excited about your plan. I'm sure we are going to be able to get your wants and needs met (*be specific*) and avoid what we discussed about (*concerns*). I'll see you on _________.

In presenting your plan you will focus on how you are going to help the prospects achieve their goals. Use the words, thoughts, and concerns and any other elements you learned about the prospects, their communication style, their buying style, and their personalities. Since the majority of buying decisions are based on emotion, get the prospects back to any emotional concerns raised in your meetings. Continue to seek positive feedback and answer any objections or concerns as they arise. While being compelling about the plans you have developed, avoid anything pushy or aggressive.

After your initial remarks, ask your prospects if they are ready to review their plan. Use language like "Our plan" and "When the three of us . . ." as you discuss various points, whether a recap of their situation or your recommended asset allocation and the reasons for your recommendation. Get agreement on all key points and/or decisions one at a time.

Use the word "because" to share your reasoning. For example: "I recommend X *because* ____________." Where appropriate, ask, "Do you see how this will address ____________?" Note the prospect's response. The word "because" is powerful. "Research shows that when the word 'because' is inserted in a repetitive script in an attempt to influence a lot of different people, compliance goes up consistently by 32 percent. . . ."[8]

- Say to your prospect, "After careful analysis we have decided on a 30/60/10 mix of equities, fixed income, and cash *because* you stated a major concern about preserving your assets, getting income of $24,000 a year, while participating to some degree in the growth of the equity markets."

- Assuming agreement, you might say, "And to contain risk, we're going to invest your fixed income in only highly rated securities *because* we want to limit risk. How does that sound?" (Or, "What will this mean to you?")
- Assuming agreement, you might say, "And we are going to invest your equities in five highly rated funds or exchange traded funds (ETFs) representing all major equity styles *because* we want to limit overlap and also contain risk. How does that sound?"

Don't use the word "proposal"—use the word "plan." Proposals are for consideration; plans are for actions to be taken. Plan your approach in advance and understand that if you get bogged down you can use a technique called "pattern interrupt." The intent is to change the mood, the situation, a thought or behavior, or any tension or negative or unresponsive pattern. The plan should be by sections, with each recommendation addressing a specific need or want or concern.

As you complete the review of your game plan, seek feedback and concerns. For example: "What would you say are the three most important benefits?" Up to this point you should have been getting positive responses along the way. It's now appropriate to ask, "Are there any questions you want to address that I may not have covered?" Pause for a response and answer any questions. If there are none, it is appropriate to say something like, "If our plan is on target, I suggest we get started. It's simply a matter of signing this account agreement and transfer form. Once the assets are transferred but before we make any investment commitments, we'll have another discussion. I very much appreciate you for selecting me as your advisor. I look forward to a long and fruitful relationship and helping you meet your financial goals and in any other area in which I can be of service to you."

Some FAs would of course like to get to a close in two meetings by combining meetings one and two. This is not recommended. If you are in a hurry, don't rush. You want to take your time and show your professionalism and the care you take in putting a wealth management plan together. Of course, many prospects don't make a decision even in three meetings. It often takes more time and meetings to get prospects ready to make changes in their financial matters.

Action Summary | Your Intake Process

Most financial advisors we have worked with believe that if they can get a prospect to come to their office for a first meeting, they can convert the prospect into a client. This is your chance. You only have one chance to make a first impression. Make sure it's a great one. If you would like ideas for doing that, we recommend the article, "9 Ways to Make a Great First Impression."[9]

The three meeting process is an approach using the steps we have outlined. It is efficient and effective if done correctly:

- *Meeting one* focuses on building rapport and trust and uncovering needs, wants, and concerns, qualifying the prospect, and creating and assessing the prospect's interest.
- The *second meeting* will be a complete diagnostic of the prospect's current financial situation and uncover the prospect's technical needs.
- The *third meeting* is about presenting your game plan, addressing concerns and objections, and gaining the prospect's commitment to work with you.

Chapter | **Six**

Your Client Planning and Review Process

Review your goals twice every day in order to be focused on achieving them. **—Les Brown**

This chapter details a structured meeting plan for each client as part of your wealth management deliverables and your client loyalty and retention efforts. This is also part of the "consultative process."

Each client meeting needs to use a structured agenda. Objectives for all meetings need to be established, whether the meeting is simply a check-in call, a telephone-based portfolio review, or a face-to-face meeting. See Figure 6-1.

Figure 6-1 | Planning and Review process.

This process may be the most overlooked one of the six core client-facing processes. Do not take it for granted. It is an important and critical process because this is one of the limited opportunities you have to meet face-to-face with your best clients—the 20 percent to 30 percent of those who provide you with two-thirds to three-quarters or more of your revenues, your most important feedback, and perhaps your best introductions.

Client meetings create engagement and face-to-face meetings have maximum impact. Where possible, it is important to spend face-to-face time with your best clients in other settings as well, whether social, intimate events, or other opportunities. We fully understand the practical limits of time and cost. Nevertheless, it's important to be face-to-face with top clients whether in your office, their office or home, or some social setting. Harvey Mackay once said, "The most important reading you can do is on your client's desks and walls."[1] It is on the client's and prospect's turf where you learn more about their reality, what they are like, and what's important to them.

A Forbes Insights article, "Business Meetings: The Case for Face-to-Face," made these points about business executives:

- Eighty-four percent preferred face-to-face communications.
- Eighty-five percent of those said face-to-face communication builds stronger, more meaningful business relationships.
- They also said face-to-face meetings are best for persuasion (91 percent), leadership (87 percent), and engagement (86 percent).
- Face-to-face contact generates a collaborative environment, inspires, and energizes a positive emotional climate between both parties.
- Lunch or coffee meetings also build relationships and camaraderie, credibility, and trust.[2]

Face-to-face meetings are important! Having said that, it's important to recognize that meetings with clients should also be convenient. Some clients, even if relatively local, do not like to travel to their advisor's office. As our society is so mobile, we don't want to lose great clients because they move. We don't want to put in the client's minds that we *must* meet in person. Creating an in-person requirement can cause issues, even though it adds value. So, consider options where appropriate: Give clients a choice, including the option of having a telephone meeting or a videoconference. Being local is not mandatory with technologies like Skype and GoToMeeting, which can make meetings more convenient for clients.

This is the process where regular client interaction has the most depth; therefore, this is where client engagement takes place. While there are a number of definitions of "client engagement," the one by Leslie Pagel at CustomerThink is excellent: While the focus here was on the "B-to-B Customer Experience,"[3] the metrics used consist of four elements that apply directly to FAs and clients. For most organizations, the ideal definition of customer engagement is based on four factors—product usage, sentiment, involvement, and competitive status.

Product usage refers to the number of products and services you offer that the customer or client uses from your "basket" of capabilities. The more products and services used by clients the more they are committing to you (i.e., the more "engaged" they are). While more products and services increases "stickiness" because it becomes more complex to undo the relationship, the key point is that it is about the client's commitment to you. In financial services we can measure cross-sell, such as the use of services like banking and lending, insurance, credit cards if offered, and online services. It's not only about the revenues from those products and services; it's mostly about loyalty and retention.

Sentiment means how the client feels and thinks about you. How important are you to your clients' lives, including their families? Do you have a meaningful relationship with the spouse, children, parents, and others in the client's family? Are you seen as a resource for decision-making when the client wants to purchase an item that isn't in your "basket" (e.g., a vacation home or travel package or an automobile). Do you know about the health and welfare of their young children, their parents, their millennial children? Have you had a family financial planning meeting? Would they trust you for that? Do you check regularly about how they feel about your services and what more you might be doing? Do you know the depth of feeling they have about your importance to their lives? These ideas are certainly critical to HNW client retention, but at some level, you can know about most of the clients you want to retain over time through a proactive contact strategy. As an advisor you can measure loyalty to some degree by the longevity of the relationship, the answers to questions you should be asking at review meetings, formal surveys, and introductions to others. But as we always say, past loyalty is no promise of future longevity. It's all about doing the next right thing frequently.

Involvement is a very interesting metric in the advisory business. Many clients are reticent to attend events (seemingly especially in New York City), but this is a worthwhile point to note if the events are "presold" and designed for client interest. Even getting clients to in-person review meetings can be challenging, so hopefully you have presold involvement as part of your intake process. Face-to-face is where relationships develop. Will your clients act as a reference where appropriate? Would they be willing to act as a case study and engage via social media? Over time you can get a sense of their involvement. If you send them a card or a small gift, do you get a thank-you call or note? Are they willing to have you meet with them in their home or office under appropriate circumstances? Does your relationship go beyond the office? Would they be willing to introduce you to their family members and/or friends? You can clearly see these clients are "engaged."

Finally, where do you stand with regard to being your client's sole or at least primary advisor? How committed is the client to you? Do they work with a competitor and measure you against the competitor's performance? If you have done a financial plan and were able to uncover all their assets, liquid and illiquid, you can know the answer, assuming the data is truthful. If the client is not willing to share complete data it could well be that the client is not "engaged" and you have to determine if this client fits the way you choose to conduct your business. There are reasons and times you will be willing to continue the relationship and work toward "engagement," but recognize this may become an issue over time because your competitor may well be applying the same strategy.

We have not seen advisors typically measure "client engagement" in a structured/formal manner or an unstructured manner. It costs time and therefore resources, but simple measurements for those top 20 percent to 30 percent of clients can have significant value to your practice.

One of the key benefits of having "engaged" clients is that engaged clients have a higher propensity to refer, and your client meetings are key to creating engagement. Julie Littlechild, who speaks to client engagement, says, "Engaged clients meet three key criteria—a client who is satisfied, loyal, and actively provides referrals." It is in your face-to-face client meetings that you have the "right conversations" that can lead to those introductions.

Littlechild's study says the "right conversations" lead to:

- Deeper connections with clients, which are reflected in higher levels of contact (e.g., 68 percent of engaged clients expect three or more portfolio reviews/year).
- Stronger personal relationships between advisors and clients, who look to the financial advisor to lead.
- Ongoing conversation; beyond reviews, client input is solicited with respect to the business. Engaged clients are more likely to have been asked for feedback, and they are more likely to believe that feedback will have a real impact on the relationship. [4]

Relationships with "engaged clients" are more expensive than average in part because of the increased contact (as shown in Chapter 4 and discussed further in Chapter 9). The extra time and cost is an investment in your best clients and provides you the many benefits[5] you want from your best clients:

- Engaged clients are more than satisfied and more than loyal.
- Engaged clients go out of their way to show their association with you.
- Engaged clients support you during both good and bad times because they believe what you offer is superior to others.
- Engagement takes your client beyond passive loyalty to become an active participant and promoter of your solutions.
- Engaged clients will want to give you more feedback—and you should be ready to handle it!
- Engaged clients will spend more money with you over time.

To move a client toward engagement, several elements must be in place:

- Clients need to have a *written* financial plan. There are a broad range of financial plans: from a basic cash flow analysis and retirement income plan to the plan with financial goals, funding for a college education, buying a larger home, starting a business, retiring "on time," leaving a legacy, personal net worth statement, cash flow analysis, debt, savings and investing plans, retirement strategy including accumulation and distribution strategies, comprehensive risk management plans, long-term investment plans, customized asset allocation strategy, investment policy statement, performance benchmarks, tax reduction strategies, and estate plans.
- The FA needs to develop a strong personal relationship with the client.
- Clients expect and need to receive a much higher level of contact than clients who are "just" content.
- There needs to be a greater sense of ownership and control when clients are asked for, and provide, feedback on the client experience.

This level of service and relationship management has significant time and cost implications. Because of the time and cost involved, engagement is typically part of the A client experience and evaluated against the value of the client and the client's potential.

The Client Planning and Review Meeting Process

To reiterate, a key part of creating engagement is taking the opportunity to seek client feedback and introductions. (We will discuss requests for introductions in Chapter 9.)

There are a number of attachments as part of this process. We will discuss each attachment in context of the process. This process is designed not only to inform clients about their portfolio but also to:

- Determine any changes that have taken place in their lives that may have affected or could affect their finances and/or plans and/or wants and needs.

- Continue the ongoing process of building and deepening the relationship.
- Ensure that the client is satisfied or, if not, develop plans and actions to improve satisfaction.
- Secure introductions to new prospective clients.

As far as scheduling your Client Planning and Review meetings, whether face-to-face or on the telephone, meetings need to be set up in advance and put on the client's and advisor's calendars. First of all, we suggest that FAs set aside an appropriate number of client meeting blocks on their Model Week and CRM calendar based on their workload calculations.

- For example, schedule a meeting every Tuesday and Thursday from 9 a.m. to 11:30 a.m. and 3 p.m. to 5:30 p.m. This allows four two-and-a-half hour time blocks for preparation, client meeting, and follow-up. Select whatever time works for you and block it on your calendar.
- The assistant can fill those times with actual client meeting times. This method limits the assistant from overscheduling the advisor, and the advisor has a structure for her or his calendar.
- Naturally these times may not work for all clients, and adjustments will be made where needed, especially for A and B clients.

Organization and structure saves time and increases efficiency. Meeting preparation time can be separated from actual meeting times as desired, as long as they are planned and blocked. Times not filled by the previous week can be released in a manner to be determined between the advisor and assistant.

- We recommend the assistant lists the meetings that are on the contact plan for the ensuing month by the 10th of that month (e.g., by April 10, May meetings are listed).
- The list is given to the advisor, who validates or modifies the meeting plan by the 15th of the month (April in this case).
- The assistant calls the clients on the list by the 20th of the month (April) and schedules the May meetings.

- The assistant sends (emails) the tentative agenda to the client by the end of the month (April in this case.)
- The assistant confirms the meetings by telephone two days before the meeting and prepares the appropriate package for the advisor after confirmation and provides the package to the advisor 48 to 72 hours in advance of the meeting. These are standards that can be modified by practice.

As desired by the practice, the assistant can ask the advisor to use a list and check off the preparation material the advisor wants for the meeting. This checklist, shown in Figure 6-2, can be modified to meet the needs of the practice.

The Client Planning and Review Meeting Process starts with planned client meetings, face-to-face or by telephone. In addition to engagement, face-to-face meetings are highly preferable for seeking introductions.

Every meeting must have a client meeting agenda. An agenda does several things, including:

- Displays professionalism.
- Gives the clients an advance view of what will be discussed so they can be both mentally prepared for what you are going to address as well as have an opportunity to modify the agenda to their wants and needs.
- Makes sure you cover everything that's important.
- Keeps you on time.
- Gives you a reminder to seek feedback and introductions.
- Sets client expectations. Too often the meeting goes too long and these critical topics are unaddressed. It's important to plan your time so that these subjects are discussed.

Figures 6-3 and 6-4 are two sample agendas for the Client Planning and Review Meeting.

Figure 6-2 | Client meeting checklist.

Street Smart Research Group, LLC
Practice Optimization for FAs

Client Meeting Checklist

- Agenda
- Most Recent Statement
- Quarterly Performance Review
- Copy of Financial Plan
- Client's Scorecard
- Client's Goals (to Guide Decision-Making)
- Current Client Fact Finder (to Ensure Updated Personal and Financial Information)
- Notes from Last Appointment
- Other Key Notes
- Actions Taken Since Last Appointment
- Outstanding Communication Information
    - Preferred Contact Information
    - Monthly Newsletter
    - Quarterly Research Overview
    - Website Access
- Other Account Statements Based on Relationship, Household, Authority, etc.
    - List
    - List
    - List
- Tax Return (Insert Years)
- Referral Form
- Discovery Sheet from Advisor Notes
- Client Goal Plan
- Insurance Policies
    - Life
    - LTC
    - Health
    - P&C
    - Other
- Other
- Other

Figure 6-3 | Client Planning and Review Meeting agenda (sample 1).

Street Smart Research Group, LLC
Practice Optimization for FAs

Planned Meeting Agenda for M/M First and Last Names

Month, Day, Year, and Location

- Review and Modification of Agenda
- Recent or Upcoming Life Events
- Review Goals, Priorities, Issues, Concerns
  - *Has anything changed regarding your goals?*
- Review Progress to Goals
  - *Are they on target?*
- Current Events and Status of the Markets
- Review of Portfolio Content and Why We are Invested in the Way It Is
  - *Questions and Answers*
- Portfolio Review
  - *Discussion of Any Necessary, Suggested, or Desired Portfolio Changes*
  - *Questions and Answers*
- Net Worth Analysis
- Additional Financial Needs
- Other (Specify)
- Meeting Summary and Next Steps
- Service Feedback
  - *What are we currently doing that you'd like to see us continue?*
  - *What aren't we doing that you'd like to see us do? or Is there one area where you think we could do a litle better in meeting your needs?*
  - *On a scale of 1 to 10 with 10 being exceptional, how would you rate our services?*
- Introduction Discussion

Figure 6-4 | Client Planning and Review Meeting agenda (sample 2).

Client Name
Agenda
July 18, 2016

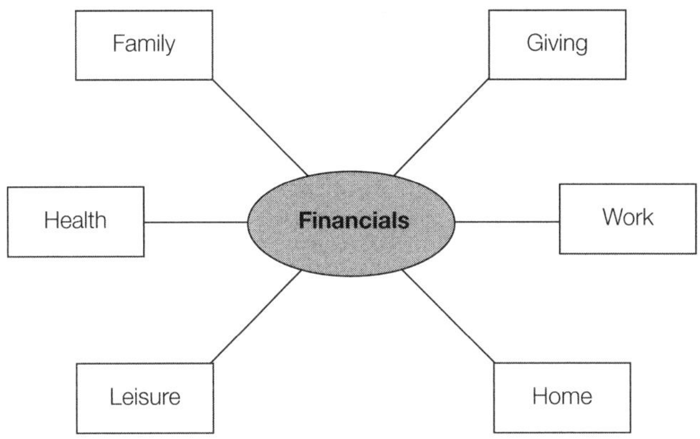

- Topics or Areas of Most Interest/Priority
- Short-Term Goals for 2016?
- Long-Term Goals for 2017 and Beyond?
- Investment Policy Statement
- Asset Allocation
- Portfolio Review/Performance Reporting
- What "One Thing" Can We Do Better for You?
- Action Items/Modifications
  - Goals ______________________________
  - IPS ______________________________
  - Asset Allocation ______________________________
  - Other ______________________________
- Suggested Next Meeting Dates

Figure 6-4 | Client Planning and Review Meeting agenda (sample 2) (continued).

Financial Planning
Potential Short-Term and Long-Term Expenses

2016			2017		
Short-Term			**Long-Term**		
$	Finance	$	$	Leisure	$
$	Health	$	$	Work	$
$	Home	$	$	Giving	$
$	Family	$	$		$
$	Other	$	$	Other	$

Annual Review
Status of Financial Needs

$	Health Care Needs	$	Financial Planning
$	Health Care Directive	$	Estate Planning-Trust/Wills
$	Income Strategy	$	Long-Term Care
$	Mortgage/Lines of Credit	$	Education Planning
$	Emergency Funds	$	Optimize SS and Medicare
$	Capital Gains Mgt. Strategy	$	Other

Annual Income Needs

$	Essential Costs	$	Desired Costs
$		$	
$	Total	$	Total

Though optional, we recommend the assistant email a note/letter and agenda to the client in advance of the meeting so they can review it and ask for any modifications they want. This also serves as a reminder. The email is intended to increase the level of importance of the meeting so clients are more willing to attend. Workload would determine if and for whom (e.g., A and B clients only) this part of the process is done. The letter shown in Figure 6-5 would be sent once the advisor has approved the meeting list. Compliance approval may be required.

The Client Planning and Review Meeting is primarily for the client's benefit—to review their current situation, discuss their goals and portfolio, and identify any changes that have taken place since the last meeting and any changes necessary based on your review. We also want to use the meeting to make sure the breadth and depth of the client's financial needs are fulfilled, as well as ensure high client satisfaction and, as appropriate, seek introductions to potential new clients.

We would like the advisor to benefit from the meeting whether it is to ensure high client satisfaction, secure introductions, or grow the relationship. We recommend advisors ask several key questions of themselves before each meeting so they have their goals clearly in mind in advance of the meeting and plan how they are going to get their desired goals met. See Figure 6-6. (Introductions, again, will be discussed in Chapter 9.)

Once the meeting is complete, the advisor would record notes in a client relationship management (CRM) system and record any potential prospects in a Prospect/Suspect Tracker (spreadsheet). The advisor would also identify actions to be taken by client and firm, assign due dates and tasks, and prepare a summary letter that is sent to the client with action items and dates to be completed. Follow-up in some form may also be required. The summary letter or email sent after the meeting would include a thank-you to the clients, with any "to-dos" and the associated due dates called out. (See Figure 6-7.) Discuss the feedback and introductions with your teammates.

Figure 6-5 | Sample letter/email sent before the Client Planning and Review Meeting.

Street Smart Research Group, LLC
Practice Optimization for FAs

March 28, 20XX

Client Name
Address
Address

Dear Bill and Billie,

First paragraphs change regularly, perhaps every 3, 6, or 12 months.

The last months have seen significant volatility in the markets and concerns in the socio-economic and international and domestic business environments. Most important as always is for investment professionals like me to ensure that my clients have the best distribution of assets to enable you to reach your goals while managing volatility and risk.

Given the changes that have taken place in portfolios due to changes in equity and fixed income values, the current environment, and laws affecting estates and investments, my colleagues and I conclude that it is more important than ever to review your entire portfolio.

This review should be conducted with an eye toward both making sure that you are not taking more risk than necessary to reach your financial goals and objectives, and making sure that your tax burden is not more than you are legally required to pay.

I look forward to meeting with you in the next several weeks. We will call you to schedule an appointment or call us at any time to schedule a time we can get together to make sure that you are optimally positioned, not just with assets that you have with me, but also to ensure that all of your assets are working in harmony together.

Attached is an agenda of the subjects I would plan to address. Please let us know if there are any other subjects of interest or concern to you.

I look forward to speaking with you soon.

FA
Financial Advisor
Private Client Group
Phone Number

Figure 6-6 | Client goal plan.

Street Smart Research Group, LLC
Practice Optimization for FAs

Client Meeting Goal Plan

Client ____

Questions

What is my business goal for this client? e.g., Improve ROA?, Gather additional data?, Gather assets away? Move to fee-based? Get introductions? Seek other business?

What is it about this relationship that would make this client willing to work with me toward this goal?

How will I go about achieving my goal? e.g., What is my work plan?

What feedback will I seek? e.g.,

- What are we currently doing that you'd like to see us continue?
- What are we currently doing that isn't valuable or helpful to you?
- Is there one area where you think we could do better in meeting your needs?
- On a scale of 1 to 10 (10 = exceptional) how would you rate our services?

Feedback is positive and I am seeking introductions—how will I ask?

Figure 6-7 | Sample letter sent after the face-to-face meeting.

Street Smart Research Group, LLC
Practice Optimization for FAs

Financial Management Group
FA Name, Senior Financial Advisor
Address
City, State Zip
email@email.com
(800) 555-5555

MONTH DD, YYYY

Dear Mr. and Mrs. CLIENT'S NAME
ADDRESS
CITY, STATE ZIP

Dear CLIENT'S NAME,

Thank you.

First and foremost, I want to thank you for being my client and tell you how much I appreciate the trust and confidence you place in me by choosing me as your Financial Advisor. I know you have many other choices you could make, so I am particularly grateful you choose me.

Meeting Summary

Second, I want to summarize our meeting of MONTH DATE. During our meeting we:

- Reviewed family, status, and financial changes during the past year and discovered you had an opportunity to roll over your 401(k) into the IRA we manage for your and you signed the paperwork. We were also able to update your financial plan with the additional data.

  Congratulations on the birth of your new grandson, NAME III. It was a wonderful gift to fund his 529 with an advance contribution of $60,000. It would be great if in 18 years his college education is covered by your generosity.

- Reviewed and validated your financial goals and determined we were on target.
- Reviewed your portfolio to make sure you understand in what we are invested and in general in the way it is invested with regard to asset allocation and asset diversification.
- Reviewed your portfolio and performance since our last meeting. We have targeted a 4.8% return base on the risk we are willing to accept and the diversification we have established. We are on target with our goals based on rational markets and have achieved a return of 6.3%. I want to make sure we understand this has been a good year for the market. We have taken some cautionary actions by moving some mid and small cap funds into fixed income securities. While this will lower our 20XX target to 4.2%, we agreed this is a much better way to manage your assets for the coming year.

Figure 6-7 | Sample letter sent after the face-to-face meeting (continued).

Name
Month DD, 20XX
Page 2

- Proposed updating your Net Worth Analysis so we can make sure the modified portfolio remains able to meet your retirement spending plans. I will call you to set a date for that meeting.
- Reviewed your additional financial needs and decided to further discuss long-term care, which we will do when we review your net worth plan.

Feedback

Third, I asked you for feedback. Client service and satisfaction are my top priorities and my structured processes ensure a proactive contact management process along with a well-thought-out investment management approach to provide the best distribution of assets to enable you to reach your goals while managing volatility and risk. I do not want to wait a year in some cases to solicit your input and make any changes that would improve the way we work together.

In order to meet this objective, we want to ensure that we have an open, ongoing dialogue through:

- Regular, proactive contact
- Our best clients tell us when we are not performing up to their expectations and while we will check in with you frequently, we encourage you to call us immediately with any questions or concerns whether it's related to account management, your statement, fees, or anything you may have heard from a colleague, friend, etc. Please call us, we are here to help.

Assistance

There are times when a family member, relative, friend, neighbor, or business acquaintance may be going through a significant life transition. I am available to help anyone you think can use me as a resource or to get a second opinion. If we can help any of the folks who are going through any of the following, please call us and we are happy to set up an appointment.

1. *Work life transitions* like retirement who may not know if they can afford to do that or have changed jobs and are not sure how to handle their 401(k)
2. *Financial life transition* like wanting a second opinion about their investments in this current market environment
3. *Family life transitions* like a change in marital status or seeking advice on funding their children's education costs
4. *Legacy life transitions* like wondering how to handle inheritance or other estate issues

I look forward to our next chat and to meeting with you again soon.

Sincerely Yours,

Name
Senior Financial Advisor
Financial Management Group

Additional Topics: General Monthly Check-In Call Discussion Topics

There are many topics that can be discussed in a check-in phone call. What you discuss depends on the client, their interests, how sensitive they are to market conditions, and your relationship and knowledge of that client, among other factors. It also depends on whether the lead advisor is calling or an assistant or junior advisor who doesn't know that client particularly well.

When the advisor makes the check-in call, she or he can do a quick review of what's going on in the markets as appropriate and ask if there is anything happening in the client's life and family you should know about. Certainly you can ask questions ("How have you been since we last spoke?") and always offer to answer any questions they may have.

Check-in calls continue to be about relationship building and having consistent communications with the client, to show you are protecting the assets they have put in your care.

Here are examples of check-in call talking points:

- Ask: "How is everything going at home? Are there any special expenses you are projecting over the next 6 to 12 months? Are there any significant changes or concerns in your life?"
- Identify key changes that have taken place in the client's financial life (e.g., job changes affect retirement plans/rollovers).
- Give a quick market status and perspective.
- Discuss a thematic topic of the month (or quarter), such as long-term care insurance (LTC) or estate planning status, depending on the client.
- Give a quick portfolio status, in line with planned asset allocation, if appropriate. For example, "We are doing well." "Everything is fine." It's better to stay away from portfolio discussions especially if this is a monthly check-in call, because we want to keep portfolio reviews to the regular schedule, from quarterly to annual, depending on the client's tier. Unless necessary, we suggest not discussing portfolio changes or new solutions because the check-in call is not

intended to be a sales call. Should clients bring up opportunities, you will of course address them.

- Gather "client wisdom"—that is, general information about contact numbers, changes in personal lives, preferences, sports, hobbies, etc.
- Ask about vacation plans. "Where are you going?" "Have you been there before?" Or, when they get back, "How was your vacation?" Check your notes.
- Gather information about the client's other advisors such as CPAs and Trust and Estate attorneys. Chapter 9 discusses Centers of Influence (COI) marketing, but here are some questions:
    - Are there times your CPA or Trust and Estate attorney may call?
    - Is it okay to chat with them in general? If they want any specific data, would we need a letter of authorization?
    - Do you highly regard this professional? Why?
    - How did you meet this professional?
    - Would you refer them to others? Why?
    - Would you introduce me?
- Establish the desire for a face-to-face meeting to conduct a portfolio review and determine if there is anything the client would like to discuss (e.g., a financial plan, their estate plan).
- Close by asking, "Do you have any other questions?"

Always thank the client for working with you.

Note that check-in calls will vary by the frequency of the call. You need to vary the content for monthly check-in calls compared to semi-annual or quarterly check-in calls. This is another reason note taking in your CRM system is important. We recommend recording notes for all client contacts. If spoken into the system or using a service like Copytalk, it can be done in one minute or less.

Every client contact is a relationship-building opportunity. Speaking to clients monthly or bimonthly about their business, their family, their children at college, their other interests, etc., is an opportunity to go beyond the business relationship with the people you never want to lose. Systematic contact, paying attention, record keeping in your client relationship management system—all are critical to your long-term success as well as to earning introductions to people they care about. This is about showing caring!

You can also use the call as a service check-in by asking one to three of the following questions about your service to make sure you are meeting your client's wants and needs:

1. Are we adding value above and beyond investment performance?
2. Is our advice helping you create a better financial future?
3. Do you feel you have a clear plan in place to meet your financial goals?
4. Are you confident that the financial plan you have in place will allow you to reach your financial goals? Are you being consistent with the savings and spending plans we discussed when we did your financial plan?
5. Do you feel we fully understand your goals for the future?
6. Are we reviewing your objectives frequently enough to understand if your needs have changed?
7. Is the short- to mid-term performance (one to five years) of your portfolio meeting your expectations?
8. Is the long-term (six-plus years) performance of your portfolio meeting your expectations?
9. Are we contacting you frequently enough?
10. Is there anything else we need to be doing to make sure you are pleased with our services?

In some cases, a sales/service assistant can make check-in calls. When an assistant makes the calls, the discussion topics we've outlined would need customization.

Action Summary | Your Client Planning and Review Process

Putting in place a structured process for Client Planning and Review delivers consistency and content, and displays competence, character, and comfort. The intent of this process is value-added contact. You want to:

- Display technical competence and know-how.
- Engender trust with ethical conduct and character.
- Engender trust with empathic skills and maturity.
- Create a positive emotional feeling so your clients can:
  - Stay informed.
  - Know they are on track to meet their goals.
  - Sleep better at night.
- Garner benefits by:
  - Creating engagement.
  - Building relationships through face-to-face contact.
  - Delivering on your promises.
  - Gathering service feedback.
  - Acquiring introductions.

Chapter Seven

Your Business Plan

Failing to plan is planning to fail. **—Alan Lakein**

If you don't know where you are going, you might wind up someplace else. **—Yogi Berra**

Your business plan defines where you want to go and how to get there. You can use the plan to monitor your progress, hold yourself accountable, and control your business's fate. A written business plan forces you to review everything at once: your value proposition, marketing assumptions and plans, operations plan, financial plan, and staffing plan. A well-executed plan can deliver the results you promise yourself. Developing a business plan is an imperative!

Prelude

The structuring of a wealth management team and business presents both challenges and opportunities. A well-run team will be efficient, achieve optimal workload and flow, fully understand the value of their time, and have a plan for long-term growth and sustainability. Over the years, we have met many teams and had a chance to study their practices. Generally speaking, teams fall into one of two categories. The first is managed chaos, where there just aren't enough hours in the day to get everything done. These teams have lots of meetings and lots of administrative work, the team leader is frequently traveling or in new client meetings, there is little scale in asset management, there is lots of trading and customization, and the feeling one gets is just overload.

The other type of team is calm. A calm team has a quieter buzz in the office. Tasks and meetings are done much more deliberately because they are planned, efficient, and effective. These teams make time for strategizing, the quality of work is high, they have a proactive service model, clients are engaged, and each team member has a defined role, to name some key traits.

What does your practice look like? Is it managed chaos or calm and effective? The key question is why are the calmer, effective teams able to manage their time more effectively and efficiently? The answer lies in the planning that these teams do in advance. These teams have a very deliberate business plan. They have decided who they want to work with and how many clients they can serve effectively, and they have a clear service definition for exactly what they are going to provide for each client. They have a set of goals, strategies, tactics, and action plans. The calm, effective teams have decided they can't run a practice without having a business plan and without planning their time well. Controlling the key variables of their desired target market(s), the number of clients, and their service commitments is critical. These teams do not have too many clients, they do not need to be overreactive, disrupting their plans, and they don't try to be all things to all clients. They plan to avoid these things.

To illustrate, let's examine this from another business's perspective. A business that can help its clients and deals well with time management is one we are all familiar with: a dental practice. Over the years we have worked with a number of dental practices, and some are managed chaos while others are very calming, efficient, and effective offices. We would all prefer to work with a dental practice that is calm, efficient, and effective. You set an appointment then receive several friendly reminders via text and phone so you are prepared for your visit. Once you arrive for your appointment, you are checked in, seated in a comfortable area where you can watch TV, read the newspaper, have something to drink, and relax for a few minutes. The staff knows all of their patients well and what they are there for, and they have a warm and friendly culture. Once your procedure is over, you are walked back to the main reception area where you can review your bill and insurance and make your next appointment. As a result, the process is professional, comfortable, and personal, which is what you want. You and the professional's time are effectively and efficiently used.

By comparison, we have known dentists who weren't quite as calm and professional. This is a different kind of practice. The furniture is old and outdated, there is no TV, no refreshments, the staff always seems too busy, and you have to wait while the receptionist is handling lots of calls, has piles of paperwork around, has a hard time fitting you into their future schedule, and seems to know you primarily through a manila folder of which there are thousands. The dentist rushes in and rushes out and always seems to be behind schedule. It's a very different environment and feeling. The chaotic practice simply has too many clients because over time it became a "volume" practice instead of a "higher end, higher touch" practice.

If you were a several million-dollar prospective financial services client, you would want to work with a professional who is always prepared and has a very well organized group. That's what this book is about, and when examining how to attract more ideal clients, the firm needs to be built and in position to properly market to and service those clients.

There are other lessons we can learn from dentists. One is that the dentist is the expert and in charge. He or she may consult with you, but ultimately you will be given a recommendation that you will most likely take. You do not see a patient suggesting that they would like a root canal when the dentist has suggested you fill a cavity and focus on proper maintenance and hygiene. Similarly, your clients look to you the same way, as the expert. Dentists are in the prevention and pain management business. A dentist will give you a plan to keep your mouth healthy and at the same time prevent pain that may arise occasionally. Your clients also look to you to keep their financial plan and portfolio healthy and to avoid as much pain as possible. We also learn that reaffirmation is important. When the dentist says "Everything looks good; see you in six months," that's a good feeling. Your clients look to you for the same assurances.

All of this illustrates that in our daily lives we get a chance to see many businesses as well as advisory practices. Pay attention to these experiences. You will notice that some businesses are very efficient and focused; some deal with a select clientele while others serve the masses; and some provide an exceptional client experience. Within your practice you can define who and how you want to provide service. Ultimately the clearer that is, the more time you will have. The more time you have, the more energy and manpower can be focused on growing the practice and other high value uses of your and your team's time.

All of this begins with the business planning process. A planned and well-run practice should be growing at 15 percent per year as measured by new clients, new assets, and new revenue. A normal practice will leak about 5 percent per year, with clients and assets leaving, so bringing in 15 percent per year of new business will help ensure that your practice is growing at 10 percent net per year. Using the rule of 72, the business should then double in size in seven years, assuming flat capital market returns. In order to achieve this level of growth a practice should have 20 percent of manpower focused on growth. Naturally you can establish a higher growth goal for your business, which will impact your plans and your resource requirements.

Purpose of Your Business Plan

A business plan is a tool for understanding how your business is put together and how to take it from where it currently is to where you want it to be in the next X years and how you plan to accomplish that. You can use the plan to monitor progress, hold yourself accountable, and control your business's fate. Writing your business plan forces you to review everything at once. A well-executed plan can deliver the results you promise yourself. For our purposes we will think of a business plan as a 12-month plan, though plans can be put in place for two, three, and five years just as well. Having said that, the longer the plan looks out into the future, the less reliable it will likely be in a dynamic world. Therefore, longer-term plans should be more generalized and goals based with larger potential steps and alternatives rather than detailed tactics. Longer-term plans are meant to be directional in nature. Business plans for financial advisors that are any longer than five years don't make a lot of sense other than as general statements about the sale of the business, for example, or succession planning, or intent to partner. Even then, they are not plans but intentions. (Companies with significant research and development or major build projects may well have longer-term plans.) The plans you make, however, including for the intermediate term, need to be updated annually, so you may be looking out five years, every year.

Business planning must be a frightening concept! If you Google "business plan," you will get tens of millions of hits. Yet no matter how much extolling of the virtues of and necessity for a business plan, it seems a minority of advisors have one, at least a good one. And, if they do, they rarely seem to review the plan and see how they are doing against the things they "promise" themselves.

One of the points we make with advisors and planners is that a classic business plan is not required by advisors especially in cases where they are not a start-up or seeking external funding or doing a deep dive into the competitive marketplace. A "business plan" for most advisors and planners is more about setting growth goals and developing an effective marketing and sales strategy for reaching of those growth goals. An effective marketing and sales strategy is about the approaches you are going to take to acquire new clients and gather new assets from both existing and new clients (e.g., introductions from clients).

While it's of value to have a handle on revenues and expenses, if you are not a start-up, it's not that difficult. In fact, for some broker-dealer advisors, there are relatively few expenses per se, and they can be estimated fairly easily by looking at last year's expenses and projecting an increase in proportion to that year's expenses and your growth goals. For example, if you pay your assistant 1 percent of gross as a bonus and last year you grossed $500,000, you rewarded him or her with a $5,000 bonus. If you are projecting a gross of $600,000 this year, you would budget $6,000 for a bonus. If you budgeted 4 percent[1] for marketing last year and hit your expense target of $20,000, this year you might budget $24,000 and make adjustments as you prefer and/or as a function of last year's overspending or underspending. If your plan calls for additional marketing campaigns not in last year's budget (e.g., monthly client intimate dinners), then increase your budget by an estimated amount for that campaign.

If you are an independent advisor with your own overhead, you know what you spent last year for personnel, equipment, rent, heat, light, power, etc., and you would use last year's numbers adjusted for any known or anticipated increases and use a similar approach for bonuses and marketing expenses. Your biggest variable may be in increased personnel costs required to grow your gross by 20 percent. This is something you should be able to determine by evaluating whether your staff seems already overloaded or at capacity. Even if they are neither overloaded nor working at capacity, you may bring in staffing in different forms and over time, such as virtual employees, interns, part-timers, or full-timers. You will also have to determine any space requirements for additional staffing.

We trust that this portion of your analysis is well within the range of your capabilities as an FA. It's easier than the marketing and sales portion of your business plan. In any case, it's best to establish your marketing and sales budget after you have completed the rest of your plan.

For many, if not most, FAs and planners, we suggest a base business plan should include the following sections:

1. A Review of Last Year (for perspective)
2. Your Business Foundations (i.e., value proposition; ideal client profile, if unique; and target or niche markets)
3. Goals (including any special or emphasis areas such as financial planning, insurance, etc.)
4. Focus Areas
   a. Marketing and Sales Strategies and Tactics
   b. Service Strategies and Tactics
   c. Operational
5. Model Week/Time Blocking
6. Marketing Calendar
7. A 90-Day Action Plan

Examples of these sections will be illustrated in the next sections. You can put together your marketing and sales portion of your business plan in one or two weekends—yes, two to four days is enough to get a base plan in place with some limited detail. My suggestion is to put your plan together starting early November and completing it by the end of that month. If you are part of a team, you should work together using a common approach. Parts of the plan can be done together (e.g., Last Year's Review, Business Foundations and Goals, Marketing Calendar, and the 90-Day Action Plan) after a couple of hours in a planning session working with a sample plan and format. Parts of the plan can be done independently and reviewed as a team (e.g., the focus areas such as Marketing and Sales Strategies and Tactics, Service Strategies and Tactics, Operations, and Model Week/Time Blocking).

When complete, your entire team should read the plan and discuss it for a couple of hours, asking and answering questions and making any needed changes. The plan should be read by your manager, if you have one, for feedback of value. Your plan is also a document that can be used by potential new employees whose feedback will also be of value.

There are, however, other views on business plans that go beyond the base plan we are recommending. In her article "Why Goals Are Secondary in Business Planning," Julie Littlechild says a goal may be "growth or income. Having that kind of goal, however, is very different from having a vision of the business and life that you want to live. I'd suggest you need both."[2] Littlechild goes on to say that a vision might include the kind of clients with whom you want to work, the kind of work you want to do, the environment in which you want to work, and the people with whom you want to work, among other items. We wouldn't argue the point of using "your vision as a filter," and as she goes on to say, "By all means, set goals, just . . . to decide if they are the right goals." For this book, we will stay focused on the elements of a marketing and sales plan based on growth goals. Establishing a practice vision would be an important component of your three- and five-year plan.

The Business Plan

There is no question that without a plan for your business the odds are high that you will wind up somewhere, but it's less likely that it will be where you had hoped. In the many years we have planned and seen plans, we observe two kinds of plans:

- One written for management that essentially says what they want you to say so they can rationalize their growth projections. Once written, these plans sit on a shelf. They are rarely if ever pulled out and reviewed or used to see where you are versus where you planned to be and/or modified based on your current reality. They are essentially ineffective as a tool for growing your business.

- One written for yourself and your team. These plans are done to guide your day-to-day efforts to get you to your desired end-state. They outline the roles and responsibilities of yourself and your team. Your action plans need to be reviewed weekly or monthly at most, and the overall plan reviewed with your team at least quarterly.

Our planning approach is essentially a marketing and sales plan. How do we get from where we are to where we want to be? We can estimate costs, but our focus in this plan is on asset growth. We start the plan with several base questions in the review of last year:

- What went well (this current year)? What were your successes and how did you accomplish them? Can and should they be repeated?
- What could have gone better (this current year)? What were your greatest concerns/hurdles? Can you overcome them in the coming year and how?
- What would your clients say about you if asked?

Figure 7-1 is a tool/questionnaire you can use to create your value proposition and better answer that last question: "What would your clients say about you if asked?"

Developing Your Value Proposition

In addition to developing your Unique Value Proposition (UVP) with material discussed in Chapter 1, you may also want to ask selected clients the following questions to help you refine your value proposition based on client input. These questions are most effective when asked in person, but it can also be done over the phone. When you speak with clients, ask them if they would be open to spending a little time answering some questions that will help you and your team become more focused so you can offer better client service. Your best clients will be willing to help.

Figure 7-1 | Section 1 Business Plan: Review of Last Year.

20XX Business Plan For:

____

Review of Last Year

What went well?

1 — Revenues up 15%

2 — Fee based business up 6 points to 63%

3 — Net new assets increased by $9 MM to $72 MM

4 — Net new households increased by 5

5 — Received 7 unsolicited referrals; closed 4

6 — Segmented book of business

What could have gone better? What were your greatest concerns/hurdles?

1 — Prospecting, i.e., use of LinkedIn, consistency in asking for introductions

2 — More consistency in client contact

3 — Developing relationships with COIs

4 — Using structured review and planning meetings with A and B clients (agenda and after-meeting letter)

5 — Use of Client Service Model/Promise

6 — Time management

What would your clients say about you if you asked?

1 — Works in my best interests

2 — Trusts my recommendations

3 — Easily accessible

4 — Proactive on contacts and determining my needs and interests

5 — Has integrity

Questions to Develop Value Proposition

1. What do you think are my and my team's greatest strengths?
2. How would you describe the service experience you have with my team?
3. How would you describe your investment experience with me and my team?
4. When you decide on a service provider, whether it's financial services, tax services, or medical, for example, what are the characteristics you look for?
5. Do we communicate with you enough, the right amount, or too much?
6. If you were to describe the exceptional client experience, what would be the most important components?
7. How would you describe the value I and my team bring to you?
8. If a friend asks you about us, how would you describe what we do for you?
9. If a friend or relative asked you why you chose us to manage your financial goals, what would you say the reasons are?
10. Name three things we can do to strengthen our relationship with you.

Take excellent notes during these conversations. They will be the foundation of your value proposition.

While not statistically accurate, we suggest having such a discussion with 10 to 15 clients and looking for common themes. We would focus on A tier clients and some B tier clients. In your A and B tier interviews you will also be seeking improvement opportunities to consider. Separately, you may want to interview some C tier clients as well to get a sense of where you stand with that group and the service model you are delivering. Some improvement opportunities may also exist.

When you are done, ask yourself and your team these three questions:

1. Did we hear anything that surprised us?
2. Can we add clear and powerful content to our UVP from what we heard?
3. Are there areas we need to improve to create an exceptional client experience going forward?

Business Foundations

To define **business foundations**, state a short version of your value proposition: Why should or why does a client do business with you as opposed to the 285,000 other choices? Defining a short value proposition is not easy. Glean ideas from Chapter 1; also consider financial life planning pioneer Mitch Anthony,[3] who, according to blogger Michael Kitces, put forth terminology for "articulating the true client-centric value proposition of financial planning." Framing the goal in the context of improving a client's "Return on Life" (ROL, as opposed to the traditional approach of trying to improve the client's portfolio ROI), Anthony suggested six key value propositions of financial planning:[4]

> *Organization.* We help bring order to your financial life by assisting in getting your financial house in order (at both the "macro" level of investments, insurance, estate, taxes, etc., and also the "micro" level of household cash flow).
>
> *Accountability.* We help you follow through on financial commitments by working with you to prioritize your goals, show you the steps you need to take, and regularly review your progress toward achieving them.
>
> *Objectivity.* We bring insight from the outside to help you avoid emotionally driven decisions in important money matters, by being available to consult with you at key moments of decision-making, doing the research necessary to ensure you have all the information, and managing and disclosing any of our own potential conflicts of interest.
>
> *Proactivity.* We work with you to anticipate your life transitions, and to be financially prepared for them, by regularly assessing any potential life transitions that might be coming and creating the action plan necessary to address and manage them ahead of time.

> *Education.* We explore what specific knowledge will be needed to succeed in your situation by first thoroughly understanding your situation then providing the necessary resources to facilitate your decisions and explaining the options and risks associated with each choice.
>
> *Partnership.* We attempt to help you achieve the best life possible but will work in concert with you, not just for you, to make this possible by taking the time to clearly understand your background, philosophy, needs, and objectives; work collaboratively with you and on your behalf (with your permission); and offer transparency around our own costs and compensation.

As Michael Kitces says, "While the words themselves are not necessarily new and unique, Anthony's use of them, along with explanations of exactly what the advisor provides, and how . . . paint a remarkably clear picture of what the intangible service of financial planning [based practice] is meant to provide. . . ."[5]

It doesn't help you to define an **ideal client profile** as affluent, nice people who take your advice, are in their 50s or 60s or older, and are willing to accept a fee-based approach. This definition gives you no specific target. You need to be targeting areas where you can focus your attention and get attention. We will discuss niches further in Chapter 9. We suggest your ideal client profile, your target market, and your niches can be synonymous. Niches are narrowly defined (e.g., not doctors, but anesthesiologists or gastroenterologists or radiologists). Individuals in narrowly defined fields tend to have a common culture and a natural affinity. They likely read the same professional journals and magazines, attend the same meetings or conference, and have more of a tendency to know others in their sphere.

Women, for example, are not a target market; retirees and pre-retirees are not a target market; airline pilots are not a target market. While there are similarities, there is no single common culture, no common way to access them, and limited shared affinity. If you narrow the focus to women executives in your geography, or working at IBM, or IBM employees retiring from New York City or Austin, Texas, you have a target market as well as a niche. Pre-retirees or retiring Exxon employees in Houston or Baton Rouge could be a niche. American Airlines or Delta Airlines pilots could be a niche. See Figure 7-2.

Figure 7-2 | Section 2 Business Plan: Business Foundations.

Business Foundations

Value Proposition/Mission Statement

We work individually with clients to understand what is important and unique to them and their families. Working with our clients we personalize plans for them that connect their current situation, values, goals, and wants and needs, with their wealth. Our goal is to translate the family's vision and dreams into a plan with a purpose. As part of this plan we focus on wealth creation, asset management protection, and identification of any risks that will mitigate their plans and ability to maintain or enhance their lifestyle and future.

Ideal Client Profile (Profession, Liquid Net Worth, etc.) — There Can Be Multiple Profiles

Professions include health care professionals, attorneys, CPAs, small-business owners, and corporate executives and managers both pre-retirees and retirees.

Investable NW = $250K minimum

Our community of clients appreciates and is willing to follow the advice of an expert. All of our clients realize that achieving their goals requires both money and planning. Our clients enjoy the simplicity, freedom, and peace of mind that comes from having all of their financial assets under the watchful eye of a single, trusted advisor. Our clients appreciate our advice and guidance. Due to the high level of client interaction and attention, our services make sense for families with over $250,000 of investable assets. Our community delegates financial matters so they can focus their valuable time and energy on the things in their life that are most important to them. Our clients want to hear the truth from us regarding their financial situation. . . no matter what.

Target Markets to Focus On:

1.

2.

3.

4.

5.

Goal Planning

Your next step is to commit to a new asset goal that will come from a combination of current and new households. You don't really need a new revenue goal as it's calculated as a function of your assets and your current or projected return on assets (ROA). You can set a goal of improving your overall ROA, though it will most likely be within 5 to 10 BPS at most of your current ROA. You can target additional revenue products like financial planning fees, annuities, insurance, or banking, if offered. For every $10,000 you project in such revenues you can lower your asset goal by about $1 million, assuming 100 BPS.

The primary questions are:

- How many new assets will come from existing clients? This will be based in part on what you accomplished in the last 12 months and your efforts in the coming months. There are some questions you need to ask that can impact this area:
  - Are your clients appropriately segmented?
  - How well do you know your clients?
  - Are you aware of any impending money in motion transactions?
  - Is your service model written and committed and highly satisfactory to your clients?
  - Have you developed a financial plan with the client?
  - Did you uncover assets away?
  - Are your service processes as efficient as they need to be?

If the answer to any of these questions is no, you have work to do here—and opportunities.

- How many new assets will come from new client acquisition? This will only in part be what you accomplished in the last 12 months. The real growth will come from the new effort you put in.
  - What did you accomplish in the last 12 months and the 12 months before that?
  - How much time do you spend on new client acquisition?
  - How much time do you need to spend on new client acquisition to hit your goal?

- Where is that time going to come from?
- How serious are you about your goal? On a scale of 1 to 10, with 10 being 100 percent committed, anything less than a 10 won't make it happen.

You need to *commit* to time blocking. After building a standard Model Week and a Marketing Calendar, you commit to and then develop a 90-Day Action Plan. See Figure 7-3.

Your next and most important steps are to define the "strategies" and "tactics" you will use to both grow assets from existing clients and new clients and improve your service strategy and operations if needed.

Focus Areas: Marketing and Sales Strategies and Tactics

There are at least 20 different marketing and sales strategies that can be used to acquire new client households and their assets. Which three or four will you use? This of course may be based on your will and skill as well as your past successes and any past failures that you can successfully overcome. About two-thirds of your new client acquisition will come from introductions from existing clients and centers of influence. LinkedIn is essentially a tactic for gathering introductions usually from existing clients. Networking, both personal and corporate, which would include "intimate events," is another strategy. If you haven't considered your "Book of Life," who you know and how you know them, it may be worth considering. While general seminars are a focus of the past, "roundtables" or "lunch and learns" inside of small businesses can be effective. Finally, "niche marketing" can be a very important strategy. For each strategy you select, you will also develop a set of tactics or steps in the process and the time frames to accomplish them, and assign who has the responsibilities for executing that strategy and set of tactics.

A critical part of the planning process is review and modification of the plan. Whether you are on a team or not, it is an imperative to take a half-day to a full day to review your progress against the plan. (We will discuss a set of weekly metrics you can use to determine progress.) Note what's working and not working, make modifications and adjustments and major changes as needed, and put together your

Figure 7-3 | Section 3 Business Plan: Goal Planning.

Goal Planning

Business Results Goal Summary

	20XX Results	20XX Goals	% Change
Assets			
Total Assets	$72,000,000	$86,400,000	20%
New assets acquired	$9,000,000	$14,400,000	—
Total households	88	100	14%
New households	5	12	240%
Qualified introductions	11	24	218%
Total revenue	$576,000	$648,000	12.5%
Fee-based revenue	$363,000	$441,000	21%

Additional Focus Areas:

Financial Planning	Will complete financial plans using XYZ software for 36 prospects and clients
Insurance	Identify all A and B clients and all prospects for opportunities
Managed Accounts	Recommend as appropriate
Centers of Influence	Identify CPAs and Trust and Estate Attorneys of top 20 clients and vet them with client

next 90-Day Action Plan. Your business plan and quarterly reviews will help ensure that you are paying attention to the broad strategies, tactics, and goals of your business as well as any details such as budgets.

Your business plan is mandatory to develop and communicate a course of action for yourself and your team. Remember, however, as Peter Drucker said, "Plans are only good intentions unless they immediately degenerate into hard work."[6]

Similar sections are completed for the other aspects of your plan within the "Focus Areas—Marketing and Sales Strategies and Tactics" section. (See Figure 7-4.) In the sample plan, they include:

- *Subsection 1:* Organic Marketing (client based). Within this section (see Figure 7-5), we suggest identifying:
    - Top 5 clients to acquire additional assets from
    - Top 10 LinkedIn contacts to approach for introductions
- *Subsection 2:* New Client Acquisition Marketing (prospecting), shown in Figure 7-6, which should or might include:
    - Meeting with prospects who were introduced by clients either as a result of client meetings or the LinkedIn process
    - Top 5 pipeline prospects to close
    - Five former clients or inherited accounts that you will commit to call on
    - Using networking approaches
    - Using intimate events and/or targeted seminars
- *Subsection 3:* Center of Influence Marketing, which includes identifying CPAs and Trust and Estate attorneys from your Top 20 clients and using the COI Marketing Strategy (discussed in Chapter 9) to vet them with clients. See Figure 7-7.

Figure 7-4 | Section 4a Business Plan: Focus Area—Marketing and Sales Strategies and Tactics/Current Clients.

Focus Areas — Marketing and Sales Strategies and Tactics

Identify Focus Areas

1. High-Level Opportunities Within Existing Practice

1. Gather assets away by conducting financial plans for all A and B clients who have not had an update plan prepared within the last 18 months
2. Conduct 3 client face-to-face meetings a week; 3 telephone meetings a week; 11 check-in calls a week based on 35 A clients, 40 B clients, and 25 C clients introducing new Client Service Promise
3. Insurance—Conduct an insurance review in context of an Estate Planning Review for all annual meetings
4. See introductions—Complete "Client Wisdom" profile seeking ways to ask for introductions
5. Use LinkedIn, connect to all clients who are on LinkedIn, update profile, use LinkedIn process to identify prospects with 24 clients
6. Gather COI information from top 20 clients and vet those COIs to identify 10 potential partners

2. Organic Marketing (Client Based)

	Tactics
Gather assets away	1. Identify clients who have not had a financial plan within last 18 months
	2. Determine which clients are ready for annual meeting and schedule, preparing them to conduct financial planning meeting
	3. Identify assets away based on financial plan
	4. Develop plan to acquire assets based on portfolios
Ensure that estate planning is addressed and insurance needs are met	**Tactics**
	1. Conduct insurance reviews for all appropriate clients during annual or follow-up meeting
	2. Meet with insurance rep/solutions provider to evaluate case and address needs
	3. Prepare case with assistance from insurance rep/solutions provider
	4. Call and meet with client to present case
Seek introductions	**Tactics**
	1. Complete "Client Wisdom" profile for all clients, identifying ways to seek introductions
	2. Identify and fill information shortfalls
	3. Determine approaches to seek introductions
	4. Script introductions requests to use at annual meetings
Use LinkedIn for prospecting	**Tactics**
	1. Link to all possible clients, prospects, and COIs as well as unrelated business contacts
	2. Follow LinkedIn script to get introductions
	3. Follow up with introductions

Figure 7-5 | Section 4a Business Plan—Subsection—Key Current Client Opportunities.

Top 5 Clients to Acquire Additional Assets From:

1.
2.
3.
4.
5.

Top 10 LinkedIn Contacts to Approach for Introductions:

1.
2.
3.
4.
5.
6.
7.
8.
9.
10.

Figure 7-6 | Section 4a Business Plan—Subsection—New Client Acquisition Marketing.

3. New Client Acquisition Marketing (Prospecting)	
Introductions from Clients	**Tactics**
	1. Complete "Client Wisdom" profile seeking clients to ask for introductions
	2. Use LinkedIn, which will require linking to all possible clients
	3.
Networking	**Tactics**
	1. Join and participate in Toastmasters
	2. Increase focus with Rotary Club
	3. Develop relationship with local SHRM Chapter
Intimate Events or Targeted Seminars	**Tactics**
	1. Monthly branch events for clients and prospects
	2. TBD, e.g., Corporate lunch and learns
	3. Top "6" client dinners with associates or friends
	Tactics

Figure 7-7 | Section 4a Business Plan—Subsection—Center of Influence Marketing.

4a. Center of Influence Marketing		
Identify 2 CPAs and 1 Trust & Estate attorney that may make appropriate partnerships to obtain introductions		**Tactics**
	1.	Identify top 10 client CPAs and attorneys and use COI Contact Strategy Part 1 to vet them with client
	2.	Use Part 2 of Strategy to personally vet COIs
	3.	Use Parts 3 and 4 to seek partnerships
Identify other than client COIs via networking groups e.g., Chambers and Toastmasters	**Tactics**	
	1.	Be on the lookout for COIs and COI contact Strategy Parts, 2, 3, and 4
	2.	
	3.	
Approach Ms. Testa for partnerships	**Tactics**	
	1.	Use Strategy Parts 2, 3, and 4
	2.	
	3.	
	Tactics	
	1.	
	2.	
	3.	

Figure 7-8 | Section 4b Business Plan: Focus Area—Service Strategies and Tactics.

Focus Areas — Service Strategies and Tactics

4b. Client Service

How are client segments defined?

Segment	**Criteria**
A	
B	
C	
D	

Describe service levels and contact strategy for each segment

Segment	**Service and contact strategy**
A	See client service models/promises
B	
C	
D	

Focus Areas: Service Strategies and Tactics

This section outlines the segments you have created as a result of your work from Chapters 2 and 3. See Figure 7-8.

Focus Area: Operations

This section outlines your plans for improvements in areas such as time management, delegation, meetings, roles and responsibilities, and perhaps a new on-boarding process. See Figure 7-9.

Model Week/Time Blocking

We made some points on time management in Chapter 4 when talking about the cost of loyalty. One of the points we made was that FAs have the following key activities that need to be addressed on a regular basis:

Figure 7-9 | Sample Client Annual Progress Summary (CAPS) letter.

Focus Areas — Operational

4c. Operational/Infrastructure Goals	
What operational and administrative priorities can you identify?	
Strategy 1: Time management	**Tactics**
	Develop Model Calendar with Time Blocking
	Track and report adherence to calendar
	Modify calendar based on reporting
Strategy 2: Delegate appropriate tasks to client associate	**Tactics**
	Order execution
	Problem resolution and tracking and reporting to FA
	Client follow up of assigned tasks and appointment scheduling
Strategy 3: Marketing meetings with client associate	**Tactics**
	Weekly planning meeting
	Quarterly progress review
Strategy 4:	**Tactics**
	1.
	2.
	3.

5. Time Management

Where do you spend your time?

	Current %	Desired %
Client Service		
Investment Mgmt/Planning		
Business Management		
Business Development		
Operational/Administrative		
Other		
Total	100%	100%

- Client and Book Asset and Portfolio Management
- Client Service/Relationship Management (including client planning and review meetings and calls, among a host of other services and deliverables)
- Marketing/Business Development (in a number of forms)
- Team Management
- Business Planning and Tracking

It is necessary for advisors to estimate the amount of time they spend weekly on Portfolio Management and schedule that on the calendar. In the following example, we label time as "Portfolio Improvement Planning." (In Chapter 4, we calculated an estimate of the amount of time Client Service/Relationship Management might take.)

We suggest handling inbound calls as shown in Figure 7-10 and a sample calendar, shown in Figure 7-11, for this segment of the business plan.

Looking at the sample calendar you can see there are slots allotted to Marketing/Business Development and some open time slots that can be used for Team Management and Business Planning and Tracking, neither of which should be excessive.

Note that on the calendar in Figure 7-11, we have scheduled two hours a day for Callbacks and Email. First of all, this is an excessive amount of time to have to spend on these activities; 25 percent of a 40-hour week would be a prohibitive commitment. These time slots are intended to address internal corporate requests, some team management and problem resolution, as well as callbacks and email handling. Having said that, the more important point we really want to make is that advisors, for the most part, should not be responding to emails and calls as they come in. It is incredibly inefficient, so we strongly suggest taking two time slots a day and getting done what's necessary at those times: emails, callbacks, critical and time-dependent issues, etc.

The next section of the plan is a Marketing Calendar, shown in Figure 7-12, which can include any number of activities such as:

Figure 7-10 | Assistant script for answering telephone.

CA Should Answer All Incoming Calls to Set Your "Importance"

- **If you are in a client meeting and you get a call, CA says:**
  - Sally (FA) is in a client meeting (in the office, in Connecticut, in "town name," or just in a meeting).
  - I expect her to be free at (next callback time, either 11:30 a.m. or 4:30 p.m.).
  - Can I have her call you back then or can I help you now?

  This is designed to show you meet with clients anywhere.

  Note that we suggest setting 2 time blocks a day for callbacks, e.g., 11:30 a.m. to Noon and 4:30 p.m. to 5:00 p.m.

- **If you are NOT in a client meeting and an A CLIENT calls:**
  - Sally (FA) is in a client meeting.
  - I expect her to be free at (next callback time, either 11:30 a.m. or 4:30 p.m.).
  - Let me interrupt her, or can I have her call you back then, or can I help you now?

  Saying you will interrupt her also states that client is important.

- **If you are NOT in a client meeting and a NON-A CLIENT calls, CA says:**
  - Sally (FA) is in a client meeting, I expect her to be free at (next callback time, either 11:30 a.m. or 4:30 p.m.).
  - Can I have her call you back then or can I help you now?

Figure 7-11 | Section 5 Business Plan: Model Week/Time Blocking.

FOR MONTH OF (Jan / Feb / March / April / May / June / July / Aug / Sept / Oct / Nov / Dec) **FOR WEEK** Number (1 / 2 / 3 / 4 / 5)

Notes Appts. for Wk ___ Top 50 Calls ___ COI Meetings ___ days ___ New Client for Wk ___ New Business Calls ___ Prospect Calls ___ Prospects ___
Fees Charged ___ Upgrades ___ Appts. Set ___ e Scripts Used ___

Times	**Monday**		**Tuesday**		**Wednesday**		**Thursday**		**Friday**	
7:00 A.M.					Breakfast meeting (COI, prospect, or client)					
8:00 A.M.	Planning week		Portfolio improvement planning				Portfolio improvement planning		COI calls	
9:00 A.M.	Email				COI calls					
10:00 A.M.	Prospect list follow-up calls		F2F client meeting prep		F2F client meeting prep		F2F client meeting prep		Prospect list follow-up calls	
11:00 A.M.	Call backs		Call backs Emails		Call backs Emails		Call backs Emails		Call backs Emails	
12:00 P.M.	Emails		Client check-in calls		Client or prosepect lunch meeting		Client check-in calls		Client telephone meeting, including prep and follow-up	
1:00 P.M.			Client telephone meeting, including prep and follow-up				Client telephone meeting, including prep and follow-up			
2:00 P.M.	Marketing and sales				Marketing and sales				Marketing and sales	
3:00 P.M.	Follow-up plans		Client F2F meeting		Client F2F meeting		Client F2F meeting		Follow-up plans	
4:00 P.M.	Call backs Email		Call backs Email		Call backs Email		Call backs Email		Call backs Email	
5:00 P.M.	6 things Review day		6 things Review day		6 things Review day		6 things Review day		6 things Review day	
6:00 P.M.										
7:00 P.M.										
8:00 P.M.										

Figure 7-12 | Section 6 Business Plan: Marketing Calendar.

Marketing Calendar

(Sample activities can include: Advertising, Emails, Drips, Newsletters, Seminars, Networking Groups, Client Appreciation, Cold Calling/Walking, Educational Events, Trade Shows, etc.)

Activities	Jan.	Feb.	Mar.	Apr.	May	June	July	Aug.	Sept.	Oct.	Nov.	Dec.

- Roundtables/Targeted Seminars
- Advisory Boards (client based and professional based)
- Networking Events (personal and corporate)
- Dinner Events/Intimate Dinners
- Client Appreciation Events
- Seminars
- Public Forums (organizations to which you do or could belong)

The final piece of your business plan is your 90-Day Action Plan, shown in Figure 7-13, which can include additional details about responsible parties, support requirements, target due dates, and completion dates.

Figure 7-13 | Section 7 Business Plan: 90-Day Action Plan.

90-Day Action Plan

	Action Steps (Task, behavior, tool, or policy I will incorporate into the practice)	Who has primary responsibility?	Support needed	Target date	Date completed
Next 30 Days					
Next 60 Days					
Next 90 Days					

Notes

Action Summary | Your Business Plan

To develop your business plan:

- Call out the three to five marketing and sales approaches you will use as part of your client acquisition strategy.
- Detail how you will use the approaches; who will be responsible for each approach; when each approach will be started, completed, and measured; and the steps that will be taken to execute the plan.
- Define if and how you can expand the relationship with existing clients with additional solutions like banking and insurance, as well as gathering assets away.
- Know that while marketing and sales are the core of your growth goals, you must concurrently retain your current clients with a focus on your high value clients.
- Remember that a business plan is much more than a set of goals. Goals are the "What" and "How Many." For example:
  - What do I want my 20XX AUM to be?
  - What do I want my 20XX production to be?
  - How many new clients do I want to acquire?
- A business plan lays out the "How," the "When," and the "Who."
- In addition to the business plan outlining where you are and where you want to be, it defines the strategies and tactics for how to get there. For example:
  - I will establish two strategic CPA relationships and one strategic Estate Attorney relationship by March 31. This includes identifying 10 quality CPAs of my top 20 clients and 10 quality Estate Attorneys of my top 20 clients.
  - I will acquire *N* new clients by seeking introductions from two CPAs and one Estate Attorney with whom I develop a strategic relationship (following the methodology in Chapter 9 of this book).
  - I will employ the LinkedIn process (discussed in Chapter 9 of this book) with 10 of my top 30 clients with whom I am connected on LinkedIn. I will complete this project by June 30.

Chapter Eight

Metrics: Daily Game Plan

> *Measurement is the first step that leads to control and eventually to improvement. If you can't measure something, you can't understand it. If you can't understand it, you can't control it. If you can't control it, you can't improve it.* **—H. James Harrington**

This chapter details a quantitative approach for the advisor with the belief that the right actions lead to the right results. Also discussed is how to estimate your workload.

The Daily Game Plan, which consists of metrics against which to measure your daily or weekly actions and results, takes a *quantitative approach*. It is our preference to take this pragmatic approach. There are four elements that we suggest and discuss in this chapter:

- Specific Client Contact Plan
- Model Week Plan
- Metrics Scorecard
- Six Most Important Things

Another approach advisors can take is a *qualitative approach*. This approach is much more of a mental approach, including components like:

- Morning Power Questions

- Inspirational Visions and CDs
- Attitude, Mindset, and Motivation

The Qualitative Approach

The subject of Morning Power Questions is not our forte, but in researching the subject we came upon an article that said:

> Tony Robbins uses his physiology to create powerful results. He's trained himself to use his emotions as a source of power in everything he does. You can do the same. By asking yourself the right questions, you can change your focus. And by focusing on "feeling our feelings," you can teach yourself to summon your most powerful emotions to support you from the start of the day and throughout your day (you'll be able to "remember the feeling.") This is a simple way to practice emotional mastery while you practice your attitude of gratitude. In the book, *Awaken the Giant Within: How to Take Immediate Control of Your Mental, Emotional, Physical and Financial Destiny*, Tony Robbins shares power questions you can use in the morning to start your day off strong with more passion, power, and purpose. [1]

We will leave Tony Robbins's thoughts at that, though we have no issue or concern about using a qualitative approach, either alone or in concert with a quantitative approach.

On another site, Jesse Lyn Stoner offers three questions "to start and end your day" that are very interesting and useful. She suggests:

> Start your day with focus and energy by taking a few moments to answer these questions.
>
> 1. What will give me joy today?
> 2. What am I excited about accomplishing today?
> 3. Who needs my help today?"[2]

To end your day, she says:

> Your day will take on greater meaning and will end on a better note if you take a few moments to answer these questions before you go to sleep.

1. What am I proud of?
2. Who do I love?
3. What am I grateful for?"[3]

These questions tie well into the quantitative approach. "Try these questions, see how they work, and find the questions that work best for you," she says. "Consider open-ended questions, rather than questions that have only one right answer or that can be answered with a simple 'yes' or 'no.' The most powerful questions are those that expand your thinking." (If you are interested in more of what Stoner says, you can review her website at http://seapointcenter.com/.)

You can also research "Morning Ritual." A colleague, Joe Lukacs, is an expert in the qualitative approach, having a long history with it and a background with Tony Robbins. You can find Joe at www.practicepower.net.

The Quantitative Approach

William Penn said, "Time is what we want most, but what we use worst." How do we spend our limited time wisely?

Too many of us do not plan how to use our time well in advance of the spending of it. This can result in a feeling of uncertainty about your productivity. Too many people seem to walk out of their offices at night, looking back at their day and wondering "what happened." A way to avoid that is to have an action plan and stick to it throughout the day. In fact, successful advisors start each day with an excellent daily game plan and a set of daily outcomes. We need to come to the office every day with clarity about what we want to accomplish. We can if we have a Daily-Weekly Game Plan as a cornerstone of our success and our Model Week.

We know we are responsible for and accountable for our results, but at times we don't take a good look at the actions we need to take to get the results we want. The road to results runs through the actions we take. However, FAs are so tied up in the day's calendar, between planned and unplanned events and issues that arise throughout the day, that they often don't focus on specific targets to measure actions against, and they rarely have an accountability plan in terms of metrics or individuals with whom they share these metrics and are held accountable. We therefore need to discuss accountability action metrics as well as measuring results. This will enable us to determine if we are taking the correct actions or need to make course corrections over time.

Your metrics plan should reflect your written business plan and contact plans as well as your personal development plan. It should be consistent in terms of approach and needs to be executed daily in a consistent manner. It is understood that it may have to be somewhat flexible to take advantage of opportunities. A successful Daily-Weekly Game Plan needs specifics to make it work for you. The plan should address:

- How many client reviews need to be done and where?
- How many phone calls do I need to make, by type?
- How many marketing contacts do I need to make?
- How many prospect appointments do I need to set?
- What has to be done to be a level 10 tomorrow? (Use a scale of 1 to 10, with 10 being top.)

Client contact is based on your segmentation and a workload planner, as discussed in Chapter 4 (see Figure 4-3, "Meeting and call volumes for our hypothetical book of business"). That table can be used to calculate workload.

In the example used earlier, the FA needed to have three face-to-face meetings a week, four telephone portfolio review meetings a week, and 12 check-in calls a week to satisfy the contact plan. These numbers become part of the "metrics scorecard," where you post your actions in order to bring you the results you want. Right actions deliver right results.

Figure 8-1 shows two parts of an Excel spreadsheet that address the areas that should make up your metrics scorecard.

On page 1 of the spreadsheet we suggest you quickly record your Daily rating (AM/PM) about how you subjectively feel about the quality of that portion of your week. You are likely to believe you had a better portion of the day if you did some business, so we suggest you rate the

Figure 8-1 | Weekly metrics scorecard.

Street Smart Research Group, LLC.
Practice Optimization for FAs — Metrics Scorecard

Business Metrics	**Week of:**	**/**	

Rating	**AM**	**PM**	**Notes (1 to 5 with 5 = Exceptional)**
Rating — Monday			
Rating — Tuesday			
Rating — Wednesday			
Rating — Thursday			
Rating — Friday			

Action Metrics	**Weekly Target**	**Actual**	**Notes**
Check-in calls with clients			
In-person meetings with clients			
Telephone meetings with clients			
Introductions requested			
Introductions received			
Calls to retail prospects			
LinkedIn prospect calls			

period "Exceptional (5)" if you closed some business or "Poor (1)" if you felt that part of your day was unproductive in terms of how you felt you used those four hours. This is a 30-second analysis that is essentially a gut reaction. What you will be looking for are patterns so you can think about why any particular day or part of a day is either positive or

Figure 8-1 | Weekly metrics scorecard (continued).

Street Smart Research Group, LLC.
Practice Optimization for FAs — Metrics Scorecard

Telephone meetings with suspects			
In-person meetings with new prospects (Discovery call)			
In-person meetings with prospects previously seen (2nd, 3rd, or 4th call)			
Prospects added to pipeline			
COI contact			
Referrals from COIs (by COI)			

Results Metrics

Results	Goal	Actual	Notes
Gross revenue/ production			
New clients			
New assets from new clients			
New assets from existing clients			
Most proud of this week?			
What could have gone better this week?			

negative. Short notes will help. After a few weeks to a couple of months perhaps you can find a pattern that can be changed if it is negatively affecting you and your performance.

The rest of the metrics scorecard, the Action metrics, asks you to record the planned actions for the week and how well you executed against those planned actions: Did you conduct the meetings and make the calls? Did you seek introductions and receive any? In the Notes column, you can list the last name of the client you met with, called, and/or sought and received introductions from. In your CRM system, you should be recording notes on every contact. Your focus and work plan should reflect your goals and the nature of your business and experience.

On page 2 of the spreadsheet we emphasize prospects and Centers of Influence. If you are not prospecting for client acquisition, it will show up here, and you have an opportunity to take action. In any one week, your prospecting and COI activity might be light, but if you are not doing prospecting or COI activity over any period of time, these records will tell you that quickly.

As with client calls and meetings, in the Notes column, you can list the last name of the prospects and COIs you met with or called. In your CRM system, you should also be recording notes on every contact with a focus on A and B tier clients.

You can also record your Results metrics, which should be reported on your firm's system. If you choose to, your assistant can post the weekly scorecard to an ongoing tally by week to give you a view of what your numbers are year to date and for the year.

Finally, at the end of the week answer two questions:

- What are you most proud of this week?
- What could have gone better this week?

Over time, answers to these questions will help you. At a high level, an experienced advisor's time distribution might look something like this:

- Client and prospect contact and preparation for contact (~40 percent to 50 percent)
    - Check-in calls
    - Telephone portfolio reviews

    - Face-to-face meetings
- Client acquisition efforts (~20 percent to 25 percent)
- Other (~25 to 35 percent)
    - Practice administration (~10 percent)
    - New client services (~5 percent)
    - Portfolio management and administration (~10 percent to 20 percent)
    - COI contact and preparation for contact (~2 percent to 3 percent)

Daily Time Log

If needed, to determine the amount of time you actually spend on each major task, you can keep a daily time log. This is something advisors do not like to do and that's understandable. However, if you are serious about getting your practice under control, it's an activity worth considering. You can do it yourself or hire someone to watch you and constantly ask, "What are you doing now?" The log is best kept for a month, especially if your activities vary during the month. Month end and month beginnings are often different from the weeks in between. If that is not true with your practice, two or three weeks may be long enough to use a time log. You need to record activities in half-hour time increments to tell you what you really do, and you must be rigorous and record enough detail. See Figure 8-2.

The Six Most Important Things

The last tool we want to mention is the Six Most Important Things worksheet, because the day is won or lost in the first hour of the day!

The intent here is to make it a habit to do the most productive thing you can at every given moment. To do this, we suggest that at the end of each day, you write down the six most important things you have to do the next day, in order of priority, and then follow that list in order. We also suggest noting what else you work on, including nonwork-related items. See Figure 8-3.

Figure 8-2 | Daily time log worksheet.

Daily Time Log Worksheet

Circle Day M T W T F Date / /

Time	**Task**	**Notes, including time on task and how it benefited your business**
7 AM		
8 AM		
8:30 AM		
9 AM		
9:30 AM		
10 AM		
10:30 AM		
11:00 AM		

Figure 8-3 | Six Most Important Things worksheet.

Six Most Important Things

Date MM/DD/YYYY

Priority	**Task**	**Notes, including time on task and how it benefited your business**	**Follow up no later than**
1			
2			
3			
4			
5			
6			
Other			

Action Summary | Metrics: Daily Game Plan

- Develop a quantitative metrics plan.
- Quality actions lead to quality results.
  - While you need to hit your numbers, it's the actions you take that will drive the numbers.
  - An action is seeking an introduction.
  - Results are receiving introductions, securing a meeting with a prospect, and converting the prospect to a client.
- This book is about how to create actions and convert actions to results.

Chapter | **Nine**

Business Development

> *Enchantment is the purest form of sales. Enchantment is all about changing people's hearts, minds, and actions because you provide them a vision or a way to do things better. The difference between enchantment and simple sales is that with enchantment you have the other person's best interests at heart, too.*
>
> **—Guy Kawasaki**

There are at least 20 business development approaches that can be used by financial advisors to acquire new clients and their assets. We will mention a number of those approaches but focus on the key approaches that experience and data show need to be part of your client acquisition strategy.

Introduction to Business Development

The objective for business development is not growing the number of clients, but growing your number of profitable clients. Chapter 4 discussed the need to balance the cost of the services to be delivered in support of client retention and loyalty with the value of the client to the business. This chapter focuses on how financial advisors can acquire those profitable clients. Many advisors see this as one of their top challenges. As we will repeat, most every advisor has said, "If I can get them into my office, I can close them." This chapter is about how you can get prospects into your office.

We detailed the client segmentation process and how to effectively and efficiently service your existing clients to increase client retention, loyalty, and advocacy. The challenge of getting more profitable clients in part starts with that segmentation process. Once you have your 80/20 analysis, a key question is, "How do you create another 20?" In our example in Chapter 2, we showed a sample book that actually yielded a 65/20 result—that is, 65 percent of revenues came from 20 percent of our clients. In that example, 34 A-level clients accounted for about 44 percent of revenues and 28 B-level clients accounted for about another 20 percent of revenues. Note that in this example we understand this book consists of too many D clients and that skews the 80/20 data, but that does not change the point we want to make. The top 34 relationships average almost $1 million in investable assets, so this advisor may want to focus on replicating his or her A tier, so would need to add perhaps 34 new $1 million (or greater) relationships over a reasonable period of time (e.g., three years). Each of these 34 clients averages about $7,000 in revenue. Depending on costs (which can be estimated using the methodology proposed in Chapter 4), these 34 clients may be identified as highly profitable. The B clients average about $4,000 in revenue and about $360,000 in investable assets. In the business development processes we will discuss, these will be your targets, with a focus on A-level prospects.

Malcolm Gladwell, an author we like, refers to a "tipping point." The tipping point feels like a snowball rolling down the hill in order to build positive momentum. As the advisor focuses efforts on working toward acquisition of "top" clients, it will become more effective over time. Eventually growth will hit a critical mass and then start building on itself. A client base and "top client" growth can eventually hit a "tipping point," so it's important that the growth momentum has you focus on that top part of your book; those clients are the ones you want to replicate.

As you explored your client segmentation, you also noted some of the characteristics of those top clients such as likability, trust (that they have in you), whether they introduce you to prospects, and their growth potential. Also note their life stages, professions, interests, etc., as we will discuss further with the Client Wisdom approach to introductions. Note your largest retail and institutional relationships as targets. In essence, you are creating your "ideal client" profile. One legendary branch manager was fond of advising advisors that each year they should acquire a new number-one client. We believe this is an exciting goal and suggest that a growing and dynamic book should focus broadly and create not just one new client, but a whole new portion/segment of the book over time.

Once you have identified the types of clients you currently have, you can create a plan for the types of clients on which you want to focus. To succeed, the question to answer is: "What do these top clients want?" Following the process in Chapter 6, Your Client Planning and Review Process, you have discussed your Client Service Model with those clients and determined which of your deliverables are of value to those clients. For every client the answer may be a bit different, but the aggregate of clients' wants and needs will likely tell us the most important items to highlight in order to earn and maintain their loyalty and advocacy and trust and to know where to focus our business development efforts.

As you do the work entailed in identifying the types of clients you have and want, you are also helping to determine the value of your practice. You understand the cash flow and revenue generated from your client base. You also know the quality of the cash flow, whether fee-based or transactional. You also know the age of clients, how assets are managed, how diverse the client relationships are in products and family generation, how long the client has been with you, the advisor, and so on. You can also consider your depth of services and the quality of those services. In this book, we spend much of the time discussing best practices around efficiency, effectiveness, and quality of services. Figure 9-1 may help an advisory team evaluate how they perform and where to target their resources. As we move into more detailed discussions of business development approaches, use Figure 9-1 to guide your efforts.

For your current top tier clients, retention, loyalty, and advocacy are driven by the quality of services you provide, which are balanced with the revenues you receive for those services. By quality of services we include the depth of the services you provide, such as described by a true set of wealth management deliverables and the customization and personalization you provide for those clients. Your business development efforts focus on those clients who want the model of business

Figure 9-1 | Profitable clients matrix.

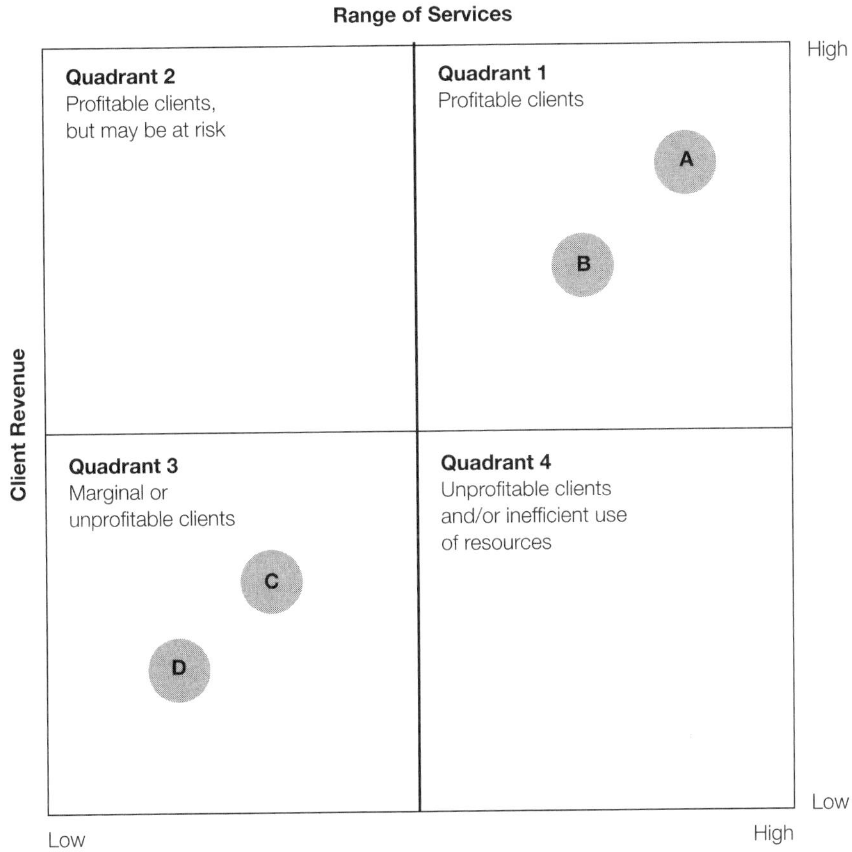

you have chosen for your practice. Each client and prospect, whether A or B (Quadrant 1 in Figure 9-1), needs to be evaluated in terms of their wants and needs in context of your business and the likely direction of their potential business over time. Do they want, need, and warrant the level of effort you and your team are investing to fulfill those clients' wants and needs?

The same questions are also true for Quadrant 3 clients. Do they warrant the level of effort you and your team are investing to fulfill their wants and needs? Do any have the potential to become Quadrant 1 clients? If not, options need to be considered in both the cases of current clients and your business development efforts. It would be very rare that you would invest such efforts for Quadrant 3 prospects.

For Quadrant 4 clients and prospects, these are investors whose revenues are relatively low whether because of low investable assets, fee sensitivity, or lack of desire to make you their sole or in some cases primary advisor. Yet you are delivering high-quality services to them, or they will likely demand high-quality services. You are probably working too hard and this almost always entails an ineffective and inefficient use of resources. You cannot afford to continue to maintain these clients and certainly do not want to invest your business development efforts in prospects like these. Your "intake process" is the point in time to ensure that this situation is avoided.

Your Quadrant 2 clients and prospects are investors whose revenues are high or relatively high; however, they may not want the business model you have chosen for your practice. These could be high-risk clients and prospects because you may not have the opportunity to deliver the high-quality services and value you typically deliver to your Quadrant 1 clients. Unless you are willing to set up a lower fee schedule, the wants and needs of these clients and prospects may be better met by other advisors who don't do what you do. In our view, different fee schedules are a slippery slope and could put you on a path for clients and prospects to choose from a menu of separately priced deliverables. This is not likely a good business model and is difficult to manage. While these investors may be profitable or even highly profitable, they may be shorter-term clients. You will have to decide if you really want to invest your business development efforts in prospects like these. Again, your "intake process" is the point in time to ensure that there is a fit between your business model and the wants and needs of these investors.

Each of the six core client-facing processes that we have discussed is about retention, loyalty, and advocacy, as well as about cost and therefore profitability. Your business development efforts need to be in context of these factors. You must also define your target client in context of the characteristics discussed and your skills, experiences, and passions or aspirations. It is also critical that your team be properly staffed and trained to service well the target clients you aspire to acquire.

Client Introductions for Business Development

Let's delineate between "introductions" and "referrals." Up until several years ago the term most people used to acquire prospective clients from active clients was *referrals*. That is, a client provides names of people to their FA who might be potential new clients. In fact, they could just as well have introduced you to their friends or family members at social events, over a meal, or at a business event. Until a short time ago, referrals didn't distinguish between providing a name and providing a face-to-face introduction.

The industry now prefers to use the word *introductions* and differentiates the term from referrals. An article on Wealth Management.com[1] states:

> Asking to be introduced to someone that's connected to one of your affluent clients is the polar opposite of asking an affluent client for a referral. Yet because advisors have been taught for so many years to ask for referrals, they tend to think of referrals and introductions as being one-in-the same. They are not!

At least today they are not. Then again, we have seen titles change over time while functions stay the same or close to the same. We change the definition to suit the times, whether it's investment advisor, investment consultant, financial advisor, and today wealth manager. There are important differences in what we do, but the function and its explanation are more important than the name.

The referenced article goes on to say, "By asking for an introduction, you are helping your client help you by identifying a specific person you'd like to meet." While this may not always be true, an introduction is a more focused request. It is also attempting to get a face-to-face introduction or meeting, whether over coffee, a meal, or at a social or business function. You may say to your client, "John, you've mentioned your parents wanted to discuss their financial situation. I'd love to do that. Why don't we set up a lunch or dinner meeting so we can talk in an informal setting?" An introduction can also be made by email, but that is not as effective as an in-person introduction.

A referral, on the other hand, is often made in the form of the advisor asking a client for prospective clients, in a nonspecific manner; for example, "John, if you know *anyone* who could benefit from the kinds of service I provide to you, I would appreciate a referral." If you ask for a referral in a general way, the client may reply, "Why don't you call Jim Smith," but more likely may respond by saying, "I don't know anyone," or "Let me think about it." If clients do give you a name, they may or may not allow you to tell Jim that they told you to call. In either case, referrals done this way are not as effective as introductions and are not recommended.

Despite years and decades of hearing that advisors should ask for introductions (née referrals), they still have difficulty doing it. One article stated that "while 83 percent of consumers are willing to refer a friend after a positive experience, only 29 percent actually take the time to do so. . . ."[2] On the other hand, Julie Littlechild reports that "58 percent of clients say they were motivated to refer in order to help a friend while 38 percent said they want to help the advisor build his/her business."[3]

From a 2015 Spectrem study:[4]

> When asked to rate their overall level of loyalty, affluent investors rated themselves quite high—at an 83.26 on a 100-point scale. However, when asked how often they refer others to their financial institution, only 9 percent of affluent investors answered "very often." In fact, 30 percent indicated they never refer others to their financial institution.

Other studies support high percentages of clients saying they would provide introductions to their advisors, if asked, yet the vast majority of those same clients claim they had never been asked. "If statistics are to be believed," says one, "then 85 percent of advisors do not ask clients for referrals. Only 15 percent of clients voluntarily offer referrals without advisors asking for them."[5]

A Google search of "referrals" can yield millions of hits. Even Googling "financial advisors asking for referrals" yields over 75,000 hits. It's not for lack of information or knowledge that advisors don't ask for introductions or referrals. Most advisors go about seeking introductions in a very ad hoc fashion. The secret to success with introductions is to move away from an ad hoc introduction/referral process to a structured introduction/referral process. Surprisingly few FAs have an established introduction/referral process or know what drives introductions. A survey on referrals by Janus Labs found:

- Client loyalty plays a major role in getting introductions.

- Almost 70 percent of clients identified as "loyal" may refer within the next year while less than 1 percent of "moderately satisfied" clients are likely to do so.
- Clients identified as "loyal" made 5.6 introductions in the last year while "moderately satisfied" clients made almost no introductions in the last year.
- Less than 11 percent of surveyed advisors on average proactively seek introductions.

Creating and identifying loyal clients is key to a successful introduction process. While most FAs might think that all of their clients are loyal, the Janus Labs survey revealed that only about 12 percent of investors surveyed are truly loyal to their primary FA. We have discussed how to create loyalty in Chapter 3.

This data shows that getting introductions to new prospective clients from current clients certainly has its challenges, though the interest in doing so remains very high. Rather than discussing the data and the issues in securing introductions, this section will discuss how to develop and use a structured process for securing introductions from clients to prospective clients and several methods for doing so.

Getting introductions is a function of you, your client's satisfaction, and your client's engagement. Starting off with you, the right mindset can result in more introductions, but it's more than simply asking a few clients for introductions on a periodic basis. You need an attitude and a way of thinking that needs to be ingrained into the DNA of your entire business. You need to train yourself to see all client relationships and strategic partnerships as opportunities for increased introductions, as well as needing a systematic process for getting clients to introduce you to prospective clients. You need to be referable in terms of the value and services you deliver. Hopefully we have addressed that up to this point.

In "Think Referrals," the SunAmerica Client Referral Program[6] identifies five key components of a referral mindset: being Committed, Focused, Collaborative, Systematic, and Confident.

In context of what we have addressed so far in this book, you need to be **committed** to implementing the six core client-facing processes, as they will provide an exceptional client offering. Every one of the six processes is **focused** on building relationships through trust and engagement. The six processes are the framework and intended to be highly **collaborative**, by taking an ask approach and delivering value. While there may be more of a focus on high-value clients, every client has a Client Service Model or Promise and an intake and Client Planning and Review process.

All six core client-facing processes are structured and **systematic**. That's their design level and what processes are. Asking for introductions in an appropriate manner for each individual client is built into the agenda as part of the Client Planning and Review Meeting process. The Client Service process is also aimed at earning introductions. The intent of the six core client-facing processes is to provide organization, structure, and consistency to give advisors the **confidence** they are doing the right things and in the best interests of their clients. These processes can give advisors the confidence they are delivering outstanding value and that, if well executed, little if anything will fall through the cracks.

If you believe in and deliver the six core client-facing processes we have been discussing, you will have the mindset for success in seeking introductions. Your clients will be well satisfied.

Client engagement is a relatively new term that seems to have gotten traction in the last several years, in part due to Julie Littlechild's "Anatomy of a Referral: The Economics of Loyalty," a study done in December 2010. In that study, Littlechild says that "the 'Engaged client' [is] one who meets three key criteria—a client who is satisfied, loyal, AND actively providing referrals." The question becomes what drives "client engagement," because as a result of engagement clients become more willing to provide introductions. The study points to the answer as:

- Working with the right clients
- Having the right conversations
- Asking the right questions[7]

Figure 9-2 is a representation, a framework, for the types of clients with whom we might work well, the conversations we might have that

Figure 9-2 | Framework for engaging the right client.

Right Clients	Right Conversations	Right Questions

• Values
• Communication style
• Personality
• "Offer" aligns with needs
• Investment philosophy
• Planning important
• Play a central role in financial life —QB/CFO
	• Deeper connection
	• Higher levels of contact/more expensive
	• 68% of engaged clients expect 3+ portfolio reviews/year
	• Stronger personal relationships
	• Look at FA to lead
	• Provide positive feedback
		• Actively involved in providing input
		  ◦ Advisory boards
		  ◦ Surveys
		  ◦ Meetings
		• Greater sense of ownership and of control when asked for feedback
		• Believe that feedback will have impact

Source: Julie Littlechild, "Anatomy of a Referral: The Economics of Loyalty," December 2010.

move clients toward engagement, and the questions we might ask so that advisors can build practices that engender loyalty and engagement and deliver the elements that result in introductions.

The right clients share your values and have values you share—namely, what do you care about and why? Is it about people, family, community, or is it about money? How do you both feel about resources and frugality? How does honesty and trust fit into their and your values? People have different values, and while we are not suggesting rights and wrongs, we are suggesting your discovery process should determine if your prospect's set of values fits with your set of values, because that's part of what leads to engagement. From your intake process to your financial planning and client planning and review meeting processes, you have the opportunity to determine whether you and your prospects and clients share communications styles, personality types, and expectations. We do not expect you to seek clones of yourself but people with whom you can be open and honest in ways that bring mutual trust.

When you share your belief system in conversations, do your prospects and clients want, even more than need, what it is you offer? Do they share your approach to investments? Are they open to your financial planning[8] and wealth management approaches, and will they include you as a central player in their financial lives? If you cannot work with your clients in a manner that allows you to do your best job for them, how deep a connection can you really have? Yes, it's more expensive because these depths take more time for discussions and in the execution of the processes we have discussed. These approaches lead to stronger relationships and a leadership role in the financial lives of your clients, and you know they do because you are asking your clients for feedback and they are providing it. Clients can provide that feedback in a number of ways, but minimally at your annual planning and review they and their feedback are an important part of the direction you set for your practice.

Most advisors want to grow their businesses with higher-value clients and work with fewer of them. What we are talking about is a direction in which the advisor's practice should travel over time. Of course, these are aspirational goals, but the sooner the better. Having said that, even for advisors who are just starting out or working with "middle-class millionaires" or the "mass affluent" or any other group, this discussion is about deciding how you want to work and who you want to work with. If you want loyal, "engaged clients," this is an approach that works.

We want to restate that we recognize you may have many clients and limits on your time and affordability. Nevertheless, these things are mandatory only for the clients you want to retain—namely, your A clients at least and many of your B clients.

Client Acquisition Through Introductions

There are several approaches to acquiring introductions from clients:

- As part of your client face-to-face planning and review meetings
    - Utilizing the principle of "aided recall"
    - Letting the client know the types of financial issues where you can provide help
- Using the LinkedIn approach

The introduction conversation is best done in person and after getting positive client feedback. Note that the meeting can take place in your office or the client's environment. Harvey Mackay is quoted as saying, "The most important reading you can do is on the walls of your client's office or home."[9] For your very best clients, think about client home visits, a convenient way to also include clients' spouses in your meeting.

Using the Principle of "Aided Recall" at Review Meetings

Feedback, which is part of your client meeting agenda, needs to precede any discussion of introductions. The agenda includes three of the following six questions to solicit that feedback. Three questions don't get burdensome, so select the three you believe give you the feedback you need. Choose any of the six questions below that may work better for you:

1. What are we doing that you'd like to see us continue?
2. What aren't we doing that you'd like to see us do?
3. On a scale of 1 to 10, how would you rate our service to you?
4. What are we doing that isn't valuable or helpful for you?
5. Do you understand your portfolio and why it's invested the way it is?
6. Is there anything else you can think of that we can improve on?

If you get feedback that suggests your client is not fully satisfied, a 7 or less on a 10-point scale, the next step is to dig into dissatisfaction and determine if and how you can resolve it. That's your focus at that point and *not* securing introductions. You need to get a rating of at least an 8, preferably a 9 or 10, before you go into a discussion about introductions.

Assuming you receive positive feedback you can move into the introduction process using the principle of "aided recall." Aided recall means prompting respondents (clients) by inducing an association of ideas (or people) to help them recall other individuals who are the same or similar to them. For example, an employee of Exxon (or any firm) should more easily be able to identify others who are also employees of Exxon, especially in her or his own department. Saying, "George, I enjoy working with you. I'm very pleased you're so satisfied with our services. I wonder if there are any other Exxon Petroleum Engineers like yourself who you might be willing to introduce us to?"

Similarly, gastroenterologists likely know or may be part of a practice with other gastroenterologists, so the same approach using the principle of aided recall applies. "Nancy, I enjoy working with you. I'm very pleased you're so satisfied with our services. Would you be willing to introduce us to one or two other gastroenterologists in your practice? Perhaps we can meet for dinner one evening?"

American Airlines pilots are likely to know other American Airlines pilots. Note that we did not just say airline pilots or, in the previous example, we did not say doctors. That's too general. There is a need to be as specific as possible by specialty (e.g., gastroenterologists, urologists, cardiologists, dermatologists, etc.). You get the idea. Of course there are medical practices with multiple disciplines, so in those cases you can use the same approach. For example, "Bill, I enjoy working with you. I'm very pleased you're so satisfied with our services. Would you be willing to introduce me to one or two other professionals in your practice?"

The aided recall approach improves the probability of acquiring introductions, assuming you have received positive feedback from your client, because it narrows the question so people's names and faces easily come to mind.

You would use questions as appropriate and specifically defined for each client, but again narrow the request, so the client understands exactly who we would like to be introduced to. Here are a few more examples:

- "You mentioned your parents and siblings. If I can be of service I would appreciate meeting with them. Is that something you would suggest?"
- To an anesthesiologist: "I enjoy working with you and would love the opportunity to be of service to other anesthesiologists like yourself. Would you be willing to introduce me to one or two anesthesiologists you work with (or know)?"
- To a farmer: "I enjoy working with you and would love the opportunity to be of service to other farmers. Would you be willing to introduce me to one or two farmers you work with (or know)?"

- To any client: "You mentioned your friends Mary and Bill. Are they folks we should know?. . . Would you be willing to introduce me to them?"
- To any client: "You mentioned your friend Joe who you went to the ballgame with. Is he someone I should know?. . . Would you be willing to introduce me to him?"

As opposed to aided recall there is "unaided recall." For example, "Who do you know who might be able to take advantage of the types of services I provide for you?" The question is huge. It is much too broad and too difficult for a client to answer. Even bringing in positive feedback is not helpful. "George, I enjoy working with you. I'm very pleased you're so satisfied with our services. I wonder if there are any others you know who you might be willing to introduce us to?" This question is difficult because people's names and faces do not easily come to mind.

You can get a visceral sense of what goes on in your mind when asked such a big question. It is difficult to reply to and is essentially forgotten once the client leaves the meeting. It just doesn't work. "Unaided recall" is a research method in which a respondent is given no assistance in answering questions regarding a specific topic: "What are names of some banks in your area?" This is as opposed to an "aided recall" question: "Have you ever heard of TD Bank?" The first question, though narrowed to banks, is difficult because you will most likely not recall all the banks in the area. The second question about TD Bank is a simple yes or no.

The aided recall approach is an effective way to seek introductions because clients know their family, they know their friends, and they know people who do what they do, so aiding the client narrows the group of people so that they can easily understand and recall exactly who you are asking about.

To use the aided recall approach effectively, gather information using the Client Wisdom spreadsheet shown in Figure 9-3. The idea is to identify and list clients with their indicative information on the left side of the spreadsheet (top left). This data is already posted on the segmentation spreadsheet (Figure 2-2). Start by listing all A tier clients. The right side of the spreadsheet (top right) is for data to be entered by the advisor from their current client knowledge. This is not intended, at least initially, as a research project. We suggest filling in the data that is known, taking perhaps one minute per client. (For two spouses, use two lines and take two minutes.) Fill out the client's Occupation and Company. If they are retired, indicate what they did and who they used to work for annotated with an R (e.g., Mechanical Engineer–R, Johnson and Johnson–R). Be specific if you can—don't record that someone is a Doctor, but an Anesthesiologist; the client isn't an Engineer but a Mechanical Engineer.

As a side benefit of entering this data you will learn how much you know or don't know about your best clients. Noting how the client was acquired will also help you relate in conversation, as you can say, "You know we were introduced by the president of your firm, Jack . . . or your neighbor John . . . *or* your mother, etc. Are there other employees at (name of firm) . . . other neighbors . . . your siblings, etc., who you think I would get along with and might be able to use my help?" Naturally use only one of the "or" options that best fits the situation.

If you know the client's CPA and/or Trust and Estate attorney note that, too. We will discuss that in the section on Center of Influence (COI) marketing. If you believe the client is "engaged" based on the earlier discussion in this book, note that as well.

Figure 9-3 | Client Wisdom spreadsheet.

			Profitability Indicators		
Tier	Name	No.	Assets	Revenue	ROA
		1			#DIV/0!
		2			#DIV/0!

Client Wisdom Data									
Company (Note whether Retired = R or Current = C)	Occupation / Profession (Note whether Retired = R or Current = C)	Schools Attended	Vacation Travel Interests	Organizations / Club Memberships	Hobbies / Passions	How was client acquired?	Know CPA?	Know estate attorney?	Engaged Advocate Yes / No
FA Defined	FA Defined	FA Defined	FA Defined	FA Defined	FA Defined	FA Defined	FA Defined	FA Defined	FA Defined

Now you have a set of data that can be used for asking questions in order to acquire, or at least seek, introductions using the "aided recall" approach: "I enjoy working with you and would love the opportunity to be of service to other executives at FIRM (*or* other Mechanical Engineers at FIRM) like yourself. Would you be willing to introduce me to one or two executives (*or* Mechanical Engineers) you work with?" For "client wisdom" based on travel, organizations or clubs, or hobbies and passions, you will want to dig further and find out more information so you can complete the request. Where do they travel to and with whom? What clubs or organizations do they belong to and how involved are they? What are their hobbies and passions and are they solo or group activities? Separately, it will be of value to know their family members, from parents and grandparents to children to siblings. Some FAs build family trees for and/or with their clients. Some use software for building those family trees. Now you can be prepared to seek introductions using aided recall. The process begins at client intake. You would likely have already built a strong relationship with that client before building that family tree.

Acquiring clients and assets means finding good (nonaggressive) ways of seeking introductions that work for you. The "Anatomy of a Referral" study by Julie Littlechild makes a point of saying, "Despite the fact that 58 percent of engaged clients say they are fundamentally motivated to refer in order to say 'thank you' to their advisor, few take action unless there is a clearly stated need on the part of a friend or family member." This is shown in Figure 9-4.[10]

Figure 9-4 | Referral study.

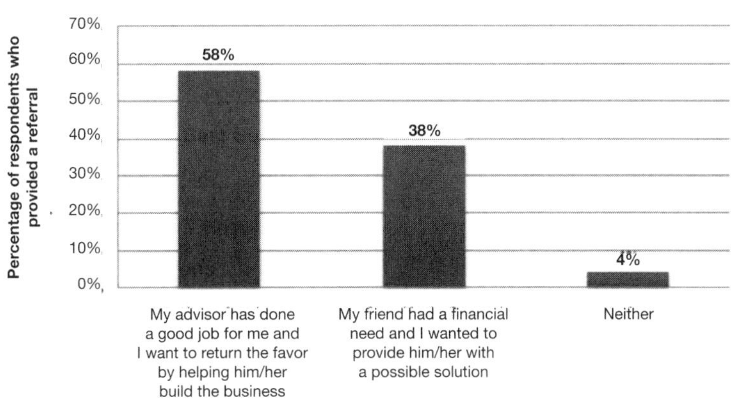

Source: Julie Littlechild, "Anatomy of a Referral: The Economics of Loyalty," December 2010.

The study makes the point of saying that a better approach than asking for an introduction is

> to help clients to spot a good referral opportunity so that they recognize the opportunity to share your name . . . the opportunity might involve a client speaking with a friend who has lost a spouse, a colleague who is selling a business, or a family member who is hoping for early retirement. The need triggers the opportunity for a referral; your clients need to recognize that need. . . . If you can help your clients understand the kinds of problems you can solve and provide them with the 'triggers' for a referral, then you are the first person they will think of in those situations.

This option is then to speak with clients about the types of clients you best serve so that when that situation arises, they can identify a prospect. Let your clients know on whom you focus, in advance, in a prepared but somewhat casual manner. For example:

> By the way, Ed, I'd like you to know my focus in case you run across situations where I can help people you know. Lately I have found a number of situations where there are . . .
>
>> Families who want to protect their assets and make sure they are able to retire the way they want. *OR* . . .
>>
>> Recent divorces or individuals who have passed away and left behind single heads of household who are concerned about a secure current and future financial situation. *OR* . . .
>>
>> Airline pilots who need to put themselves into a position where they can have a secure financial future after they retire. *OR* . . .
>>
>> Corporate executives who have complex financial needs because of a number of different sources of wealth.
>
> If you happen to hear about such situations, I am happy to be a resource for them.

Tailor the "who" (families, single heads of household, airline pilots, executives, etc.) and the "what" (ability to retire, secure their situation, etc.) based on the person you are speaking with and your niche, if you have one. It's best to limit your statement to one or two specialties so that your client can retain what you said and recall it when a friend or family member raises the concern. Don't try to say you do everything for everybody, otherwise you may wind up doing nothing for nobody.

In these cases you are not directly asking for a referral. You are "planting a seed" so your client knows what you do and whom you do it for. When a client's friend, neighbor, or colleague mentions a concern, your hope is that your name immediately comes up—your seed has sprouted. You can also see that knowing a lot about your clients and their families can be very important to your introduction efforts. Use the family tree, where appropriate, to understand where family introductions can come from.

What we are looking for in these cases are life changes that may also create "money in motion" opportunities. There are at least four basic money in motion categories:

- Work Life Transitions
- Financial Life Transitions
- Family Life Transitions
- Legacy Life Transitions

There are a number of types of transitions within each area. For example, with work life transitions there can be plans to retire, the sale of a company, a layoff, or a change in jobs. In doing a bit of research, you can identify which situations are most prevalent. For example:

- Every year, almost 4 million people are retiring.[11]
- As of March 2017 there were 5 million total separations, little changed from July.[12]
- A typical U.S. worker now lasts 4.2 years on the job.[13]
- Every month, 2 million Americans quit a job.[14]
- In 2015, 5.25 million existing homes sold and 510,000 newly constructed homes sold.[15]
- There are 800,000 new widows/year (13.6 million total in the United States).[16]
- There are 877,000 divorces and annulments/year.[17]

As an aside, we do not suggest divorcees as a primary target niche unless you are a Certified Divorce Financial Analyst (CDFA), as there are many unique and complex issues associated with divorce such as the short-term and long-term effects of dividing property, analyzing pensions and retirement plans, and recognizing the tax consequences of different settlement proposals. There are issues beyond those that most FAs deal with on a regular basis. However, once through the divorce, single, mature heads of household can be a good niche market.

Put your request in context of the transition on which you want to focus. For example:

> "If any of your colleagues at ABC are contemplating retirement, I'd love to chat with them."
>
> "If any of your friends have recently left their job, I'd love to chat with them."

Be prepared in any of these requests to relate a situation where you were able to help another person and how you did that. As an example:

> "I recently worked with a client's uncle who was laid off from his job. The gentleman had some savings but was concerned about his ability to support himself and his family if he didn't get a job with equivalent income. What we did was a complete financial plan and identified his shortfalls and what he would need in terms of income from another position. In this case the gentleman always wanted to change fields but that would have required taking a lower-paying job in an area he had always wanted to explore. This was his opportunity, so we estimated his income needs, what kinds of position he could afford to take, what had to be done about his budget, options for his older children's college expenses, as well as looking at his portfolio, and we were able to put together a life plan that would work for him."

Figure 9-5 is a summary of a number of key life transitions. While you can put your request in writing in a letter to clients, it's best shared as part of one or more discussions.

To reiterate one last point on this section: We don't want just names and phone numbers seeking referrals—we want "introductions." This means, "Would you be willing to introduce me over coffee, lunch, breakfast, or dinner?" If we cannot get an in-person introduction, we

Figure 9-5 | Key transitions.

The Types of Client I Best Serve

Are you or a family member, relative, friend, neighbor, or business acquaintance going through any of the following life transitions? We can help if you or others are (or expect to be) going through any of the following:

1. **Work Life Transitions**
   a. Is retiring soon?
   b. Has started or sold a company recently?
   c. Has been laid off from their current employer?
   d. Has changed jobs recently?
2. **Financial Life Transitions**
   a. Is purchasing or selling a home?
   b. Is struggling with their investments and trying to decide what to do in this current market environment?
   c. Needs more income from their investments?
   d. Is unhappy with their current financial advisor?
   e. Is worried about saving for college for their kids?
   f. Is concerned about having enough money for retirement?
   g. Has inherited some money recently?
3. **Family Life Transitions**
   a. Has changed their marital status?
   b. Had a spouse or significant other pass away recently?
   c. Has young children or grandchildren?
   d. Is concerned about aging parents?
4. **Legacy Life Transitions**
   a. Has talked about how to leave some inheritance for their children?
   b. Is looking for ways to reduce their taxes?
   c. Is interested in charitable giving?
   d. Is concerned about their estate plan?
   e. Owns their own business and wants to establish a savings plan for their employees?

can ask the client to introduce us via a personal email, so the prospect is at least expecting a call from us. You would tell the referrer you don't want to call the person referred "out of the blue" and make them wonder why someone gave out their name. Ask if they would mind sending an email to the person they are referring to you. Here's a sample you can provide:

> Peter, my financial advisor [insert NAME] is a very valuable resource for me and a member of the local community. He's a very good person who treats his clients like friends rather than just as a client and offers great personal service and a unique set of deliverables because he is very selective in working with a fixed number of families who are concerned about their financial well-being.
>
> He doesn't want to call you "out of the blue" and make you wonder why I gave your name out. I thought a quick introduction by email would be OK. He will email you to suggest you set up a quick phone call to explore the possibilities. If you are interested, he'll follow up with you, and if you are not interested, he'll back off immediately. I hope you will take his call; he's a terrific and knowledgeable person with a unique way of approaching financial and investment planning.
>
> Thanks, Bill
>
> If you copy me on the email I will know that it has gone out so I can follow up with an email to them (and I will copy you, so you know I've followed up). If they are interested, I'll *carefully* pursue their interest. If they are not interested, I'll back off immediately. I will do nothing to pressure them or in any way make you regret you introduced me to them. How does that sound?[18]

Introductions from Clients Using the LinkedIn Approach to Client Acquisition[19]

LinkedIn has been shown to have significant potential for those financial advisors using the platform specifically and social media generally. A 2012 LinkedIn survey (in partnership with FTI Consulting) found that:

- 62 percent of financial advisors actively prospecting on LinkedIn over the past year converted new clients from that process.
- 32 percent of the financial advisors who converted new clients from LinkedIn had $1 million or more in new assets under management from new clients.
- There are 5 million "affluent investors" with $100,000 or more in investable assets, and 73 percent of them use LinkedIn to research investment decisions.
- The "ultra-affluent investors" with $5 million or more in investable assets are 157 percent more likely to trust articles shared on LinkedIn and 37 percent more likely to trust information shared by their LinkedIn network.
- Finally, 52 percent of affluent investors say that they would interact with financial advisors via social media, but only 4 percent currently are being engaged by financial advisors online.[20]

Recent data states that "during the most recently reported quarter, LinkedIn had 450 million members."[21] This is up about 123 percent from Q4 2012, when there were about 202 million members. (In 2016, Microsoft acquired LinkedIn for about $26 billion.)

The data and recent experience suggest the use of LinkedIn by FAs makes great sense as a prospecting tool. This is an opportunity to know more people, and prospects, that you wouldn't ordinarily know. The power of LinkedIn for advisors lies in their second-degree connections. The number of first-degree connections you have is not as much a factor as how many second-degree connections you have in your network. However, the more first-degree connections you have, the more second-degree connections you will likely have in your network.

There are a couple of "principles" to follow to operate successfully in LinkedIn. Disconnect from all financial industry colleagues/competitors and focus on connecting with all your clients, prospects, friends, family members, and appropriate COIs (e.g., CPAs, attorneys, and insurance professionals if they are not competitors). People who are working are more likely to have broader networks than those who are not working. If you can find your health practitioners on LinkedIn, I would certainly connect with them as well as any small-business relationships you have in your potential niche areas. Be cautious with whom you connect and focus on people you really know. For prospecting, there is little value in connecting with strangers. Again, do not connect with other advisors unless they are on your team. We do not want them to have access to your second-degree connections.

Once you have connections, you need to begin reviewing your network. In other words, you are reviewing your connections' connections. Do not spend endless amounts of time reviewing all of a connection's 500+ connections. Review their connections until you find a set of names that stick out as potential prospects. (We will get more specific in the process outline that follows.) Prospect names should stick out based on title and location and perhaps their work history and the job they have. We may assume that senior partners, C-Suite executives, doctors, dentists, senior executives, and others have a good income. We don't know if they are good savers, but we have a rational starting point.

Remember that we only selected a set of names that stuck out. Your connections may have many great connections. You can go back to your connections a small number of times. Our view is that we can go back to your first-degree connections perhaps only two or three times in total.

We want a list of names so that it is probable that your first connection will know a few of them (their first connections) well. There are individuals on LinkedIn who connect with too many people, including many who ask to connect with people they don't know or do not know particularly well. There is little value to that, but some people like to collect connections. If someone has 300, 400, or 500 or more connections, it is unlikely that person knows all of them well. Remember Dunbar's number (see Chapter 2).

Here is a process to follow when prospecting:

- Decide with whom you (the financial advisor) are comfortable using this approach.
  - FA and client must be connected.
  - FA has a good relationship with the client.
  - Client probably has a "good number" of connections.
- When you have decided whom you will use this approach with, then decide how many names you will ask the client to review.
  - Varies depending on the number of client connections.
  - Process users identify a range of connections between 10 and 30 people; 15 is the most common number and is what we suggest in order to identify three or four possible candidates. More than that might be imposing.
- Next, go through the client's connections (your second-degree connections), if they are visible, to decide which of those connections could be qualified introductions.
  - If the client's connections are not visible, you cannot use this process with this client.
  - Identify the 15 or so names that have the characteristics that might make good prospects.
- Advisors should use this approach only two or three times with any client or friend.
  - FA can search by title in the client's connections or company or job type.

    - FA makes sure the client is geographically desirable.

- Prepare a first email from you (the advisor) to your client (first-degree connection). A sample email could read something like this:

> Brian (Client Name),
>
> I spoke with Robyn (client's wife) last week. Congratulations on your new house, I'm sure you are very excited. It sounds like the deal of the century. [This opening paragraph is an example of a personal note, a pleasantry.]
>
> Anyway, the reason for this email is that I was on LinkedIn a few days ago and I got caught up reviewing your connections. You actually have several people that stuck out based on . . . (e.g., titles). I wanted to ask you if you would mind if I made a short list of names and send it over to you. I just wanted to see if we could have a quick conversation to see what "intelligence" you have on these individuals . . . if anything?
>
> Thanks,
>
> Rob (Advisor Name)

- Send the email.
- Follow up with a call to the client and get his/her agreement to review the names.
    - Thank the client and let him/her know you will put together a note with names and set up a short chat.
    - Ask what a good date and time is for a short chat and make an appointment.
- Prepare for a conversation with the client. For example:
    - Send a second email to the client 10 minutes before the scheduled call time saying you will call in a few minutes.
- Make the call (a recommended script follows).
    - After any small talk and thanking the client for his/her time, review the names.
    - Eliminate names the client doesn't know very well.
    - Ask questions about people the client knows, to further cut down on names.
    - Discuss intentions to call these people and ask for permission to use the client's name.

> Hi Brian,
>
> I really appreciate you taking a few minutes to go through these names I emailed to you. Do you have the list I sent over?
>
> I know I sent over *N* names. We are going to make this quick. If you're like me, you may be connected to people you don't know very well on LinkedIn. So, the first thing I want to do is eliminate/cross-off anybody that you do not know very well . . . so who should I delete?
>
> Okay, so that leaves us *X* names. I want to continue to eliminate some more possibly. Obviously you know me and my personality and you know these individuals very well. Out of these remaining connections, is there anyone that you think would be a clash of personalities? [*Note:* As you go through the names, ask how your client knows them, how long they have known them, whether there is something in particular you should know about them.]
>
> Thanks for taking the time to go through these connections. I really do appreciate it. I just wanted to explain to you my intentions with these individuals. I may send them an email, but I am most definitely going to call them to introduce myself. My goal in the call is to see if they would be open to a 10–15 minute conversation. At the end of the day, either they will be open to it or they will not. If they are open, great . . . either I can add value to what they are doing or I cannot. Since you get along with these individuals, you wouldn't mind if I mentioned your name either in the email or on the phone, so I can get my foot in the door easier, would you?
>
> Do you happen to have any of their phone numbers handy? [*Note:* You may prefer to ask your client (Brian, in this case) if he would be willing to send the email introduction, using the sample letter we previously provided.]

Summary: Keys to "Client Engagement"

To increase the possibility of acquiring introductions using any of these approaches it is of significant value to have an "engaged client." We have discussed in depth how to create engagement. In summary, the keys to client engagement, satisfaction, and loyalty are in your processes.

Engaged clients receive a more holistic offer and your intention to be their financial quarterback or personal CFO. Is your offer focused on financial planning and true wealth management? Is it more likely to cover your client's full financial life? Are you delivering the higher level of contact your engaged clients expect, including at least three or more meetings a year? Do you have a strong personal relationship with your clients? Are they actively involved in providing input to you?

Client engagement is a fairly "simple" concept but implementation requires hard work. With perhaps 10.1 million households in the United States with $1 million or more in investable assets[22] and perhaps 285,000 competitors,[23] well-executed and consistent service can be a differentiator, but the "zone of affection" requires every team member's efforts.

The number-one driver of trust is "following through on promises . . . . The foundation of trust is built one brick at a time based on the consistent and ongoing evidence that you are trustworthy."[24]

In our business, you build this trust when you. . .

- Conduct formal plan and portfolio reviews.
- Reassure your clients through personal, informal communication.
- Offer educational activities, such as workshops.
- Contribute to or follow general articles about the markets or other financial topics.
- Acknowledge that you, as the advisor, value the relationship in ways that don't directly relate to the business relationship.
- Focus on understanding personal financial goals during review meetings rather than looking only at portfolio returns.

Getting introductions is about four things:

1. Delivering on your promises
2. Believing you deserve introductions for the quality work you do
3. Having a process
4. Executing, executing, executing on a consistent basis

COI Marketing Strategy for Client Acquisition[25]

Introduction

Over the years, Prince & Associates asked hundreds of FAs how they sourced their best clients. In 2000, 25.7 percent got their best clients from other clients, but by 2003 that had dropped to just 14.2 percent. Whereas with professional referrals, 69.7 percent got their best clients in 2000, but it had risen to 81.4 percent by 2003.[26]

Whether these numbers still reflect the current reality is not critical. It is critical to understand that professional referrals (or introductions) remain an important source of business growth opportunities. Many advisors have been challenged to develop the quality relationships that have resulted from professional alliances and referrals. Prince works primarily with the very high net worth marketplace, which has some differences from the high net worth and mass affluent marketplaces. Nevertheless, the points made and the approaches therein are highly valuable. Pursuing quality professional alliances is a high-value marketing and sales approach. (You can also get a good introduction in *The Middle-Class Millionaire*.[27])

To support the thesis that professional referrals (or introductions) remain a solid source of business growth opportunities, Matt Oechsli of the Oechsli Institute (www.oechsli.com) wrote an article[28] that ranks the top 5 "marketing activities used to acquire $1 million+ clients." In rank order they are:

1. Referral Alliances (e.g., CPAs, attorneys, etc.)
2. Personal Introductions
3. Indirectly Generated Referrals (word-of-mouth)
4. Social Prospecting and Networking
5. Intimate Client Events

The thesis of *Rainmaker* is that "if you want the wealthy as clients, you must go where the rich go to look for you. 68.9 percent of the affluent find their primary FA through their attorney or accountant. Allow us to put it this way, if almost 70 percent of the wealthy find their primary FA through their attorney or accountant, why would you look anywhere else for them?" [29]

The authors go on to say that while many of the "Elite 1200" advisors they collected data from employ a variety of methods to acquire new clients, they have all built strong relationships with other noncompeting professionals who provide them a steady stream of high-quality, prequalified, wealthy referrals. The principle noncompeting professionals they partner with are accountants and attorneys.

> What we are talking about is creating a meaningful strategic partnership between the advisor and a carefully chosen select number of professionals, usually attorneys and/or accountants.

> A *True Partnership* means that they are more than just one of a number of FAs being recommended; they are the first and often the only FA to be recommended. This is the essence of a strategic relationship compared to a strategic alliance.

Importantly, they state, "So, in the end, what we find derailing the success of FAs is that they chose not to succeed, by failing to intention success. They're unwilling to make the effort to ratchet up their practice."[30]

Rainmaker's authors also state:

- For middle-class millionaires, "first in importance are referrals from other professional advisors they employ—accountants and attorneys (54.2 percent). Then comes a referral from another client of the financial advisor (30.1 percent)."
- For women of wealth (743 in the study), they found "advisor referrals were the principal way these affluent clients selected a financial advisor." Professional referrals are used by almost 70 percent of women of wealth.
- "When professionals make referrals of their affluent clients, there is also a very good chance those referrals will turn into new affluent clients for FAs."

They further state that while financial incentives are important, the value add you can bring to strategic partners via direct incentives (fee and revenue sharing) is not likely to provide enough or the right kind of incentives to interest a strategic partner. Nevertheless, providing reciprocal referrals will remain very or extremely important even though one-for-one referral scenarios may not happen.

However, indirect financial incentives are not limited, and they are valuable to accountants, attorneys, and other professionals. These indirect financial incentives include:

- Help with practice management
- Insights into alternative compensation structures
- Marketing support and ideas

Step 1: Why and Who to Identify as Potential COI Partners

In a CEG Worldwide study[31] of more than 2,000 FAs industrywide, 61 percent reported that such referrals were the source of their best five new clients in the previous year. Coming in a distant second were referrals from existing clients, cited by 23.4 percent of surveyed FAs. CEG Worldwide notes that:

> In the study by Russ Alan Prince of more than 1,400 clients with at least $1 million in investable assets, 54.2 percent named referrals from professional advisors such as attorneys and accountants as an important way to find their primary FAs. Trailing behind in importance was referrals from existing clients of the FA cited by 30.1 percent of those surveyed.[32]

There are many types of professionals who would make excellent strategic partners. Two types stand out with particularly high potential:

- CPAs and accountants who work for individuals and families in the FA's target market(s). These professionals can make quality alliance partners.
- Attorneys, primarily estate and wealth protection attorneys, who work in the FA's target market. They can also make valuable strategic partners.

While strategic alliances with CPAs and attorneys can develop into powerful relationships that result in business introductions, you have additional options among other professionals:

- Life insurance specialists working in the high end of the market can have good relationships with individuals in your target market. They may also have relationships with other professionals serving the affluent, like private client attorneys, that can lead to additional opportunities.
- Association executives who lead organizations in your target market may be open to exploring ways to better serve their clients through an alliance.

- Business brokers may be open to an alliance because some of their largest financial transactions can be the sale of the FA's business. Business brokers know that some transactions may not be completed because the potential seller is not sure what to do with the proceeds. Your financial planning and investment services can be very helpful to the business broker and seller of the practice.
- Some investment bankers who facilitate mergers and acquisitions may welcome an alliance that helps clients invest equity that has been released. Broad-based wealth management services can provide a set of excellent services.
- Consultants who work in your target market may have contacts they can leverage to help you while building their own businesses.
- Property and casualty agents who focus on clients with multimillion-dollar homes, jets, or specialty autos, for example, also may have good affluent client relationships.

The professionals in your target market areas have several things in common:

- They work with affluent clients in the same areas as you.
- They may have built trusted, long-term relationships with their clients.
- They want to grow their businesses.[33]

Special attention is almost always focused on CPAs and Trust and Estate attorneys. However, you can build alliances with almost any type of professional advisor with these characteristics.

"With so many choices," the CEG Worldwide study asks, "how do you begin to narrow your options?" As a first step, create a profile of what your ideal strategic partner would look like. Although you may not identify an individual who perfectly matches this profile, it will help keep you on track toward the ideal through your discussions with candidates.

CEG Worldwide's profile for the ideal CPA firm might look like this:

- Highly respected regional firm.
- Three to 20 CPAs in the firm. (To this CEG recommendation we add that it may be more appropriate to work with smaller firms with, say, one to five CPAs because they may not be as inundated by requests from FAs to form "strategic" professional partnerships.)
- 150–300 clients per CPA.
- Principal specializes in your target niche.
- Principal is marketing oriented and has an entrepreneurial outlook.
- Firm is client-centric, focused on the best interest of its clients.
- Firm sincerely wants to help clients solve their problems and achieve their goals.
- Firm is open to working with other professional advisors.

The profile for the type of attorney you decide to work with might look like this:

- Works extensively with affluent clients.
- Works extensively with other professional advisors to the affluent.
- Specializes in trusts and estates, including wealth protection.
- Has an entrepreneurial outlook and is marketing oriented.
- Is interested in growing the firm's business in innovative ways.
- Has the best interest of clients in mind.
- Sincerely wants to help clients solve their problems and achieve their goals.
- Shares your commitment to client service, integrity, and professionalism.[34]

Before searching for CPAs and Trust and Estate attorneys from external sources, start with those professionals who are used by your clients. With your profile of the ideal strategic partner, you can prepare a master list of candidates including your client's CPAs and Trust and Estate attorneys. For additional candidates, you can turn to various local and national websites and organizations. You can also phone the heads of your local and state CPA societies to ask for assistance in identifying leading firms in your market.

From your master list, identify the top ten possibilities. In the case of CPA firms, CEG recommends, you can assess the whole firm, though your primary contact would hopefully be the managing partner. For attorneys, you can look at the individual attorney, not his or her entire firm. [35]

Contact the potential partner directly to discuss joint opportunities for working together and schedule an exploratory meeting. These can be difficult calls for FAs to make but referencing a joint client can smooth the way as would an email to the professional from the client. Professionals need help with business development and also face challenges in growing their businesses. Depending on conditions, some professionals may be preconditioned to work with FAs. Therefore, some will be willing to meet with you.

"Once you have these initial meetings scheduled," CEG Worldwide notes, "you will be ready to begin the strategic alliance consultative process, which allow you to determine the right strategic partners and to launch your alliances effectively."[36]

Other Points of Interest from the CEG Worldwide Study[37]

- "About one-third of surveyed firms use an internal model. That is, they provide . . . financial services and products through one or more employees or partners at the firm. A sizable majority of the firms (65.4 percent) use a collaborative model, whereby they provide financial services and products through employees or partners and through strategic arrangements with financial services providers outside the firm."
- "The most common type of outside provider used by collaborative firms is the turnkey asset management program (TAMP). More than six in ten of surveyed collaborative firms rely on TAMPs for portfolio management and support. About half of collaborative firms (51.5 percent) provide clients with referrals to select financial services professionals to access financial services and products, while about one-third (31.3 percent) have created formal strategic al-

liances or joint ventures with one or more financial professionals."

- The COI relationship "rests on the foundation, which must have four key elements:
  - *Integrity:* Are both partners principled, trustworthy, and reliable? Will you be able to fully trust one another?
  - *Chemistry:* Do you connect with each other on both a professional and personal level? Do you have genuine rapport?
  - *Empathy:* Do you understand one another's issues and challenges?
  - *Competence:* Do both partners have the professional experience and technical expertise required to capably address their clients' challenges?"

Step 2: Vet Potential COIs with Your Clients

The objective of this part of the strategy is to get an initial idea of the capabilities and "quality" of the professional. Quality can be a subjective attribute and may be understood differently by different people. The "quality" you will be looking for in this and the other steps of your COI marketing strategy can include: character, excellence, worth, value, skill, and responsiveness. In general, you are seeking a professional who is fit for and well suited to the purpose he or she was hired for, as well as for you and your business.

The COI may or may not be the absolute best in his or her field but needs to be competent to meet your clients' needs and be relatively cost-effective. Does this professional communicate well and have a good attitude? Is the person enthusiastic about what he or she does? Is the person certainly ethical with high integrity and friendly? Is this someone you like and could work with?

If you are in the early stages of your career and have no or few clients within the primary geographic area in which you work, you will have to "hunt" for professionals with whom to build a relationship. The LinkedIn approach, as previously addressed, may be another source for you. The first set of professionals to vet should be the professionals who work with your top 10 to 20 clients or so, including:

- Primary connections
  - The CPAs they work with in preparing their tax returns
  - The Trust and Estate attorney they work with in preparing their will
- Secondary connections
  - The banker or mortgage broker they work with in obtaining a mortgage
  - The real estate agent they work with in buying a home
  - Other professionals where specific expertise is needed

If you find your client is highly satisfied with the professional you will likely want to interview that professional to establish a relationship and perhaps even choose to work with them yourself. This is someone with whom you should go to the next step.

If your client is not highly satisfied, you can then identify highly satisfactory professionals to that client once you have that group in place.

Over time you may want to know the names and contact information of most, if not all, of your top clients' other advisors, though you will develop a "strategic relationship" with only one or two professionals in any one discipline. With some minimal effort you can maintain contact with most of them through your automated drip marketing system. An example of an automated drip marketing system is a set of emails to an individual or group of individuals based on specific timelines or user actions. Such an approach can allow you to keep in touch with the individual or group based on specific events. This might include when a client or prospect logs onto your website or requests an article from your site. The emails can be pre-written and may be personalized. An automated drip marketing system can also include sending out compliance-approved newsletters, company-written materials, and special compliance-approved announcements. Depending on your team structure you may have some minimal contact with more than your "strategic" professional relationships.

Requesting COI Information from a Client

FA to client:

- We are always getting calls from CPAs and estate attorneys (or other professionals you are vetting). We want to make sure we have the names of your CPA and estate attorney so we can respond to any of their questions with your permission.
    - If client does not have a CPA and/or an estate attorney, this may be an opportunity to provide a referral to one. Ask if they would like a recommendation.
    - If client has a CPA and/or an estate attorney, record their names on your COI contact list and in your CRM system.
- May I ask you a few questions to get a sense and background of your CPA and/or an estate attorney, from your perspective?
    - Assuming yes, ask questions such as:
        - What type of business do they have?
        - How did you meet this professional?
        - How do you feel about the work they've done for you?
        - What are their costs, and do they seem in line with your other experiences?
        - What do you see as unique about that professional that made you pick them?
        - In what areas are they particularly strong?
        - Do they have any weaknesses?
        - Are they responsive?
        - Do they have a specific type of client they work with (e.g., individuals, small businesses, and corporations)?
        - And, most important: Would you recommend this CPA and/or estate attorney to others in your family and friends? Why?

You should record all COI data in whatever database system and/or CRM system you use. This will also be the base for recording conversations with the COI. Some financial advisors also keep a notebook by COI with a page for each client they have referred to that COI. They also keep a section and page for each client that COI referred. This notebook is then used for follow-on conversations with the COI as appropriate.

Step 3: First Call to a COI

At this point you have gotten a positive indication from your client and/or searches that this COI is worth contacting based on information available to date. You are now going to speak to an initially vetted COI.

The objective of this part of the strategy is to introduce yourself and get a very quick sense of the COI through the conversation, but it is primarily designed to get an in-person appointment with the COI. We suggest the COI be geographically proximate to you so that your travel is easier and any clients will likely be close as well.

Make sure you have Googled the COI, reviewed their website if available, and reviewed their LinkedIn page and any other social media data or other information you can find to learn about that person and firm.

The response you will get is most often positive or at least courteous. The COI may well have been contacted by many advisors in the past. The professional may also be associated with one or more other advisors. If this COI is one you would *really* like to have as a partner, your approach could convince them that you are an advisor they would also like to partner with and that you are serious about establishing "strategic" professional relationships. You can indicate you are talking to several professionals and would like the opportunity to meet, if they are willing and interested.

They most likely know what you want, but they also need introductions. This is why we suggest that in some or many cases it may be more appropriate to work with smaller firms—for example, the firm with one to five CPAs, because they may not be as inundated by requests from FAs to form "strategic" professional partnerships. You may also want to work with less established COIs who are still hungry for business.

If you cannot get an appointment with this COI now, and not likely going forward, determine if this COI will be open to some degree of continuing contact, perhaps a couple of times a year, and if the person is open to being included on your drip list. Cordiality at a minimum is needed and you will of course invite the COI to feel free to contact you if you can be of service. Send him or her an electronic business card (VCF) and follow up with an email thanking them for speaking with you and inviting them to stay in contact. If you can connect on LinkedIn, you may want to do so, assuming they are not a potential competitor.

Script to Establish the Meeting with the COI

COI NAME, this is (NAME).

- Our joint client, Mr. and/or Ms. (NAME) thinks very highly of you. We've been working together for N years and have a great relationship, so I am particularly pleased that (CLIENT NAME) recommended you.
    - Do you have a few minutes to chat?
    - Assuming yes, keep going.
    - If no, ask when a good time to call back is.
    - If you are blown off, you can drop it or ask the client to call so the COI will take your call. However, you may be better off dropping it here if the person is unfriendly.
    - Proceed as you would with someone you cannot get an appointment with. As suggested previously, send this person an electronic business card and follow up with an email thanking them for speaking with you and inviting them to stay in contact.
- If you are invited to keep going, briefly build some additional rapport with a conversation. For example:
    - How long has (NAME) been your client?
    - How long have you been in the business?
- At this point you can ask for an appointment: "COI NAME, I'd like to get together for a brief meeting with you and discuss how you do your business. There are times when I need to refer a client to a CPA/estate attorney and I'd like to find out more about you and your business. Can we meet for breakfast or lunch some time?"
- Assuming a yes, schedule the meeting: "I would like to come by your office if that works for you." A visit to their office will tell you more about the COI as well. You can get many impressions from the physical facility where the person works and the office staff.

Step 4: First Meeting with the COI

You are meeting with a pre-vetted COI for this call and one with whom you have spoken and have gotten at least a reasonably good sense that you are speaking to a COI of substance based on your research and conversation.

The objectives of this part of the strategy are to:

- Understand the COI's capabilities and services and evaluate the individual based on some of the previously discussed criteria, your client feedback, and your research.
- Briefly talk about your business from the standpoint of why you are in the business, the types of clients you work with, and the kinds of problems you address and solve. This is where storytelling applies. Keep it short because this call is about the COI.
- Start to build a relationship if there is rapport and a meeting of the minds.
- Begin to enter into the process to establish a joint referral/business relationship if the person is willing /interested.
- Plan the next step, which is to invite the COI to your office where this potential partner can get an understanding of what you do, how you do it, and who you do it for.

As in an initial client or prospect call, let the COI talk 80 percent of the time. The more you let people talk, the more they like you. The more you talk, the less they like you. Let this CPA or attorney sell you on their skills and services. As one blogger writes:[38]

> Cold hard truth: we're all narcissistic to some degree. Even when we may not feel like we're the hottest thing since World War III, we do like to believe that our inner lives and thoughts are fascinating. Just take a look at our social networks as we fill our days with Facebook status updates, Instagraming everything, and tweeting about every aspect of our lives. . . .
>
> But believe it or not, there's a reason for this beyond everyone being profoundly self-involved: as it turns out, talking about ourselves literally makes us feel good. Scientists have found that talking about

> ourselves activates the same pleasure centers of the brain that are associated with food and money. So in short: we are our favorite subjects because goddamn it feels good to talk about ourselves. And since this fits in with the reward theory of attraction, getting people to talk about themselves is a valuable part of getting people to like you.
>
> . . . You [also] have to be an active listener, taking what they say and bouncing it back by asking the right questions.

Obviously you would have had some opening rapport conversation such as the ever-typical "How are you?" or "Thank you for seeing me today," or "I am looking forward to learning about you and your business." But you also need to have an interview plan (see the sidebar for a list of COI interview questions). Work from a written set of questions with writing space to record answers. People you are interviewing don't mind you using a questionnaire to make sure you cover everything and record their answers.

You won't be able to ask all of these questions in the time you have. Ask the COI how much time they had allotted to the meeting and stay to that commitment. If you established rapport and you like what you have seen so far, and the COI does as well, you can address more questions as time goes on. This is intended to be a long-term relationship.

Highlight the questions that are most important to this interview. Few interviews go exactly as planned, as one question may open up a topic line you had not planned on. During the interview—and in fact in any subsequent conversations—as you listen to the COI's answers, think about how you can add value to that person and/or his or her business. This is of course always a good idea when speaking with clients and prospects and when networking.

COI Interview Questions

1. What are your goals for your business?
   - *a.* Short term and long term?
   - *b.* If we were sitting here 5 years from now, what would you like to have seen happen? (Note: You are looking for their aspirations and desire to grow their business. If they are looking to put it on cruise control, they are not likely the best strategic partner.)

2. Are there any particular problems you have in your profession/running your business?
   - *a.* Plans to solve? (Increase income would be an example.)

3. What are your favorite types of cases to work on, and why? (Where does their interest lie?)

4. What types of cases are the most profitable to you? Have you ever quantitatively analyzed them? (Do they know who their best clients are?)
   a. What professional types are your dominant client groups? (You are looking for a pattern of opportunity associated with a professional group.)
   b. What issues do they voice to you as their major financial concerns? (You are looking to shift into a conversation about specific clients where you can offer solutions to their problems, and even to gain a client introduction.)
   c. What issues do you perceive them as having? (With this question you can hunt for wealth management interests.)
   d. When you look at your business owners, what level of revenue makes for your best client?

5. How did you initially build your business?

6. Where do your new clients come from?
   a. What are the top five sources and why? (Good information to know, but this question is a way to also find out how heavily any other advisors are feeding them clients. There is a possible opportunity to reverse-engineer their COIs, delivering significant value.)
   b. Have you worked with financial advisors in the past?
   c. What has been your best and worst experience working with a financial advisor?
   d. What could we offer that would differentiate us as financial advisors?
   e. What makes an ideal client for you—e.g., how would I recognize a great prospect for you?
   f. How many new clients do you usually get in a year?

7. What are you doing to get more referrals, and/or what problems are you encountering? (What if anything are they doing systematically to get more clients or more business from existing clients?)

8. Who is your toughest competition and why? (This question is a way to diagnose where they feel their firm could improve by looking at who they envy and why.)

9. What financially related problems are your clients bringing you? (You are looking to identify issues with their clients that you may be able to resolve.)

10. What kinds of marketing do you do? What have you found to be most successful? (Make an inventory of any efforts.)

11. What kinds of networking groups are you involved in? (Inventory active groups to possibly join.)

12. What personal goals do you have? What are you doing about these? (Explore wealth management opportunities with them.)

13. Do any products or services in particular trouble you? (You are looking for product landmines that you want to avoid.)

14. Do you mind if we spend a few minutes discussing how we do our business? (Be prepared to answer questions as appropriate about any of the following.)
   a. What's in your pitch book
   b. Your processes and service model
   c. Your communications process

   d. Your investment philosophy and approach
   e. Your differentiation

15. In Conclusion
   a. Would you be interested in working together in a way that could mutually benefit us?
   b. How do you feel about someone like me working with you?

16. Discuss next steps such as another meeting, a planning session, a test client, or perhaps using the COI as a test client at no cost or any expectation, of course. Consider offering a financial plan for the COI, preferably with real data but even partially real data could be helpful.

You will not likely have time to ask more than a half dozen questions, so plan your time accordingly. You will want to spend a few minutes on point 14 and ask the big questions on point 15.

Source: This is a version of questions from Brett Van Bortel, coauthor (with Russ Allen Prince) of *Rainmaker: Strategic Partnering with Attorneys and Accountants to Create a Pipeline of New Affluent Clients* (Erlanger, KY: National Underwriter Company, Summit Business Media, 2006). Our additional explanations are in parentheses. There may be other questions you will want to ask as the conversation develops.

http://www.thinkadvisor.com/2006/08/01/building-the-cpa-alliance.

The three stories told here are from Ellen Uzelac, "Building the CPA Alliance," Research Magazine, August 1, 2006, http://www.thinkadvisor.com/2006/08/01/building-the-cpa-alliance. Reprinted and excerpted with permission from Think Advisor, © 2006 ALM Media Properties, LLC. All rights reserved.

If after your interview there is continuing interest you will move to the next step. If not, you will determine if this COI will be open to some degree of continuing contact, perhaps a couple of times a year, and if the person is open to being included on your drip list. Cordiality at a minimum is needed. Invite the COI to contact you if you can be of service. Send an electronic business card and follow up with an email thanking them for speaking with you and inviting them to stay in contact. If you can connect on LinkedIn, considering potential competition, do so.

Plan the next step, which is to invite the COI to your office, where they can get an understanding of your facilities, your support staff, the tools at your disposal, and your team and management.

Step 5: A COI Visit to Your Office

At this point you have determined that the COI is not a competitor. You have directly asked that up front if it's not clear from their website.

If they have a referral relationship with other FAs you have also asked if they are willing to consider you as a second source, if that is acceptable to you. At this point they are probably not yet a "strategic" professional relationship.

You have by now gotten at least a somewhat positive response from a qualified COI with whom you have begun to build a relationship. They have left the door open on the question of whether they are considering entering into a "strategic" professional relationship. (*Note:* If you have not gotten a positive response from this COI you may want to dig further into why not. If you don't get a positive response and you can't find out why, the best you may be able to do is have a cordial, positive, but non-referring relationship.)

If everything has gone well to this point, the objective of this part of the strategy is to continue to build on the relationship by inviting the COI to your office, where they can get an understanding of what you do, how you do it, and who you do it for. It is important that they accept your invitation and commit to a visit.

In essence, this is a sales call at this point. The "sale" is the COI's agreement to a visit. However, you must be cautious and not be salesy, as this may not go over well. COI relationships must be nurtured. An alliance can take months, even a year or longer to establish. Don't become impatient or expect quick results.

If the COI does not commit to a visit, you will have to decide whether to continue to pursue a "strategic" professional relationship. You will have to determine how open this COI will be to continuing contact. Does not committing to visiting your office indicate a lack of desire to develop a "strategic" professional relationship? If yes, you may want to drop further attempts to develop that relationship and move on. If maybe, but not now, you may want to maintain contact such as a call two or three times a year and see if they are willing to visit at a future time. Keep dripping if it's of value and the COI is open to being included. (*Note:* An email is NOT a substitute for a call.)

As said, cordiality at a minimum is needed and you will invite the COI to feel free to contact you if you can be of service. Send the COI an electronic business card and follow up with an email thanking them. Connect on LinkedIn if appropriate.

The Strategic Value of the COI Visit

As John Bowen of CEG Worldwide notes, "Most advisors have all kinds of challenges forming strategic relationships because they don't have a clear, compelling value proposition to bring to the CPA [and Trust and Estate attorney]. They may have a good business model but so often what they do is come up to the CPA, as they would a client, and try to impress them with their investment or technical knowledge. Much like clients, CPAs can't tell the difference between advisors. What they want is an understanding of how the CPA does business and how the advisor can provide them with a coordinated financial offering. They are looking for people who can provide insight, who can be looked at as a business partner. This is more than just a good-old-boy referral network."

"I'll bet 80 percent of brokers and advisors would say, 'CPA alliances are part of my marketing strategy.' What happens is they end up signing up a lot of CPAs and not doing a lot of business with them," says Chip Roame of Tiburon Strategic Advisors.

Continuing, Roame says, "Why such a high failure rate? It's simple: the lack of a systematic approach."

"Everybody wants to meet more clients through referrals; they all know it's the best way. But most don't have a systematic approach to it," according to Bill Cates of Referral Coach International. "There's a lot of fear and mistaken assumptions that keep them from developing that business. And the solutions are pretty simple, really."

In *Rainmaker*,[39] the authors state "a strategic partnership is a relationship, and building it right, from the foundation up, requires time and thought. The two basics are personal integrity and technical expertise."

The COI visit to your office is your opportunity to communicate your views and values. You must communicate your ethical and personal standards. In your visit you will want to:

- Introduce all of your staff.
- Illustrate that you and your team are client-centric by discussing your "Client Service Model" or "Promise."
- Discuss that you have a fiduciary perspective. If you are a fiduciary certainly discuss that fact. Some firms are technically not fiduciaries, however; a fiduciary is a person or business that holds a legal or ethical relationship of trust with one or more other parties. With a new Department of Labor (DOL) rule you have additional legal fiduciary responsibilities.
- Outline the tools and technologies you have in support of your clients (e.g., your financial planning tools, your CRM, etc.). Show a sample report with the types of recommendations you provide.
- Go through a sample analysis of how you have helped solve a client "problem" using a client example (keeping client specifics confidential).
- Show the COI the processes you use to interact with clients to illustrate your systematic approach. (You can find a description of these processes at www.financialadvisorsuccess.com.)

You can also discuss the types of situations where you have helped clients resolve their wants and/or needs in life transition circumstances as listed in Figure 9-5. In essence, you are sharing your "compelling value proposition," which includes your people, your skills, your experience and expertise, what you deliver to your clients, and the tools, processes, and approaches you bring to the table. Illustrating your technical expertise should come as an offshoot of everything we have discussed thus far, rather than being a focal point.

Step 6: Plan Next Steps with the COI

At this point you have hopefully impressed the COI. The fact that the COI has visited your office is positive. As with client meetings, as your next steps you will want to:

- Summarize your meeting, reiterating the points you tried to make and your value proposition.
- Seek feedback, asking questions about what they liked, what you might have addressed that you didn't, and any suggestions they have.

Although the COI is now moving toward a "strategic" professional relationship, the relationship must continue to be nurtured over the coming months and longer. The objective of this part of the strategy is to:

- Continue to build on the relationship.
- Develop how you can jointly work together in a way that could mutually benefit the COI and yourself.
- Plan on a next meeting, perhaps over a meal, to develop next steps.

You will want to offer to become a resource for the COI's practice, providing an ongoing education on investment-related subjects and keeping them updated on the markets and resources available to your wealth management approach. These next steps can be addressed at the same time as the Step 5 meeting or in another meeting after a week or so.

Script for Working with a COI and Other Ideas

- Are you comfortable enough with who we are to consider some next steps? (Assuming a positive response, continue to explore other topics.)
- At this point, we've agreed to continue exploring working together. What are your thoughts on the ideas I have suggested?
- Let's set up another meeting to:
    - Brainstorm plans for working together on a test client.
    - Review our "Offerings for Strategic Partners." (See Appendix 2 for a list of potential offerings you would want to discuss in another meeting.)
    - Serve as test clients for one another, at no cost and without any expectation, and consider a financial plan for you and your spouse or partner. You could prepare my tax return with the same agreement.

- Discuss conducting a marketing event together, where we can both invite clients and both speak at the event.
- Explore ways to work together such as through roundtables, teleconferences, newsletters, appreciation events, etc.
- Send clients various materials, such as each other's newsletters, client magazines, equity and fixed-income information, research, or tax tips. (Perhaps ask a subset of clients what they would like and deliver it.)
- Establish a plan for continuing contact such as a call, lunch, or visit perhaps every 30 to 45 days. (You'll want to schedule a breakfast or lunch meeting every three or four months with each of your "strategic" COI relationships.)

In Conclusion

These final words of advice are excerpted from the *Rainmaker* Keynote Summary.

- "Many advisors don't come close to the level of knowledge they have about their potential strategic partners as they do with their investor clients. In other words, advisors know the attorney or accountant is their client, but they don't engage in the kind of relationship management they would with a top investor client."
- "Do all the things you do with your BEST investor clients, and move it over to attorneys and accountants—your 'strategic partners.'"
- "You do not need a lot of partners to significantly increase your income. In fact, the research on this point reveals a striking fact. The average number of partners for the 'Elite 1200' is 3.9. Perhaps even more interesting is that it never goes above 5. In fact, when advisors try to work with more than 5, their production began to go down. Why? It appears that they could not feed all of these strategic partnerships adequately and began to backslide into 'affiliations.'" [It is difficult, in other words, to develop and maintain the type of *close* "strategic" relationships with COIs that you will need to get them to provide quality introductions.]
- The guidelines for a "strategic" relationship include having a:
    - Good personal relationship
    - Relationship that adds value to both businesses, including revenue growth
    - Solid and continuing joint business arrangement
- If the COI does not meet these criteria, move on.

- "The Elite 1200 . . . turn 180 degrees, from an approach of "Let me tell you about me" to "What can I do for you?"[40]

Plans are only good intentions unless they immediately degenerate into hard work.
—Peter Drucker

Appendix 1: Metrics

- Track all components of your "strategic" professional relationships.
  - Your referrals to your "strategic" professional relationship:
    - Who did you refer?
    - When did you refer your client?
    - What happened (e.g., did the COI get the client's business)?
    - What was the resultant business value?

    Ask your client for their perspectives on the professional.
  - Referrals from your "strategic" professional relationship:
    - Who was referred to you?
    - When were you given a referral?
    - What happened (e.g., did you get the client's business)?
    - What was the resultant business value?

Provide a nonconfidential overview of the client and thank the professional, whether or not business was achieved.

Appendix 2: "Offerings for Strategic Partners"

- Professional Financial Planning
- Portfolio Analysis
- Estate Planning
- Banking and Finance Services
- Fiduciary Responsibilities and Compliance
- Practice Management

(More detail can be found at www.financialadvisorsuccess.com.)

Appendix 3: The Types of Clients We Best Serve

The same conversation you have with your clients about life transitions (see Figure 9-5) you can also have with COIs. It's another opportunity to bring up stories about any relevant and appropriate situations where you helped solve a client's financial situation. According to Jonathan Gottschall, author of *The Storytelling Animal*:

> Science backs up the long-held belief that story is the most powerful means of communicating a message. In business, storytelling is all the rage. Without a compelling story, we are told, our product, idea, or personal brand, is dead on arrival. In his book *Tell to Win*, Peter Guber joins writers like Annette Simmons and Stephen Denning in evangelizing for the power of story in human affairs generally, and business in particular. Guber argues that humans simply aren't moved to action by "data dumps," dense PowerPoint slides, or spreadsheets packed with figures. People are moved by emotion. The best way to emotionally connect other people to our agenda begins with "Once upon a time . . ."[41]

Book of Life for Client Acquisition

Many advisors, especially when they are new to the business, have put together a list of all the people they know or have known for the purpose of creating a "suspect" list. A *suspect* is defined as an individual or organization with the potential for needing a particular product or service you provide. They are potential clients who may have been introduced to your product or service (e.g., a known investor) but have not yet rejected your offer. They are not as strong a candidate as a prospect because the advisor may not have met with them as yet (at least with respect to business) but would like to meet them and have a business discussion.

A *prospect* is defined as a potential client qualified on the basis of buying authority, financial capacity, and willingness to buy. These prospects are also called sales leads. They must have been willing to meet with the advisor or have met with the advisor to be a qualified prospect.

The "Book of Life" spreadsheet (see Figure 9-6) is focused on who the advisor knows or knew, such as friends and family but not limited to those groups. The advisor would list what she or he knows about them. Essentially filling out the list is an exercise in self-brainstorming but can be made easier by thinking in categories.

Advisors may have already explored this area but may have not been formal about it. We recommend not culling the list while putting it together by "assuming" anything about the person's financial situation or their potential interest. We recommend just posting names and whatever is known about the people at this moment. They may or may not be client-worthy, but they may know people who are client-worthy.

The purpose of this exercise is to record everyone the advisor knows, formally, in writing. Note whether you might or could or do like them as individuals.

The individuals are alive as far as you know, but you do not need to know all the information that is included on the spreadsheet. If you do not know their contact information, age, or their interests or where they work or what they do, that's fine. Record what you know and leave the rest blank. The missing information can be researched later if necessary. If all you know is the name and how you know them (source of name), that's fine. Record and move on.

You will likely have many more opportunities to look for your "Book of Life," including:

1. Family
2. Country club
3. The Rotary or similar organizations and clubs to which you, as an advisor, belong (or will belong)
4. Any "ethnic" based organization to which you many belong, e.g., Italian-American, African-American, etc.
5. Religious affiliations
6. Executives and key persons at previous places you worked and the clients, supporters, and suppliers you may have met affiliated with that firm
7. Small businesses (but find sub-niches in this area where you can focus your skills, such as law firms, auto body shops, auto parts distributors, etc.)

8. Medical/dental practices you know and/or use
9. Employees affected by layoffs
10. School classmates
11. Friends and their families
12. Organizations and charities in which you have a real interest
13. Hobbies and other life interests
14. Racquetball, tennis, polo players or other sports enthusiasts or venues you know where people are likely to have money
15. Golfers
16. Parents of your children's friends
17. People who might be expected to retire soon
18. People who mentioned that they have just moved their business to another advisor and to check back with them in a year or two
19. People likely to sell their business
20. People who may not make good clients but could be good for getting introductions
21. People who have changed jobs and may have an IRA account that can be rolled over
22. People who may inherit wealth
23. People you have met on various occasions in your role as a financial advisor
24. People associated with specific companies that are creating wealth
25. People who are part of your social network
26. Others

Even though Dunbar's number suggests that humans can comfortably maintain only 150 stable relationships, theoretically, the average American may know as many as about 600 people.[42] In addition, according to Funders and Founders,[43] individuals may interact with as many as 80,000 people in a lifetime. Our suggestion is to target 250

Figure 9-6 | Book of Life spreadsheet.

Name	Contact Data (Email/Phone)	Age	Relationship	Source of Name How You Know the Person	Current Advisory Firm	Estimated Assets	Potential Contraints

Leverage	Leverage	Leverage	Leverage	Leverage	Leverage	Leverage
Industry / Position	Company / Occupation	Schools Attended	Vacation Travel Interests	Organizations / Club Memberships	Hobbies Passions	Engaged Advocates

people for your "Book of Life" spreadsheet (Figure 9-6), but you do not have to do it all at once.

Similar to the Book of Life, Matt Oechsli refers to an individual's "Spheres of Influence" and suggests the client's Spheres of Influence include family, friends, colleagues, neighbors, and organizations, recreational and professional.

Niche Marketing for Client Acquisition

Niche marketing[44] is not so much a marketing approach as it is a context for marketing. Niches represent a specific pool of individuals who are targetable prospects. These individuals tend to have similar challenges that could be unique to the group; they represent a business opportunity and should complement your specific strengths and personal interests. Examples of niches with these characteristics are general dentists and general medical practitioners (e.g., GPs or internists). These professions tend to be tied to a chair or examination room and have appointments back to back in many if not most cases. In many cases medical and dental insurance puts stresses on incomes, resulting in high and/or growing patient loads. These niches represent a business opportunity because their income is well above average. It would be helpful for advisors to have the experience of having worked in the field or to have clients already in these fields from whom they can gain knowledge in their issues and concerns.

Niches generally respond predictably to your marketing activities and financial solutions. Advisors have indicated physicians in particular are at times challenging because of their self-confidence. They are also a challenge to get time from, yet they have been sought after by many advisors.

Other important niche characteristics are much more narrowly defined (e.g., not doctors, but anesthesiologists or gastroenterologists or radiologists). Individuals in narrowly defined fields tend to have a common culture and share a natural affinity. They likely read the same professional journals, attend the same meetings or conferences, and have more of a tendency to know others in their sphere. You want niches to be active communicators if possible and be affordably accessible.

Women are not a niche, retirees and pre-retirees are not niches, airline pilots are not a niche. The commonality among women, retirees, and pre-retirees is just not there. There is no single common culture, no common way to access them, and there is no shared affinity as a larger group. If, however, you narrow the focus to women executives in your geography . . . or to IBM employees retiring from New York or Austin, Texas, . . . or, for that matter, to women retiring from IBM in New York City, you have defined niches. There are myriad and diverse niches. For example:

- There is an advisor who loves fishing and his dad was a professional bass fisherman. He made a career working with professional fisherman.
- The first client for an advisor out in California was an executive at Disney. The majority of his client base worked there.
- An advisor in New Jersey was a studio musician before entering the business. His niche became studio musicians.

There is practically no limit to niches. Advisors have successfully focused on niches such as oral surgeons; plastic surgeons; orthodontists; airline pilots from specific airlines; engineers in a specific company; office supply executives; Indian physicians; Pakistani, Greek, or Italian businessmen; Redimix contractors; and the list goes on.

The reason niche marketing is a context rather than a marketing approach is that advisors can seek introductions within the niche from one client to another in that niche. In some cases COIs specialize in the same niches in which you may be interested, so you would use your COI marketing strategy with that group of COIs. You can focus your LinkedIn searches on specific professions or organizations and, if you hold intimate events, you can invite a client to dinner and ask him to bring one of his friends in that same niche. Putting people into groups can create a feeling of proprietorship and relationship with that group. This feeling is an important element to your business development efforts. It can make you feel a level of comfort and confidence as you move forward. You have made a type of investment in the group and the individuals in that group. In essence, you can attain a sense of ownership so you can have more confidence in prospecting in that group either proactively or reactively. Your investment in a niche by preparing yourself to work with that group is an important step. Invest yourself by reading about the group in publications they may be reading, understanding their demographics and psychographics, interviewing group members and COIs who work with them, joining their organizations, and networking with them. In addition, identifying group members who may be prospects and researching them will also prepare you for marketing to the group and individuals within the group.

There is also the belief that niches provide higher assets under management, especially for higher-level producers. The profitability should also be higher because marketing costs are lowered, the prospecting is easier, the pipeline is larger, the closing rate is higher and quicker because of natural trusted relationships, and the referral flow is better because of word-of-mouth.

Commonality within your marketplace makes you the master of the trade and enables you to spend your time better and be more focused. However, for a niche to be productive, it must generally have at least 200 to 300 prospects in your access area who are well-to-do and well positioned from an income perspective. Ideally, the target market should be definable—for instance, it may be a group that meets regularly, reads the same publications, or attends the same meetings, etc. Most important, the advisor should have a level of comfort in working with the selected targets.

As an advisor, you may have more niche opportunities than are practical. Pick three that fit, that you like, and where you have an "entry point" via contacts and/or knowledge to leverage practitioners or employees (e.g., law firms, medical/dental practices, firms you have previously worked for). Your entry point needn't be limited to practitioners and individuals; if you have a focus on 401(k) plans that can be a product-based entry point.

Putting people into groups can create a feeling of proprietorship and relationship with that group. This feeling is an important element to your business development efforts. It can make you feel a level of comfort and confidence as you move forward. You have made a type of investment in the group and the individuals in that group. In essence you can attain a sense of ownership so you can have more confidence in prospecting in that group either proactively or reactively. Your investment in a niche by preparing yourself to work with that group is an important step. Invest yourself by reading about the group in publications they may be reading, understanding their demographics and psychographics, interviewing group members and COIs who work with them, joining their organizations, and networking with them. In addition, identifying group members who may be prospects will also prepare you for marketing to the group and individuals within the group.

From a marketing perspective, niche marketing allows the advisor to become an expert in how to reach prospects in the niche rather than relying on a more helter-skelter, one-off approach to finding prospective clients. It also allows the advisor to develop a marketing plan tailored to that niche based on in-depth knowledge of the niche's wants and needs. A custom-designed approach enables advisors to leverage their marketing efforts to reach prospective clients in that niche.

From a planning perspective, niche specialists leverage their time and solutions by offering the specific financial needs of the niche so the advisor becomes an expert in the financial services to meet them. The advisor does not need to know everything about all the solutions the business offers, but needs to know well how to meet the needs of the niche. For example, an advisor who is expert in the 401(k) plans of modest-sized companies in her area may have an excellent niche. In addition, knowing the benefit plans of two or three local companies and having a common solution set simplifies planning and increases expertise.

The advisor can leverage high net worth prospective clients' need to be introduced by someone they know and trust. Niche marketers have focused and leveraged access because people in the selected niche may know each other and interact. When their talk turns to investing, the financial advisor wants her or his name to come up as the expert who knows many other high net worth people who all basically have similar financial needs. While the advisor won't know hundreds of different clients very well, she or he can be unique within that niche. The ideal goal is to become the "broker of record" in the selected niche.

Additional Marketing and Sales Approaches for Business Development

Following are a few words about other effective approaches FAs can use to develop and grow their businesses. A solo advisor can undertake only so many efforts. Those efforts should include introductions from clients and professional alliances, LinkedIn, and possibly your "Book of Life." As a member of a team you may be able to use other approaches by sharing the marketing workload so you can do some strategic networking, undertake more "intimate events," conduct targeted roundtables, have a drip program, speak at public forums, and/or develop and manage client advisory boards. All these efforts can help in business development.

Additional resources we recommend:

- *Millennial marketing.* You can find our article "Millennial Marketing: Why It's Viral and How to Shape It" at www.financialadvisorsuccess.com or at http://horsesmouth.com/millennial-marketing-why-it-s-vital-and-how-to-shape-it. If you are not a member you can join with a free trial.

- *Strategic networking.* Financial advisors need to get involved in organizations within the community that attract those with high net worth. Networking is the process of developing and maintaining quality relationships that may enrich your life and help you achieve your goals. It is about giving first and realizing that we learn from everyone we meet. An excellent book we recommend is *Million Dollar Networking* by Andrea Nierenberg (Herndon, VA: Capital Books, 2005).

- *Intimate client events.* These are small gatherings to which clients are encouraged to bring friends, and where the overt purpose is solely social, not business focused.
- *Targeted roundtables.* These private events tend to focus on a group of people that one or more of your clients may be part of. Using your Client Wisdom worksheet (see Figure 9-3) you can identify companies your client works for where you can offer a "lunch and learn" event or an after-work event. You can also conduct roundtables if your client is part of a social group.
- *Drip programs.* Extensively used and worthwhile, drip programs keep your name in front of prospects. It's rare that advisors will acquire clients from these mailings, so follow-up phone calls are required where you can ask about people's interest in the material you are sending or if they would prefer different material.
- *Speaking at public forums on a range of corporate compliance-approved topics.* Speaking engagements are another way of getting recognition of what you do and how you do it. Your internal marketing areas may provide prepared presentations on a host of subjects.
- *Client advisory boards.* Sitting on the board are top clients and members of your team tasked with giving you feedback on services, marketing, and other aspects of your business and potentially sharing ideas on how you can grow your business. Client advisory boards can be powerful tools for building relationships with top clients, capturing detailed client feedback, and growing business.

Action Summary | Business Development

There are many business development approaches that can be used by FAs to acquire new clients and their assets. In Figure 9-7, we have listed 18 of them, and throughout this chapter we have detailed five of the most effective approaches for acquiring new clients. **LinkedIn** is actually another form of getting **Introductions from Clients**. We know that many FAs find securing **Introductions from COIs** to be a challenge. We are not suggesting it's easy, but it can be extremely worthwhile especially if you use the structured approach outlined in this book and limit your strategic relationships to the right four or five professionals.

Figure 9-7 | Business development approaches.

Business Development Approaches	
Effective Approaches	**Less Effective Approaches**
Introductions from clients	"Seminars"
Introduction from COIs	Cold walking
LinkedIn	Cold calling
Book of Life	Telemarketing
Niche marketing	Direct mail
Networking (Pers./Corp.)	TV/Radio
Intimate events	
Targeted roundtables	
Drips	
Public forums	
Beneficiary campaign	
Advisory boards	

Your **Book of Life** is a form of warm calling, which can be effective and a good way at least of getting started and developing your craft. As coaches to financial advisors, we have known clients whose family members tell them they just purchased insurance or had an estate plan put together without discussing their actions with their close relative, the FA, because they didn't really know what they did/could offer as a financial advisor. Naturally some relatives and friends will say they would rather not have you in their business, but most of us hope our relatives would at least trust and respect us more than a relative stranger.

Niche marketing is or can also be an extension of Introductions from Clients and actually is a very exciting approach. Determination of potential niches starts with your Client Wisdom spreadsheet (see Figure 9-3).

Chapter **Ten**

The Benefits of Implementation

Advisors rightly want to know how to justify the expense of making changes in their businesses, especially if they decide to hire a coach. The benefits are addressed in this chapter, but at the end of the day, 50-plus years of experience says justification is a state of mind.

While there is some research suggesting asset and revenue growth can be attributed to working with a business coach, perhaps the biggest benefit is difficult to measure. In financial advisory practices, most FAs tend to work individually, even if part of a team. As part of a team, advisors can at times work with their partner to bounce ideas off one another. With solo-preneurs it's difficult. There is a great benefit for advisors to share ideas with another individual to:

- See if plans make sense from another perspective.
- Find out what other advisors are doing in similar situations.
- Brainstorm new ideas and consider other options.
- Share confidentially.

In essence, when another individual is your partner you have an informed, knowledgeable teammate, an independent voice who cares as much about your business as you do. The difference between success and failure is often small. That gap can be narrowed with a business coach.

Statistically accurate metrics on the growth of assets and revenue over a significant period of time (e.g., several years or more) for multiple advisors is limited. One article said, "The Oechsli Institute claims that the average coaching client brought in over $19 million in assets over the past 12 months, added 21 new clients and increased advisory fees by nearly 22 percent."[1] It is difficult to evaluate specific benefits without knowing the situation, including the baseline in these cases. Neither of the other two firms described in the same article quoted any quantitative benefits.

In another article from 2011, Matt Oechsli's research showed that "advisors who are consistently acquiring wealthy clients are a distinct minority, and most other advisors are eager to learn how to replicate that success."[2] He "defined 'elite' advisors as those who have acquired five or more new $1-million-plus clients over the past 12 months." Only about 10 percent of FAs reach this level, with only 1.5 percent acquiring 10 or more million-dollar clients. The rest of the "elite" acquired five to nine new $1-million-plus clients while about 50 percent of FAs acquired one to four new $1 million-plus clients and 40 percent acquired none. (These FAs were not part of the Oechsli program.)

We can point to cases in our own experience where FAs have increased production by 50 percent in little more than three years while they also grew AUM by 83 percent. However, one of the reasons it is difficult to suggest an anticipated increase in growth rates is because it depends on too many variables: the advisor, the markets, the length of service of the advisor, the client base, and mostly the depth of execution the advisor puts into implementing the recommended processes. While case studies are available, they are usually one-offs and don't represent statistically accurate assessments.

Most of the literature states benefits in the form of qualitative improvements. We have no doubt, though, that you will grow your assets, revenues, and client households, and have an excellent ROI in doing so, if you:

- Formally segment and analyze your book and clients.
- Develop a realistic and complete business plan.
- Implement the six defined processes.

- Execute several business development approaches.
- Track your actions and results.
- Clearly define and state the value you deliver.

You will also be more efficient as well as effective while being able to be more consistent in what you do and how you do it. You will have the time to implement an effective set of marketing and sales approaches for improved client acquisition efforts. You will be less overwhelmed, less stressed, and have a more manageable practice. You will maintain or improve your client retention.

Overall, implementation of the contents of this book would provide:

- More structure around what you do, when you do it, who you do it for, and how you do it.
- A focus on what is important to you.
- Ideas on what is working for others.
- An opportunity to be held accountable if you implement these processes with a capable, experienced accountability partner. On a scale of 1 to 10 (10 being high), you need a laser focus to be at a 9.5 or better. That's where accountability comes in.
- A better understanding of your unique areas of opportunity.
- A clear roadmap of how to take your business to the "next level."
- An increase in client loyalty.
- Deeper and more profitable relationships.

A coach who is experienced in working with FAs would be of value in the customization and implementation of these processes. Let's look at some benefit data.

In their article "The Neuroscience of Leadership," David Rock and Jeffrey Schwartz write:

> You've probably had the experience of going to a training program and getting excited about new ways of thinking, only to realize later that you can't remember what the new ways of thinking were. Were

> the ideas no good in the first place? Or did you just not pay enough attention? A 1997 study of 31 public-sector managers by Baruch College researchers Gerald Olivero, K. Denise Bane, and Richard E. Kopelman found that a training program alone increased productivity 28 percent, but the addition of follow-up coaching to the training increased productivity 88 percent.[3]

The International Coach Federation (ICF) is a well-known professional organization that has more than 60 chapters worldwide. ICF states that the benefits of using a coach include "fresh perspectives on personal challenges, enhanced decision-making skills, greater interpersonal effectiveness, and increased confidence. And, the list does not end there. Those who undertake coaching also can expect appreciable improvement in productivity, satisfaction with life and work, and the attainment of relevant goals."[4]

According to the ICF, "Coaching generates learning and clarity for forward action with a commitment to measurable outcomes. The vast majority of companies (86 percent) say they at least made their investment back." And 99 percent of companies and individuals who hire a coach are "'Somewhat' or 'Very Satisfied' with overall experience" and "96 percent would repeat the process."[5]

Another site that offers coaching says that one of the "main benefits of coaching" to the recipient is that it "generates improvements in individuals' performance/targets/goals [by] 84 percent," and among the benefits to the organization is that coaching "allows fuller use of individual's talents/potential [by] 79 percent."[6]

Coach Bill Cole (www.mentalgamecoach.com) says:

> A coach won't do the work for you, but here is how a coach can help launch you to the next level:
>
> 1. *A coach can be a confidant.* You can tell your coach things you wouldn't tell others, because a coach is trained to understand and be nonjudgmental.
> 2. *A coach can help you see your blind spots.* Everyone, even the coach, has personal areas that are out of view or awareness until someone points them out. A coach is perfectly poised to perform this critical function.

3. *A coach can provide objective feedback.* Other people may have agendas. Your coach has your best interests in mind in providing feedback and counsel to you.
4. *A coach provides another set of eyes.* Even the top performers in the world have coaches to help them see what they themselves can't see.
5. *A coach can keep you accountable.* Your coach can help you take on more responsibility by having you report weekly (or biweekly) on your accomplishments and initiatives.
6. *A coach can be a sounding board.* Your coach can be another set of ears as you talk about the things that are bothering you. As you hear yourself have a conversation new personal realizations emerge.
7. *A coach can be another source of creative ideas.* You can brainstorm and try out new ideas, behaviors, and mental processes as your coach provides a safe place to experiment.
8. *A coach can help you create your vision.* Your coach can assist you in developing your plans for success based on your values, personal strengths, background, and assets.
9. *A coach can help celebrate your successes and be a source of strength when you fail.* Your coach can be a supportive and nurturing source of energy.
10. *A coach can help you process life.* Life is a process and a good coach can assist you in reviewing and reframing what happens in your business, your sports, and your life![7]

If some of these points are goals you would like to achieve, the benefits should be apparent.

Action Summary | The Benefits of Implementation

The answer to the benefits of implementing the approaches and principles laid out in this book are based in your belief system. You will achieve these benefits if:

- These approaches and principles are what you want.
- The benefits as described are what you are looking for.
- You are willing to work hard to get them.

A Final Thought

One of our favorite business books is *The E-Myth Revisited* by Michael E. Gerber. The E-Myth, or Entrepreneurial Myth, says that most new businesses are not started by entrepreneurs who set out to build a strong business but by technicians who enjoy the hands-on work themselves.

Because of that natural bias, most business owners focus on working in their business when really they should be working on their business. There is, however, a simple and effective way to offset the E-Myth tendency. Instead of looking at the business as a one-off operation, Gerber suggests the owner should consider the business to be a prototype for a large number of franchises that will be added at a later stage. By adopting that mindset, the business owner will not only participate in the business as a technician but will also act as a manager (putting systems in place and controls) and as an entrepreneur (having a vision of how the business can create sustainable added-value for all key stakeholders). A business that is built and managed by someone who combines the approach of the technician, the manager, and the entrepreneur will have a far greater chance of future success than one guided by someone thinking like a technician alone.

Afterword

The goal of this book was to describe the structure and organization you need to put yourself in a position to effectively and efficiently grow your business. Implemented well, the processes we have discussed will put you more in control of your practice and provide the retention, loyalty, and advocacy that will be the base for that growth.

As an experienced investment advisor and senior sales executive in the financial services industry for more than a quarter of a century, we want to add a few more points about becoming a top advisor.

- Top advisors have confidence. Confidence can result from any number of things—branding, advertising, having an office and a great team, niche "domination," and depth of your client relationships, for example. These things may or may not be unique. We believe the principles and processes discussed in this book will, however, add confidence so that you know you are delivering the right services at the right time to the right clients. Process removes the ad hoc nature of service delivery.
- One legendary head of a brokerage firm used to say, "If you don't toot your own horn, then someone is likely to clog it up." In other words, successful advisory teams not only identify what they are good at, they also do a great job of marketing their strengths. You need a quiet confidence knowing you are in a strong competitive position because you deliver significant value to your clients. Yet you are always aware that competitors are working on ways to acquire "your" clients, and this drives you to consistently and continuously improve your relationships and deliverables.
- Successful advisory teams are built properly and built to grow. As Jim Collins says in *Good to Great*, successful teams have strong leaders who get the right people on the bus, the wrong people off the bus, and the right people in the right seats. And they stick with that

discipline—first the people, then the direction. Getting the right people on the team and in the right roles is critical, and clients and prospects can sense this and appreciate the value.

- Great advisory teams also possess a strong ability to relate to what clients and prospects want. As Tony Robbins has pointed out, top performers can highlight the "pain and gain" that makes humans human. Top teams realize that what clients want is to eliminate pain and increase gain. Pain can be felt not only in market declines but in poor services, lack of a plan, poor communication, high fees, and so on. Gains can also be viewed as trust, confidence, great communication, client loyalty programs, and financial planning, as well as making the most of your money.
- Leo Pusateri[1] notes that successful advisors can articulate their Value Proposition or Value Ladder. Top performers have a strong value conversation with their clients and prospects. Strong value trumps pricing and creates loyalty. The organization and structure as defined by the processes we have discussed create that value.

It may take a while to master all of these elements; however, a good initial goal is to be great at something. This will allow you to compete from a position of strength. The best are great at some aspect of the business. Jim Collins asks, "Why try for greatness? . . . They're doing something they really care about, about which they have great passion."[2]

We also asked ourselves, "Who is likely to implement our approaches?" There is an idea called "the 20-60-20 Rule,"[3] which to us applies to people, businesses, and clients. The top 20 percent are strong performers. They do their jobs well, understand what is required of them, and have the skills to deliver. You know which employees and clients are the top 20 percent. Some advisors in the top 20 percent who want to be in the top 10 percent or better will employ these approaches because they have the passion to be great. Some advisors are in the middle 60 percent and are promising talents. They are pretty good at their jobs and do "most" of what they are supposed to do. Those who have a strong desire and interest to move from the middle 60 percent to the top 20 percent will also adopt the approaches that we have expounded.

Great sports team coaches like Mike Krzyzewski of Duke and Bill Belichick of the Patriots, among others, show how serious they are.

They are students of the game—they are process-oriented, lead by example, set standards, and are creative and work hard, among many other qualities. What are your key traits? What traits would you like to further develop in order to build your resume of skills and your strategy to be great?

"Strategy is about making wise choices and then having the courage and conviction to follow through and commit to turning words and ideas into action."[4] This is the charge we leave you with.

Notes

Acknowledgments

1. Dan Diamond, "Just 8% of People Achieve Their New Year's Resolutions. Here's How They Do It," *Forbes.com*, January 1, 2013.
2. Steve Levinson, Ph.D., and Pete Greider, M.Ed., *Following Through: A Revolutionary New Model for Finishing Whatever You Start* (New York: Kensington Publishing, 1998).

Introduction

1. Philip Hersh, "Chasing Katie Ledecky," *ESPN.com*, August 4, 2016, http://www.espn.com/espn/feature/story/_/page/espnw-ledecky160804/what-makes-olympic-swimmer-katie-ledecky-remarkable.

Chapter One

1. See Michael Kitces, "Replacing the Data Gathering Meeting with a 'Get Organized' Client Experience," *Nerd's Eye View* (blog), March 14, 2016, https://www.kitces.com/blog/get-organized-meeting-alternative-to-financial-planning-data-gathering-meeting/.
2. Charles R. "Chuck" Schwab became one of the first to embrace new trading rules that opened the way to discount brokerage on May 1, 1975, when the brokerage industry deregulated commissions, acting on a Securities and Exchange Commission mandate. See http://www.sfgate.com/business/article/The-genesis-of-discount-brokerage-1975-SEC-2637815.php.
3. Pusateri Consulting and Training, "Pricing Integrity," White Paper 1, Pusateri "Pricing Your Value Unapologetically" Series, 2012, 4, https://www.pusaterconsulting.com/documents/White%20Paper/Pusateri%201%20White%20Paper.pdf.
4. Bernstein quoted in Resource Planning Group, October 14, 2014, http://www.rpgplanner.com/investment-committee_24_2845815755.pdf.
5. Steve Levinson, Ph.D., and Peter Greider, M.Ed., *Following Through: A Revolutionary New Model for Finishing Whatever You Start* (New York: Kensington Publishing, 1998), 9.
6. David Rock and Jeffrey Schwartz, "The Neuroscience of Leadership," *Strategy + Business* 43 (Summer 2006).

7. Bernstein quoted in Resource Planning Group.
8. Bob Seawright, "Five Good Questions for William J. Bernstein of 'Efficient Frontier,'" *Think Advisor*, March 3, 2011, http://www.thinkadvisor.com/2011/03/03/five-good-questions-for-william-j-bernstein-of-eff.
9. Ibid.
10. "The Psychology of Money," accessed May 21, 2017, http://www.iwillteachyoutoberich.com/psychology-of-money/.
11. Bob Seawright, "A Hierarchy of the Value a Financial Advisor Provides," *Nerd's Eye View* (blog), March 8, 2016, https://www.kitces.com/blog/hierarachy-of-financial-advisor-value/.
12. Ibid.
13. Ibid.
14. Ibid.
15. Wade Pfau, "The Value of Financial Advice," *Forbes.com*, July 21, 2015, http://www.forbes.com/sites/wadepfau/2015/07/21/the-value-of-financial-advice/#5d3e4aa03e8c.
16. Tim Duy quoted in Morgan Housel, "122 Things Everyone Should Know About Investing and the Economy," *The Motley Fool*, December 12, 2014, http://www.fool.com/investing/general/2014/12/12/122-things-everyone-should-know-about-investing-an.aspx.
17. Kitces, "Replacing the Data Gathering Meeting with a 'Get Organized' Client Experience."
18. Ibid.
19. Also see Carl Richards, *The Behavior Gap: Simple Ways to Stop Doing Dumb Things with Money* (New York: Portfolio, 2012).
20. Tia Ghose, "Why We're All Above Average," LiveScience.com, February 6, 2013, http://www.livescience.com/26914-why-we-are-all-above-average.html.
21. "What Skill Do the Most People Think They're Above Average At?" Quora.com, https://www.quora.com/What-skill-do-the-most-people-think-theyre-above-average-at.
22. Thorin Klosowski, "Why You Think You're Great at Everything, Even When You Suck," January 2, 2014, http://lifehacker.com/why-you-think-you-re-great-at-everything-even-when-you-1492423875.
23. Pfau, "The Value of Financial Advice"; Pfau cites two major research efforts: Francis M. Kinniry Jr. et al., "Putting a Value on Your Value: Quantifying Vanguard Advisor's Alpha," Vanguard Research, September 2016, https://www.vanguard.com/pdf/ISGQVAA.pdf, and David Blanchett and Paul Kaplan, "Alpha, Beta, and Now . . . Gamma," Morningstar Investment Management, August 28, 2013 https://corporate.morningstar.com/US/documents/Research-Papers/AlphaBetaandNowGamma.pdf.

24. "Number of U.S. Financial Advisers Fell for Fifth Straight Year—Report," Reuters, February 11, 2015, http://www.reuters.com/article/wealth-cerulli-advisor-headcount-idUSL1N0VL23920150211.

25. Bureau of Labor Statistics, *Occupational Outlook Handbook*, http://www.bls.gov/ooh/business-and-financial/personal-financial-advisors.htm.

26. Silverstein, "The Law of Fractional Advantage."

27. Ibid.

28. Kenichi Ohmae, *The Mind of the Strategist: Business Planning for Competitive Advantage*.

29. Katherine Vessenes, "9 Key Questions to Ask in Your First Meeting," *Horsesmouth.com*.

30. Anna Pitts, "You Only Have 7 Seconds to Make a Strong First Impression," *BusinessInsider.com*, April 8, 2013, http://www.businessinsider.com/only-7-seconds-to-make-first-impression-2013-4.

31. Eric Wargo, "How Many Seconds to a First Impression?" Association for Psychological Science, July 2006, http://www.psychologicalscience.org/index.php/publications/observer/2006/july-06/how-many-seconds-to-a-first-impression.html.

32. The Aite Group study is summarized in "New Research: CFP Certification Provides Value to Clients, Firms and Financial Professionals," July 31, 2012, CFP Board, http://www.cfp.net/news-events/latest-news/2012/07/31/new-research-cfp-certification-provides-value-to-clients-firms-and-financial-professionals.

33. Michael Kitces, "Kitces: Can Becoming a CFP Boost Income?" *Financial Planning*, September 26, 2016, http://www.financial-planning.com/news/kitces-can-getting-a-cfp-mark-boost-income.

34. William J. Bernstein, "The Probability of Success (Or, Confessions of a Personal-Finance Writer)," *Efficient Frontier*, 2003, http://www.efficientfrontier.com/ef/103/probable.htm.

35. Julie Littlechild is a speaker, consultant, and writer, and the founder of Absolute Engagement.com.

36. Julie Littlechild, "Why Defining the Value You Provide Just Isn't Enough," December 8, 2015, http://www.absoluteengagement.com/blog/client-engagement/why-defining-the-value-you-provide-just-isnt-enough/.

37. Lance Roberts, "Dalbar: Why Investors Suck and Tips for Advisors," April 8, 2015, http://www.advisorperspectives.com/commentaries/20150408-streettalk-live-dalbar-why-investors-suck-and-tips-for-advisors.

38. "Dalbar's 21st Annual Quantitative Analysis of Investor Behavior (QAIB)," 2015 Advisor Edition, https://www.bellmontsecurities.com.au/wp-content/uploads/2015/04/2015-DALBAR-QAIB-study.pdf.

39. Kitces, "Replacing the Data Gathering Meeting with a 'Get Organized' Client Experience."
40. Mark Hebner and Mary Brunson, "IFA's Quote of the Week: 40 (William Bernstein)," Index Fund Advisors, November 18, 2008, https://www.ifa.com/articles/IFAs_Quote_of_the_Week_40_William_Bernstein/.
41. Silverstein, "The Law of Fractional Advantage."

Chapter 2

1. Ben Steverman, "An Investor's Guide to Fees and Expenses 2014," *Bloomberg.com*, October 8, 2014, http://www.bloomberg.com/news/articles/2014-10-08/an-investor-s-guide-to-fees-and-expenses-2014.
2. Ibid.
3. Pusateri Consulting and Training, "Pricing Integrity," White Paper 1, Pusateri "Pricing Your Value Unapologetically" Series.
4. Patricia J. Abram, John J. Bowen Jr., and Russ Alan Prince, *Building Client Loyalty: The Case for a Wealth Management Solution*, http://www.cegworldwide.com/downloads/ebwp/wp_ceg_building_client_loyalty.pdf?elq=5891cee18dee4360a3a3ca2bc24e5f94&elqCampaignId.
5. Michael Kitces, "Dunbar's Number and How Many True Financial Planning Client Relationships You Can Really Have," *Nerd's Eye View* (blog), October 10, 2012, https://www.kitces.com/blog/dunbars-number-and-how-many-true-financial-planning-client-relationships-you-can-really-have/.

Chapter 3

1. "Investors Adopt More Hands-On Approach to Advisors, Says J. D. Power Full Service Investor Satisfaction Study," news release, April 2016, http://www.jdpower.com/press-releases/2016-us-full-service-investor-satisfaction-study.
2. TeleFaction data research; Colin Shaw, "15 Statistics That Should Change the Business World—But Haven't," *Beyond Philosophy* (blog), June 10, 2013, https://beyondphilosophy.com/15-statistics-that-should-change-the-business-world-but-havent/.
3. Shaw, "15 Statistics That Should Change the Business World—But Haven't."
4. Ibid.
5. Thomas O. Jones and W. Earl Sasser Jr., "Why Satisfied Customers Defect," *Harvard Business Review*, November–December 1995, https://hbr.org/1995/11/why-satisfied-customers-defect.
6. James L. Heskett et al., "Putting the Service-Profit Chain to Work," *Harvard Business Review*, July–August 2008, https://hbr.org/2008/07/putting-the-service-profit-chain-to-work.
7. Ibid.

8. Jones and Sasser, "Why Satisfied Customers Defect."
9. Patricia J. Abram, John J. Bowen Jr., and Russ Alan Prince, "Building Client Loyalty: The Case for a Wealth Management Solution," CEG Worldwide, LLC, 2005.
10. Sarah Chandler, "Why Do Widows Leave Their Advisors?" *Investopedia*, January 16, 2015.
11. Ilana Polyak, "For Some Widows, Breaking up with an Advisor Is Easy to Do," *CNBC.com*, October 11, 2014.
12. See Amy Fontinelle, "How Financial Advisors Mistreat Women (And What Women Can Do About It)," http://www.investopedia.com/articles/personal-finance/030314/how-financial-advisors-mistreat-women-and-what-women-can-do-about-it.asp.
13. "Listening Skills," *SkillsYouNeed.com*, http://www.skillsyouneed.com/ips/listening-skills.html.
14. Graeme Wood, "Secret Fears of the Super-Rich," *The Atlantic*, April 2011, http://www.theatlantic.com/magazine/archive/2011/04/secret-fears-of-the-super-rich/308419/.
15. Geoff Colvin, "Humans Are Underrated," July 23, 2015, http://fortune.com/2015/07/23/humans-are-underrated/.
16. Extracted from Carl Richards, *The Behavior Gap: Simple Ways to Stop Doing Dumb Things with Money* (New York: Portfolio, 2012), pp. 96–102.
17. Michael Kitces, "Goals-Based Financial Planning Is Impossible Without First Evaluating the Possibilities," *Nerd's Eye View* (blog), November 5, 2014, https://www.kitces.com/blog/goals-based-financial-planning-is-impossible-without-first-evaluating-the-possibilities/.
18. Ibid.
19. Michael Kitces, "Replacing the Data Gathering Meeting with a 'Get Organized' Client Experience," *Nerd's Eye View* (blog), March 14, 2016, https://www.kitces.com/blog/get-organized-meeting-alternative-to-financial-planningdata-gathering-meeting/.
20. Ibid.
21. Robert Laura, "Three Retirement Goals People Never Achieve," *Forbes*, October 25, 2014, http://www.forbes.com/sites/robertlaura/2014/10/25/three-retirement-goals-people-never-achieve/#11e00c0a42fc.
22. Richards, *The Behavior Gap.*
23. Noriaki Kano is an educator, lecturer, writer, and consultant in the field of quality management. He is the developer of a customer satisfaction model (now known as the Kano model). Noriaki Kano was born in 1940 in Tokyo, Japan. He received a master's degree and doctorate from the Faculty of Mechanical Engineering of the University of Tokyo. For 35 years he has worked as a professor at the Tokyo University of Science. He is the author of

the book *Guide to (Total Quality Management) TQM in Service Industries*, https://managementmania.com/en/noriaki-kano.

24. See Russ Hill, "Advice in the Age of Longevity," September 1, 2016, *Financial Advisor* magazine, http://www.fa-mag.com/news/advice-in-the-age-of-longevity-28531.html.
25. Steve Levinson, Ph.D., and Peter Greider, M.Ed., *Following Through: A Revolutionary New Model for Finishing Whatever You Start* (New York: Kensington Publishing, 1998).
26. Anne Field, "My Life as a Client: Style vs. Substance," *WealthManagement.com*, October 3, 2016.

Chapter 4

1. Michael Kitces, "When Does It Make Sense to Join with a Financial Advisor Partner?" *Nerd's Eye View* (blog), July 18, 2016, https://www.kitces.com/blog/financial-advisor-partnership-when-should-advisor-partners-merge/.

Chapter 5

1. The Three Meeting Process and verbiage in this chapter, other than as referenced from other sources, is developed from work with a colleague, Coach Joe Lukacs of PracticePower (http://practicepower.net/).
2. Bobbi Masiello, "Engaging Female Clients: An Industry Imperative," The Clarke School/Clarke Financial Group, 2013.
3. Ibid.
4. Ibid.
5. Ibid.
6. Scott West and Mitch Anthony, *Storyselling for Financial Advisors: How Top Producers Sell* (Chicago: Dearborn Financial Publishing, 2000), 11.
7. Ibid., 54.
8. Dr. Charles E. Dwyer, "Power and Influence."
9. Peter Economy, "9 Ways to Make a Great First Impression," *Inc.com*, February 20, 2015, http://www.inc.com/peter-economy/9-ways-to-make-a-great-first-impression.html.

Chapter 6

1. Harvey Mackay, *Swim with the Sharks Without Being Eaten Alive* (New York: HarperCollins, 1988).
2. Forbes Insights, "Business Meetings: The Case for Face-to-Face," 2009, http://images.forbes.com/forbesinsights/StudyPDFs/Business_Meetings_FaceToFace.pdf.

3. Leslie Pagel, "What Is Customer Engagement?" *CustomerThink.com*, August 23, 2014, http://customerthink.com/what-is-customer-engagement/.

4. Julie Littlechild, "Anatomy of the Referral: Economics of Loyalty," December 7, 2010. The study was created and conducted by Advisor Impact, New York, with the support of Texas Tech University Division of Personal Financial Planning.

   Only summaries seem to be available at this time because Advisor Impact is no longer in business. The best is at: https://www.vanguard.co.uk/documents/adv/literature/practice_management/adviser-impact-driving-referrals.pdf.

   Summaries can also be seen at: http://www.advocis.ca/pdf/Forum/May2013/cultivating-quality-referrals.pdf and https://www.aicpastore.com/Content/media/PRODUCER_CONTENT/Newsletters/Articles_2011/CPA/Feb/AnatomyReferral.jsp.

   Also at: http://www.thinkadvisor.com/2011/02/01/making-referrals-happen.

5. Kyle LaMalfa, "The Top 9 Ways to Increase Your Customer Loyalty," Loyalty Expert and Allegiance Best Practices Manager, ©2007 Allegiance, Inc. All rights reserved. http://www.tutorialspoint.com/white-papers/6.html.

Chapter 7

1. Matt Oechsli states, "The majority of elite financial advisors (57 percent) spend 4 percent or more of their gross production on marketing." He also says they budget "between 2 to 10 percent of . . . gross revenue to marketing" on a sliding scale. See Matt Oechsli, "The Marketing Budget of an Elite Financial Advisor," *WealthManagement.com*, February 25, 2015.

2. Julie Littlechild, "Why Goals Are Secondary in Business Planning," *Absolute Engagement* (blog), August 30, 2016, http://www.absoluteengagement.com/blog/growth/goals/.

3. Michael Kitces, "6 Key Value Propositions a Good Financial Planner Can Provide for Clients Seeking a Better 'Return on Life,'" *Nerd's Eye View* (blog), https://www.kitces.com/blog/6-key-value-propositions-a-good-financial-planner-can-provide-for-clients-seeking-a-better-return-on-life/.

4. Ibid.

5. Ibid.

6. https://www.brainyquote.com/quotes/quotes/p/peterdruck131070.html.

Chapter 8

1. "7 Power Questions to Start Your Day," *Sources of Light*, accessed May 30, 2017, http://sourcesofinsight.com/7-questions-to-start-your-day/.

2. Jesse Lyn Stoner, "3 Powerful Questions to Start and End Your Day," *Jesse Lyn Stoner on Leadership* (blog), April 9, 2015, http://seapointcenter.com/3-powerful-questions-to-start-and-end-your-day/.

3. Ibid.

Chapter 9

1. Matt Oechsli, "Mastering the Personal Introduction: The Old Way of Getting Referrals Has No Place in Affluent Circles," *WealthManagement.com*, October 14, 2013.
2. Leslie Kramer, "Top Reasons Why Advisors Don't Get Referrals, August 7, 2015.
3. Julie Littlechild, "Clients Who Refer Were Asked for This," June 27, 2014.
4. Spectrem Group, "New Spectrem Study Reveals That Affluent Investors Seldom Refer Their Financial Advisor to Others Despite Professing Strong Loyalty," news release, December 18, 2015.
5. Preeti Vasishtha, "Want Referrals? Then Just Ask, Many advisors do not ask clients for referrals to avoid embarrassment. Here's a plan to gain referrals," *Advisor Today*.
6. SunAmerica Mutual Funds, "Think Referrals," 2011, https://www.safunds.com/pdf/referral-program/module-1-think-referrals.pdf.
7. Julie Littlechild, "Anatomy of a Referral: The Economics of Loyalty," December 2010. The study was created and conducted by Advisor Impact with the support of the Texas Tech University Division of Personal Financial Planning and sponsorship of Schwab Advisor Services.
8. Ibid. Littlechild's study says that financial planning plays a substantial role among the most engaged clients, as 64 percent of engaged clients say they have a written financial plan, compared to 44 percent of content clients, which drops significantly with complacent and disgruntled clients.
9. Harvey Mackay, *Swim with the Sharks Without Being Eaten Alive* (New York: HarperCollins, 1988).
10. Littlechild, "Anatomy of a Referral: The Economics of Loyalty."
11. Glenn Kessler, "Do 10,000 Baby Boomers Retire Every Day?" *Washington Post*, July 24, 2014.
12. Bureau of Labor Statistics, "Job Openings and Labor Turnover—March 2017," news release, May 9, 2017, http://www.bls.gov/news.release/pdf/jolts.pdf.
13. Quentin Fottrell, "Typical U.S. Worker Has Been 4.2 Years in Their Current Job," *MarketWatch.com*, January 12, 2014, http://www.marketwatch.com/story/americans-less-likely-to-change-jobs-now-than-in-1980s-2014-01-10.
14. Alan Hall, "'I'm Outta Here!' Why 2 Million Americans Quit Every Month (And 5 Steps to Turn the Epidemic Around)," *Forbes.com*, March 11, 2013, http://www.forbes.com/sites/alanhall/2013/03/11/im-outta-here-why-2-million-americans-quit-every-month-and-5-steps-to-turn-the-epidemic-around/#450f5ff9fe2a.
15. National Association of Realtors, "Field Guide to Quick Real Estate Statistics," updated May 2017, accessed May 29, 2017, https://www.nar.realtor/field-guides/field-guide-to-quick-real-estate-statistics.

16. WidowsHope.com, accessed May 29, 2017, http://www.widowshope.org/first-steps/these-are-the-statistics/.
17. "Marriage and Divorce Statistics," Avvo.com, updated 2015, https://www.avvo.com/legal-guides/ugc/marriage-divorce-statistics.
18. These email ideas come from Bill Cates of Referral Coach International (www.referralcoach.com).
19. Thanks to Josh Feinberg of JLT Consulting for the LinkedIn material. See http://www.jltconsultinginc.com/our-team.
20. FTI Consulting and LinkedIn, "Financial Advisors' Use of Social Media Moves from Early Adoption to Mainstream," May 2012, https://business.linkedin.com/content/dam/business/marketing-solutions/global/en_US/site/pdf/wp/linkedin-research-financial-advisors-use-social-media.pdf.
21. "Numbers of LinkedIn Members from 1st Quarter 2009 to 3rd Quarter 2016 (in Millions)," https://www.statista.com/statistics/274050/quarterly-numbers-of-linkedin-members/.
22. From the 2014 Spectrem Group survey, cited in Robert Frank, "More Millionaires Than Ever Are Living in the US," *CNBC.com*, March 10, 2015, http://www.cnbc.com/2015/03/09/more-millionaires-than-ever-are-living-in-the-us.html.
23. "Number of U.S. Financial Advisers Fell for Fifth Straight Year—Report," Reuters, February 11, 2015, http://www.reuters.com/article/2015/02/11/wealth-cerulli-advisor-headcount-idUSL1N0VL23920150211.
24. Jeb Blount, "When It Comes to Trust, You Are Always on Stage," *Training.com*, August 9, 2013, https://trainingmag.com/content/when-it-comes-trust-you-are-always-stage.
25. The material in this section is in part based on or influenced by the concepts and ideas from Russ Alan Prince and Brett Van Bortel in their book *Rainmaker: Strategic Partnering with Attorneys and Accountants to Create a Pipeline of New Affluent Clients* (Erlanger, KY: National Underwriter Company, Summit Business Media, 2006). The book and study were sponsored by Van Kampen Investments.
26. https://www.invesco.com/static/us/investors/contentdetail?contentId=a1257fc1ac6d4410VgnVCM100000c2f1bf0aRCRD&dnsName=us&title=rainmaker-keynote-elite-combo.
27. Russ Alan Prince and Lewis Schiff, *The Middle-Class Millionaire* (New York: Currency/Doubleday, 2008).
28. Matt Oechsli, "Five Financial Advisor Marketing Activities You Must Master," *WealthManagement.com*, March 20, 2014, http://www.wealthmanagement.com/practice-management/five-financial-advisor-marketing-activities-you-must-master.
29. Prince and Van Bortel, *Rainmaker*.

30. Ibid.
31. The material in this section is in part based on or influenced by the concepts and ideas from John J. Bowen Jr., Paul Brunswick, and Jonathan J. Powell, "Building Powerful Strategic Alliances," CEG Worldwide Industry Intelligence Report, 2010, http://www.cegworldwide.com/downloads/ebwp/eread/SA/CEG_Strategic_Alliances_ebook.pdf.
32. Ibid.
33. Ibid.
34. Ibid.
35. Ibid.
36. Ibid.
37. Ibid.
38. Harris O'Malley (aka Dr. Nerdlove), "5 Secrets to Make People Like You," February 10, 2015, http://www.doctornerdlove.com/2014/02/5-secrets-to-make-people-like-you/.
39. Prince and Van Bortel, *Rainmaker*.
40. Invesco Consulting, Rainmaker, https://www.invesco.com/static/us/investors/contentdetail?contentId=a1257fc1ac6d4410VgnVCM100000c2f1bf0aRCRD&dnsName=us&title=rainmaker-keynote-elite-combo.
41. Jonathan Gottschall, "Why Storytelling Is the Ultimate Weapon," *Fast Company*, May 2, 2012, http://www.fastcocreate.com/1680581/why-storytelling-is-the-ultimate-weapon.
42. Andrew Gelman, "The Average American Knows How Many People?" *New York Times*, February 18, 2013.
43. Anna Vital, "Why We Live—Counting the People Your Life Impacts," Funders and Founders infographic, April 29, 2013, fundersandfounders.com/counting-the-people-you-impact/.
44. Some of the thoughts and verbiage in this section are derived from Horsesmouth. Horsesmouth, Rich Niche Prospeting: How to Uncover Your Natural Market and Start Capturing Wealthy Clients in 30 Days. Copyright 2007 Horsesmouth LLC.

Chapter 10

1. Brian Mathews, "Top 3 Coaching Programs for Financial Advisors and Planners," *Investopedia*, September 12, 2016, http://www.investopedia.com/articles/fa-profession/091216/top-3-coaching-programs-financial-advisors-planners.asp.

2. Matt Oechsli, "Marketing Tactics of Elite Advisors," Cetera Financial Group, August 2011, http://www.sterlingbridge.com/sites/default/files/users/sterling-bridge/images/pdfCovers/Marketing%20Tactics%20of%20Elite%20Investors.pdf.

3. David Rock and Jeffrey Schwartz, "The Neuroscience of Leadership," *Strategy + Business* 43 (Summer 2006).

4. International Coach Federation, "Benefits of Using a Coach," http://coachfederation.org/need/landing.cfm?ItemNumber=747&navItemNumber=565.

5. Ibid.

6. "Benefits of Coaching," http://www.abetterperspective.com/Benefits_of_Coaching.htm.

7. Bill Cole, "Why Hire a Coach? Ten Terrific Ways to a More Powerful Life," http://www.mentalgamecoach.com/articles/Article3_02.html.

Afterword

1. Leo J. Pusateri, *Mirror Mirror on the Wall Am I the Most Valued of Them All?* (Williamsville, NY: Pusateri Consulting and Training/Financial Entrepreneur Publishing, 2001).

2. Jim Collins, *Good to Great* (New York: HarperCollins, 2001), 209.

3. Patrick Sanaghan, "The 20-60-20 Rule," 2011, https://www.tarleton.edu/ORG/strategicplan/documents/leadershipdocs/The_20-60-20_Rule.pdf.

4. Paul Simister, "Stuck in the Middle of Porter's Generic Strategies," February 14, 2011, http://www.differentiateyourbusiness.co.uk/is-your-business-stuck-in-the-middle.

Index

Note: Page numbers follow by *f* indicate figures.